Little is known about the greatest poet in classical Sanskrit literature and one of the greatest in world literature. A most self-effacing writer, he has chosen to reveal little of himself in his work.

Kālidāsa probably lived and wrote at the close of the first millennium BC, though a date later by some five centuries has been assigned to him by some scholars. It is highly probable too that he lived and wrote in Ujjain, Madhya Pradesh—splendid capital of empires, a centre of culture and India's great emporium for a thousand years.

Kālidāsa is a dramatist, a writer of epic and a lyric poet of extraordinary scope. In all, seven of his works have survived though tradition has ascribed to him many a spurious work authored by later writers who assumed his style. The two works best known outside the country are the play, *Śakuntalā* and the lyric monody, *Meghadūtam*. Kālidāsa is a courtly poet; but at the same time he is a very learned poet who wears his learning lightly and with grace.

It has been suggested that Kālidāsa was a high court official who was sent on embassies by the Emperor Chandra Gupta II to other royal courts; and that *Meghadūtam* was written during a long spell of separation from his wife when he was residing at the Vākataka capital of Nandhivardhana, near the 'Rāma's hill of the poem, as adviser to the widowed Queen Prabhāvatī Gupta, daughter of the emperor, who was ruling the kingdom as regent for her infant son.

Kālidāsa's work is instinct with Śiva's presence. The blend of the erotic and spiritual that characterizes Śiva-mythology, is reflected in the poet's work. A mystic feeling for the transcendental combines with a sensuous feeling for beauty in Woman and Nature.

*

Chandra Rajan studied Sanskrit from the age of nine, in the time-honoured manner, with a pandit. She was educated at St. Stephen's College, Delhi University, where she had a distinguished academic record and took degrees in English and Sanskrit Language and Literature; later, she did some post-graduate work on W.B. Yeats at King's College, London. Trained early in Carnatic music, she studied Western music, specializing in opera, at New York, when her husband was posted there on a diplomatic assignment.

Chandra Rajan has taught English Literature at Lady Sri Ram College,

Delhi University and at the University of Western Ontario, London, Canada.

Her book, *Winged Words* (Macmillan), an anthology of poetry from Jonson to Eliot, with a critical introduction and annotations, was widely prescribed at the pre-university and first year university levels. A book of poems, *Re-Visions*, was published in 1987. She is currently working on translations of Kālidāsa's other poems and on a novel based on certain crucial episodes from the epic *Mahābhārata*.

KĀLIDĀSA

THE LOOM OF TIME

A Selection of His Plays and Poems

Translated from the Sanskrit and Prakrit
with an introduction by
Chandra Rajan

PENGUIN BOOKS

Penguin Books (India) Limited, 72-B Himalaya House, 23 Kasturba Gandhi Marg,
New Delhi 110 001, India
Penguin Books Ltd., Harmondsworth, Middlesex, England
Viking Penguin Inc., 40 West 23rd Street, New York, N.Y. 10010, U.S.A.
Penguin Books Australia Ltd., Ringwood, Victoria, Australia
Penguin Books Canada Ltd., 2801 John Street, Markham, Ontario, Canada, L3R 1 B4
Penguin Books (N.Z.) Ltd., 182-190 Wairau Road, Auckland 10, New Zealand

Copyright © Chandra Rajan, 1989
Reprinted 1990
All rights reserved

Typeset in Taxila by Tulika Print Communication Services Pvt. Ltd., New Delhi
Made and printed by Ananda Offset Pvt. Ltd., Calcutta

This book is sold subject to the condition that it shall not, by way of trade or otherwise, be lent, resold, hired out, or otherwise circulated without the publisher's prior written consent in any form of binding or cover other than that in which it is published and without a similar condition including this condition being imposed on the subsequent purchaser and without limiting the rights under copyright reserved above, no part of this publication may be reproduced, stored in or introduced into a retrieval system, or transmitted in any form or by any means (electronic, mechanical, photocopying, recording or otherwise), without the prior written permission of both the copyright owner and the above mentioned publisher of this book.

Om
yakṣasvarūpāya jaṭādharaya
pinākahastāya sanātanāya |
divyāya devāya digambarāya tasmai
yakārāya namah śivāya ||

Contents

Acknowledgements

I first wish to thank my husband, Professor Balachandra Rajan, and my daughter, Professor Tilottama Rajan, for the unfailing support and encouragement they have given me in my work. In spite of their teaching and other academic responsibilities and the demands of their own writing, they have both found time to read large portions of the translations in this book. They have given generously also of their time, listening to me talk interminably about Kālidāsa and Sanskrit literature in general—a far cry from their own fields of specialization and interests—offered comments and suggested the possibility of other perspectives. I am indebted to them in a deeper though less tangible way—for the wide-ranging discussions we have had over the years on literature, Aesthetics, and Art in general. For all of this I am grateful.

I have had wide-ranging and thought-provoking discussions and exchange of views on many aspects of India's arts and culture with Dr Lokeshchandra, art-historian and Director of the International Academy of Indian Culture, Delhi; and also availed myself of the facilities of his library; for all of this I express my appreciation.

I thank my friend and former colleague, Malati Varma, who read parts of the translations in their first draft and suggested slight changes in the rendering in a few places.

A word of thanks to Laksmi Kannan for prodding me out of an abysmal apathy.

The positive response of two friends and former colleagues at the University of Western Ontario, Professors Ross Woodman and Kent Hieatt, both of the English Department, to parts of the first draft of the translation of *Meghadūtam*, were important to me as representing the response of *readers outside the culture.*

Laurie Consaul, Asst Curator of the Herbarium at the University of

Western Ontario, was kind enough to help me with the identifications of some of the trees mentioned by Kālidāsa.

I wish to thank the staff of the Inter-loan section of the Weldon Library, University of Western Ontario for the promptness and efficiency with which they procured out of print tests or xeroxes of these for me.

I wish to thank Damini Singh for the patient hours she spent on getting the manuscript ready for the press and for the care with which she has done it.

I thank Sri Abdul Nazar, who did most of the typing and re-typing with care and cheerfulness of spirit. I also thank my brother who did some of the small things which are of great help in making life a bit easier when one is strapped for time.

Finally I wish to take this opportunity to remember with affection and respect two persons who are no more. Firstly, my grandfather, Dr P.S. Chandrasekhara Iyer, an eminent physician but more importantly a fine scholar of Sanskrit, who early inculcated a deep love in me for Sanskrit and its great literature and who opened the doors of its rich treasure-house of myth and legend to me in my childhood. Secondly, my first teacher of Sanskrit, Sri Ramasetu Sastrigal, who led me, an ignorant nine-year-old, into the Kālidāsan world, pointing out its varied beauties and laying out the subtleties of the poet's language when we first started our exploration of this fascinating world with the invocation to Śiva-Śakti that opens Kālidāsa's great epic, *Raghuvamśam*:

May the Parents of the Universe
Pārvatī and the Supreme Lord
eternally con-joined as Word and Meaning
grant fittest utterance to my thoughts.

Āśvina 18, Vikrama 2046 *Chandra Rajan*
(10 October, 1989)
New Delhi

Abbreviations

ASU	Allahabad University Studies
AV	*Atharvaveda*
BM	Bharata Mallika—seventeenth century commentator on *Meghadūtam* (*The Cloud Messenger*)
BNM	*Bharata-Nātya-Manjarī*
BORI	Bhandarkar Oriental Research Institute, Poona
comm.	commentary
IP	*Indian Philosophy*
JUB	*Journal of the University of Bombay*
KS	Kashi Series, Chowkamba Press, of the *Nātyaśastra*
Kumāra	*Kumārasambhavam*
Māl.; Mālavikā	*Mālavikāgnimitram*
Manu	Institutes of Manu
Mbh.	*Mahābhārata*
Megh.	*Meghadūtam*
MNG	*Nātyaśastra*, ed. with tr. by M.N. Ghosh
NS	*Nātyaśastra*
R	*Raghuvamśam*
Rām.	*Rāmāyaṇa*
Ṛtu.	*Ṛtusamhāram*
RV	*Ṛgveda*
S, Śak.	*Abhijnānaśākuntalam; Śakuntalā* for short
SB	Śata-patha Brāhmana
Skt	Sanskrit
Urvaśī	*Vikramorvaśiyam*

Key to the Pronunciation of Sanskrit Words

***Vowels*:** The line on top of a vowel indicates that it is long.
a (short) as the *u* in b*u*t
ā (long) as the a in f*a*r
i (short) as the i in s*i*t
ī (long) as the ee in sweet
u (short) as the u in p*u*t
ū (long) as the oo in c*oo*l
ṛ with a dot is a vowel like the i in first or u in fūrther
e is always a long vowel like a in m*a*te

ai as the i in p*i*le

o is always long as the o in p*o*le

ow as the ow in *o*wl

The *visarga*, two vertically lined points ':' is translitrated into roman as an 'h' and sounded like the 'h' in 'loch'; e.g. pramattah, bhartuh, Duhṣanta.

Also note, the final'i' in feminine nouns are long in the nominative case but short in the vocative case; e.g. Vetravatī and Vetravati (when she is addressed by name).

Consonants: K is the same as in English as in *k*itten

kh is aspirated

g as in *g*oat

gh is aspirated

c is ch as in *c*hurch or *c*ello

ch is aspirated

j as in *j*ewel

jh is aspirated

ṭ and ḍ are hard when dotted below as in *t*alk and *d*ot

ṭṭ is the aspirated sound

ḍḍ is aspirated

ṇ when dotted is a dental; the tongue has to curl back to touch the palate.

t undotted is a th as in *th*ermal

th is aspirated

d undotted is a soft sound—there is no corresponding English sound,the Russian 'da' is the closest.

dh is aspirated

p and b are the same as in English

ph and bh are aspirated

The Skt v is an English w

There are 3 sibilants in Skt: S as in *s*ong, Ṣ as in *sh*over and a palatal Ś which is in between, e.g. Śiva.

Key to Prose Passages in the Play

Lines of prose in the play are referred to using points and plus and minus signs; e.g. 1.20.+16-18 refers to lines 16-18 *after* st. 20 in Act 1; 3.36.-2,3 refers to lines 2 and 3 *before* st. 36 in Act 3.

A Note on Texts and Translations

Kālidāsa's works have unfortunately come down to us not in their original form, but in several recensions (divergent versions of a text) current in different regions of the country. The ancestry of the recensions is not clear. But it is evident that after his lifetime, Kālidāsa's poems and plays became subject to alterations, the reasons for which are again not clear. It is not uncommon for this to happen in the history of Sanskrit literature. Many factors would have contributed to the process of the *one true text* becoming diverse recensions. The manuscripts of the works, none of them contemporaneous with the author, belong to one or other of the recensions. They display a bewildering variety of readings; the length of the texts themselves as well as the number and order of the verses in them vary; interpolations present a problem. Some of the variants are substantive enough to warrant a somewhat different *reading* of the text, as in the case of *Abhijnānaśākuntalam* (*Śakuntalā* for short).

The translations in this volume differ in their textual basis from the great majority of other translations. The texts of both *Meghadūtam* and *Abhijnānaśākuntalam* follow the Eastern Indian (Bengal) recensions to which insufficient attention has been given. Even though the Bengal version is not the one translators most frequently use, the bibliographical arguments for it, and for *Śakuntalā* in particular, are not unequal to those for other texts and, as I shall endeavour to show, there are strong aesthetic arguments for it.

The text of *Śakuntalā* has been handed down in four main recensions: Eastern or Bengal, Southern, Kashmir and Devanāgarī (Northern). Which of these comes closest to the play as Kālidāsa wrote it and as it was staged during his lifetime is difficult to determine, to say the least. Dileep Kumar Kanjilal attempts this difficult task in his critical edition of the play, *A Reconstruction of the Abhijnānaśākuntalam*, 1980. He finds motifs, images and word-clusters specific to the Bengal Recension echoed in later plays, such as Harṣa's. He also examines the Prakrit verses and finds them correct grammatically and metrically in the Bengal text and indicating where they are not in other texts, argues for its superior authenticity. Pischel who edited the play according to the Bengal Recension, in 1877 (reprinted in the Harvard Oriental Series, 1922, after his death), is of a similar opinion.

The Devanāgarī Recension of *Śakuntalā* with Rāghava Bhatta's commentary was published by the Nirnaya Sagar Press, Bombay, in 1883. It is the shortest text of the play and the one frequently translated. The Bengal Recension, which I have translated, is a longer version, containing 35 more verses and a number of additional prose passages. My translation is based on the critical edition produced by Kanjilal, already referred to. In his introduction, Kanjilal writes that he has reconstructed the play on the basis of the oldest extant manuscript, an early twelfth century Newari manuscript in the possession of the Asiatic Society, Calcutta, supported by other Bengal and Śāradā manuscripts, two of the latter not having been utilized before. The differences between the Pischel and Kanjilal editions are few and minor. I have adopted one Devanāgarī variant in my translation as being more appropriate in the context. In 7.7.2, the Bengal Recension reads *aga*, meaning trees, while the Devanāgarī has *ara*, the spokes of a wheel. This might be an example of the kind of error a copyist of manuscripts could have made.

One can argue that the Bengal text is more satisfying, aesthetically. The longer and more numerous prose passages and the additional verses, result in a smoother narrative and fuller characterization. The differences between the two recensions are found mainly in Acts 1 and 3; they are particularly significant in the love episodes which the Devanāgarī treats in a rather perfunctory manner.

The Devanāgarī text (D) seems to make somewhat abrupt transitions in some places, giving the impression of something missing at that point. For example, it does not contain the lines at the end of Act 1, where Anasūyā asks Śakuntalā to hurry up and come with her and Priyamvadā, as well as Śakuntalā's response about the numbness in her thighs—a deft touch which conveys the sudden physical impact an overpowering emotion might make. Again, in Act 2, the Devanāgarī text does not have st. 8 which seems to be an appropriate response to Mādhavya's wry comment preceding it. The conversation regarding the *untimely blossoming* of the Mādhavī bush is not included either (1.20.+14–30). This passage is important because it foreshadows Śakuntalā's marriage and characterizes it at the same time.

The Bengal text devotes more space to the development of the love of Śakuntalā and Duhṣanta, in Act 3. It presents the courtship as well as the conflict in Śakuntalā's mind in some detail. Stanza 40 at the end of Act 3 reveals something of the complexity of the King's character. The first three lines bring out one aspect, the pleasure-loving and philandering side to his nature, and it articulates his *carpe diem* philosophy—seize the moment before it flies away beyond your reach. But it concludes on a different note, when Duhṣanta says, 'My heart, in the beloved's presence, stands somewhat abashed'. A man of the world, assured and poised and a great King who has fallen in and out of love many times, has had his way presumably and got what he wanted, Duhṣanta now stands dumbfounded before the innocence and purity that Śakuntalā represents. By sharply abbreviating a long section of verse and prose starting at st. 26 (20 in D) which concludes with the important stanza discussed above, the Devanāgarī text makes a crucial omission. It further omits the delightful prose passage of four-cornered banter which follows st. 23 (st. 18 in D).

The King in the Bengal text is more fully drawn. He is a man of words as well of deeds, more so than in the Devanāgarī text. He loves as passionately as he fights furiously. And he is a man who is in love with love as much as he is in love with a girl; a man who talks about love and being in love in a highly self-conscious manner. And how beautifully he speaks about it all! By presenting Duhṣanta in the first half of the play as a passionate lover, courtly and gallant—too gallant for the liking of the simple hermit girl who mistrusts such gallantry, and as it turns out with good reason—Kālidāsa draws a sharp contrast between this man, debonair, noble and even considerate at times, and the cynical, harsh and cold King of Act 5.

Śakuntalā is also drawn more finely in the Bengal text. The final section of Act 3, already referred to, reveals another side to her character; she is not wholly innocent of the ways of love. Seeing through the King's flimsy stratagems to get close to her, she indicates that she too can play at this ame, though not with his expertise. The Śakuntalā of the Bengal text also shows some of the fiery spirit of her ancestress in the epic. Both the hero and the heroine are more idealized in the Devanāgarī text; they are more interesting in the other.

The minor characters come across better in the Bengal text. Priyamvadā has more lines given to her, providing more scope for her bubbling sense of fun and her readiness to tease both Śakuntalā and the King. Mādhavya's sharp wit, always reaching out to deflate Duhṣanta's ego and undercut his highflown statements, has more room to play around.

The captions at the end of each Act seem to be a feature of the Bengal Recension. They are not found in the Devanāgarī texts of the plays, though the epic *Raghuvamśam* and the long poem *Kumārasambhavam* have captions at the end of each canto. In *Śakuntalā*, the captions for the first two Acts, 'The Chase' and 'The Concealment of the Telling' are notable. They contain an element of symbolism. The chase is a central motif in Act 1; the King is not merely chasing a deer, he is after a girl. The deer is closely associated with Śakuntalā through imagery and it leads the King into her world, which I have characterized in the introduction as the 'green world' as opposed to the gilded world of the court. The chase motif is picked up in Act 2 where we come across several phrases pertaining to the sport of hunting: the hunter's skill; his elation when he gets the quarry; knowledge of 'the changing responses of fear and anger of woodland creatures'. (Śakuntalā reminds the King in Act 5, that during his stay in the Hermitage, he once described her and her pet fawn as kin, both 'creatures of the woods'.) All of these phrases conveying as they do the sense of dominance over the prey and gaining possesssion of it, characterize the initial attitude to and relationship of Duhṣanta with Śakuntalā.

The interesting point to note about the caption to Act 2, 'The Concealment of the Telling' is that it is parallelled by another concealment in Act 4, the concealment of Durvāsā's curse by Śakuntalā's friends. The first concealment in Act 2, moves the plot forward; the second introduces the complication. The theme of concealment has ramifications in the play.

The translation of *Meghadūtam* in this volume is based on the text of the poem on which the early seventeenth century Bengal scholiast, Bharata Mallika wrote his highly informative and sensitive commentary, *Subodhā*. I have used the critical edition of this text with commentary, produced by

J.B. Chaudhuri. The differences between this critical edition and the critical edition produced by S.K. De for the Academy of Letters (Sāhitya Akādemi, New Delhi) are few and minor. The text of the poem established by Mallinātha, the fourteenth century scholiast from South India, contains a longer version. This text has had wide acceptance and is the one frequently translated. The verses in Mallinātha's text which have not been accepted as genuine by Bharata Mallika (or by De) are placed in Appendix IV.

I have used the Nirnaya Sagar Press edition of *Rtusamhāram* with Maṇirāma's commentary—a rather perfunctory commentary.

We now come to the matter of translation and the translation of Kālidāsa's texts specifically. Translation is like serving two masters at the same time. Languages do differ widely in their grammatical and syntactical structures and though one hopes to meet the demands of the source and receiving languages in a balanced manner, it is a fact that compromises have to be made one way or the other. We endeavour to provide the best approximation to the original not only within the limitations set by our own abilities but more so within those set by the receiving language.

Sanskrit is a highly inflected language; and it has some distinctive features which indeed constitute some of its strengths; for example, the extensive use of compound words and prefixes, and an array of synonyms with slight nuances of meaning that colour the expression of what is being said. The inflexional structure and the use of compound words give the language a tightly knit compactness which is of importance in poetry; this compactness suffers some dilution in translation. Because Sanskrit is a highly inflected language, word order is not of special importance as it is in English; punctuation is minimal consisting of a vertical stroke (|) to mark the end of the second quarter of a stanza and two vertical strokes (||) that correspond to the period in English. Inversions are frequent, with the predicate often separated from subject and object by long clauses consisting of single compound words, with their sub-units linked alliteratively, not only for euphonic but other poetic effects as well. This lends the language a musical quality difficult to convey in another language. This is especially true in the case of poetry which was and still is chanted or sung and not read silently.

Compound words are also able to project images with immediacy: for example the word, *paruṣapavanavegotkṣiptasamśuṣkaparnāh*(*Ṛtu.*: 1.22) conveys strongly the picture of wild winds and their force and energy: by splitting the compound word into its sub-units we have the following:

paruṣa—pavana—vega-utkṣipta—sam-śuṣka—parnāh
violent—winds—by great velocity—hurling-up—shrivelled-leaves

Compound words can also articulate ambivalences (see notes on *Megh.*).

Puns, proverbs and certain kinds of wordplay especially those dependent on sonic resemblances or identity are almost untranslateable; for example, the phrase *dhanuṣ-khanḍam ākhanḍalasya*, the literal meaning of which is—a fragment of the bow wielded by the fragmentor (breaker)—we need notes to make the point clear. However this is a difficulty present in all translation; for example, in the following line from Keats: 'Thou *still* unravished bride of quietness', something is bound to get left out in translating it into an Indian language; specifically, one would be hard put to find a single word to convey both senses of the word 'still'.

Kālidāsa's poetry like much of Indian art is stylized. The stylization is not a rhetorical procedure but part of the self-awareness with which the verse shapes itself. The translation therefore, to be *faithful*, has to somehow contrive to be stylized and readable; to steer clear of a literalness of rendering as well as an identification of readability with contemporaneity. It has been my endeavour throughout this volume of translations to be faithful not simply to *what* the poetry says (its paraphraseable meaning) but also to *how* it says what it says. That would be to respect its way of perceiving itself to create artifacts of the imagination. To accomplish this with some degree of success, inversions are unavoidable at places, and also the occasional passive construction which is frequent in Sanskrit. I have used these sparingly.

The translation of the prose in the drama poses its own brand of problems. Kālidāsa uses several dialects (*prākrits*) current in his day. It is not possible to differentiate between them by style or through diction. Therefore, there is an unavoidable ironing out of the rich variety of speech of that age into one flat prose.

But I have attempted some slight differentiation in another area. There are several levels of speech in the play, depending on the occasion, private or public, and on the relationships of the speakers to one another, and here some differentiation is possible.

*

Nature has a life of its own in Indian thought; it enshrines centres of power, radiating holiness, plenitude, beauty. For this reason, I have refrained from using the neuter form of the English pronoun. A hill is therefore a 'he' and a stream is a radiant 'she'.

I have translated only a few of the names of the flora in the Kālidāsan landscape. While there are several kinds of lotuses mentioned, each with its own distinctive name in the original and each beautifully evocative, I have reluctantly used the generic term 'lotus'. I have however, retained the Sanskrit names for many other flowers, trees, shrubs and vines mentioned or described, for two reasons. Firstly, English equivalents are not readily available (except botanical terms) and identifications are not always definitive. Secondly, the Sanskrit names form part of the poetic effect in certain passages; they frequently sound like the roll call of epic heroes and their weapons.

> Beauty, Genius of Blossom-Time, forsaking
> the Kadamba, Kutaja, and Kakubha,
> the Sarja and the Arjuna,
> now dwells with the Saptaparṇa.
>
> (*Rtu.*: 3.3)

Here, the poet seems to be having some fun at the expense of the epic poets.

On the other hand, I have translated nearly all of the epithets of Indra in *Meghadūtam* and *Śakuntalā*, because the meaning of a particular epithet chosen by the poet has a specific significance in the context: for example, in *Śak.*: 6:30, the epithet for Indra, *Śata-kratu*, The Lord of a Hundred Powers, serves to enhance Duhṣanta's own glory; in *Śak.*: 7:1 Indra is called Marutvat—He who is accompanied by Storm Winds (*Maruts*), again glorifying Duhṣanta; Ākhaṇḍala, The Breaker of Dark Clouds (dark forces) to let light shine through, suggests in the context that the dark delusion clouding the King's memory is destroyed through Indra's power or compassion.

The translations are accompanied by a long introduction, notes, an annotated glossary and appendices. The introduction suggests ways of looking at the three works in this volume singly and as a group. These are however not exhaustive for want of space. Still, an attempt has been made within a brief compass to relate these works in a meaningful way and trace a pattern of development in the poet's *oeuvre*. The myths that lend an added depth and resonance to a work, especially *Meghadūtam*, are briefly recounted in Appendix II. An in-depth analysis of a verse from *Ṛtusamhāram* which is the earliest of Kālidāsa's works, has been included as part of the notes to show how the poet's multilayered imagery functions as an integral part of the structure.

The notes and glossary should be of some help in bridging gaps in communication by explaining the numerous mythological and metaphysical allusions in the poems and the play. They also point to the possibility of multiple readings of a line or passage; in most cases a translation can convey only one of the possible readings.

Because Kālidāsa's works emerge out of a philosophical context (as all great works of art do) and returns us to it, some information about religious and metaphysical concepts, both Vedic and Śaiva, is unavoidable. It has been kept to a minimum.

The presence of all this background information in no way implies that Kālidāsa cannot be read with pleasure and delight without this explanatory apparatus. The response to great poetry (and poetic drama) is the immediate response to it as poetry. While it is true that the Indian and the European intellectual traditions are different, emerging as they do, each from its own world view and intimately interwoven with it, the two worlds of these traditions ought not to be treated as totally opaque to each other. If an educated Indian is able to *read* and enjoy the Greek tragedies and Tolstoy in English translations, which is the only way for most of us who have neither Greek nor Russian, we can safely assume that English readers (both within the culture and outside it) who have no Sanskrit can appreciate and enjoy Vyāsa, Vālmīki and Kālidāsa, through translations of their works into English. With numerous hurdles to negotiate in the course of translation, it is a matter of satisfaction that translations can 'carry over' much of the power and beauty of the original. The notes and annotations are simply a means to enable the reader to explore the depths and reaches of Kālidāsa's art and *taste* its full flavour—*Rasa*.

Introduction

> I give power and knowledge to him I love:
> I invest him with Holy Power:
> I make him a sage, a seer.
>
> (*Rgveda*, 10:125:5)[1]

I

Kālidāsa's status as the major poet and dramatist in classical Sanskrit literature is unquestioned.

> Once, when poets were counted, Kālidāsa occupied the little finger; the ring finger remains unnamed true to its name; for his second has not been found.[2]

That is high praise. Kālidāsa's accomplishment is distinguished not only by the excellence of the individual works, but by the many-sided talent which the whole achievement displays. He is a dramatist, a writer of epic and a lyric poet of extraordinary scope. In his hands the language attained a remarkable flexibility, becoming an instrument capable of sounding many moods and nuances of feeling; a language that is limpid and flowing, musical, uncluttered by the verbal virtuosities indulged in by many writers who followed him; yet, remaining a language loaded in every rift with the rich ores of the literary and mythical allusiveness of his cultural heritage. By welding different elements to create new genres, his importance as an innovator in the history of Sanskrit literature is clearly established. The brilliant medieval lyric poet, Jayadeva, in praising Kālidāsa as *Kavi-kula-guru* (Master of Poets), conveys his recognition of this aspect of the poet's greatness. Bāṇa, the celebrated author of the prose-romance, *Kādambarī*, exclaimed:

Who is not delighted when Kālidāsa's perfect verses spring forth in their sweetness, like honey-filled clusters of flowers?

thus drawing attention to the exquisite craftsmanship of the poet's verse. For nearly two millennia, Kālidāsa's works have been read with deep appreciation, widely commented upon and lavishly praised. It would be safe to assume that the poet enjoyed success, fame and affluence during his lifetime. We sense no hint of dissatisfaction in his works, no sign of bitterness at not receiving due recognition. Yet, we do not possess any information about him, his life and the times in which that life unfolded and fulfilled itself. All we are left with are a few legends. The poet has drawn a veil of silence round himself so complete that even his real name is unknown to posterity.

No name is affixed to the poems and the epic; they have come down to us virtually anonymous. What information we possess is derived from references to them by later poets[3] and writers[4] and the commentaries written on them and from inscriptions.[5] The name is met with only in the plays, where in each prologue, the author styles himself as Kālidāsa. Like others in Sanskrit literature, this name is descriptive: Vyāsa, meaning 'the compiler', is the author of the *Mahābhārata*; Vālmīki, 'he who emerged from the anthill (*valmīka*)', of the *Rāmāyana*; similarly Kāli-dāsa means the votary or servant of Kālī. Kālī is time in the feminine (Kāla is time); the concept of Time as a creative principle is as old as the Vedas.[6] We can then translate the name Kāli-dāsa as 'the servant of Time', a phrase that prompts us to explore its significance.

Kāla and Mahākāla are among the many names given to Śiva, the Absolute; the many names given to godhead are descriptive of its different aspects and functions as seen in the world of phenomena and apprehended by the human consciousness. Formless, eternal, One, Śiva is pure consciousness, the changeless reality behind the manifold changing world that is brought into being by his inherent power or Śaktī—cosmic energy. Kālī is one of the many names of Śakti; the names descriptive of the creative power are the feminine forms of the words pertaining to the many aspects and functions of the unitive godhead: Śivānī, Bhavānī, Kālī, Mahākālī, derived from Śiva, Bhava, Kāla and Mahākāla, define the feminine, creative aspect of the One. In iconography this concept is imaged as Ardhanarīsvara—the Lord whose one half is woman. Śiva and Śakti are therefore one indivisible Whole.

The natural consequence of the poet's reticence is that a number of legends have gathered round his name. One of them presents him as a simple, unlettered Brahmin youth of uncommon beauty and grace of manner, who was orphaned at six months and brought up by the driver of an ox-cart. Through devout prayer and worship of the goddess Kālī, he obtained profound learning and the gift of poetry and is said to have assumed the name of Kāli-dāsa—'the servant of Time' or 'the servant of Creative Power'.

Legends surround the name and fame of many ancient writers. A popular legend speaks of the transformation of the author of the *Rāmāyana* from a cruel highway robber to a great and holy sage. It is said that, repenting of his misdeeds, the robber performed severe austerities over such a long period of time that his body was buried in an anthill that formed round it. Emerging from it finally enlightened, he assumed the name Vālmīki. The description of an ascetic in Mārīca's hermitage seems to contain an allusion to this legendary happening (*Sak.*: 7:11). Rather than dismissing them summarily as apocryphal, such legends are better read as metaphors for the divine inspiration that is seen to lie behind poetic composition and as underlining that powerful vision and extraordinary felicity of expression that some poets possess more than others. They are perceived as being born again touched by the divine fire; the new name is assumed to indicate this and identifies their initiation into their calling. The legends surround them with an aura of the miraculous that sets them apart as vehicles of the Holy Power of the creative word, *Vāc*.

Some Sanskritists in fixing Kālidāsa's dates, have theorized that his works contain veiled references to his patron, King Vikramāditya of Ujjayinī with whom Indian tradition associates the poet, and base their identifications of this king accordingly. If this were the case, it would be reasonable to assume that the poet may well have left a few clues about himself, his family and birthplace in his works that we could all then set out happily to discover. But he has not. All this points to something of significance; that it was the poet's deliberate decision to strip his texts of all biographical detail, veiled or otherwise. In its turn, this decision must be seen as indicative of Kālidāsa's attitude to his writing. It suggests that he did not choose to situate it in his individual personality and relate it definitively to his own life and times, but projected himself as a medium, a voice. The poet has effaced the authority of his own voice from his texts. It is open to the reader to see this self-effacement from a metaphysical point of view as a transference of authority to a voice beyond Time, to 'the voice of Silence'[7] that shaped the universe: or to perceive the texts as situated within time and responsive to cultural shifts in the course of time but not fixed in any specific context. The name Kāli-dāsa would relate equally to both meanings of the word *Kālī* in the name: Creative Power and Time.

To look at the first of the possibilities: *Vāc,*[8] the Śakti or inherent power of the Supreme Spirit in the Vedas, speaks through the poet who has constituted himself as a medium. And in so doing, Kālidāsa places himself in the ancient tradition of the Vedic poet-seers who saw themselves as speaking the Word and uttering the Truth. Looking deep within, into the depths of their consciousness,[9] they saw the light that never was on sea or land and expressed the vision they discovered there 'for all ages to come'.[10] The Word reveals the unseen through the seen,[11] using the language of metaphor, and links the transcendent with the transient. The poet, *Kavi* (from which the word *kāvya* for poetry is derived), establishes communion between the two worlds, between men and gods.[12]

The second possibility is particularly useful in the interpretation of Kālidāsa's plays by enabling the reader to adopt readings other than or in addition to the strictly historical one that places them in the framework of the poet's milieu and the poetics that were current in his age. There is more in a great work of art than can be compassed in any single mode of interpretation that sets out to explore its significances.

A classic does not simply belong to its own time. The very definition of a classic implies the recognition that it speaks to all ages, despite the complex ways in which it relates to and reflects the specific circumstances of the world in which it originated. A classic work must carry within itself the potentialities for relevance to future generations of readers in different cultural contexts. The very lack of biographical detail, the self-effacement of the author, frees his texts from a specific context with its own social and literary codes. Drama, which is the most socially-oriented of literary forms, comes across with an immediacy to audiences, even when their responses are shaped and ordered by social and literary codes different from those in which it was imbedded. While placing *Śakuntalā* in a particular set of poetics is no doubt useful and interesting as providing a historical *reading*, it is more illuminating and rewarding to see the play's accomplishment as lying in the manner in which it escapes the constraints of those poetics even as it acknowledges them.

II

Kālidāsa's dates have not been established conclusively. Three dates have been put forward, none of them even remotely exact, and spanning centuries:

(i) The second century BC, the period of the Śuṅga Empire which held power roughly from 184 BC to 78 BC over most of northern and central India, ruling from Pātalīputra, the imperial capital (modern Patna). Kālidāsa is believed to have been the court-poet of Agnimitra Śuṅga who ruled as his father's viceroy at Ujjayinī, the second and western capital of the empire. He is the hero of Kālidāsa's first play, *Mālavikāgnimitram,* a romance with a historical basis.

(ii) The first century BC, in the reign of the celebrated Vikramāditya of story and legend who ruled at Ujjayinī and is believed to have founded the Vikrama era (still used in the country) in 57 BC to commemorate his victory over the Śaka (Scythians) invaders of Malwa. A long and persistent Indian tradition associates Kālidāsa with this monarch, making him Vikramāditya's court-poet.

(iii) The fourth to fifth centuries AD, during the period of the Gupta Empire, in the reign of Chandra Gupta II, who assumed the title of Vikramāditya, or the Sun of Valour, after he had completely overthrown the Śaka power in western India.

These dates are discussed briefly in Appendix I.

It is only too obvious that Kālidāsa's birthplace is not known for certain. Various regions in the country have laid claim to the honour of being the poet's place of birth. It is clear though, from reading his works, that the greater part of his life must have been spent in Malwa (ancient Avanti); and that in the deepest sense, Ujjayinī, of which he writes with such affection and pride, was the poet's own city. 'Indeed, you would have lived in vain', says the Yakṣa to the rain cloud, admonishing it not to miss the chance of a visit

to Ujjayinī glowing in splendour
like a brilliant piece of Paradise
come down to earth with traces of merits
of dwellers in Paradise returning,
the fruit of their good deeds almost spent.

(*Meghadūtam*, st. 30)

The two poems in this volume reveal an intimate knowledge of the region of the Vindhya mountains. The poet describes the topography of the Vindhyas and the Malwa region with a loving exactitude as if the landscape lay on the palm of his hand. Malwa, in central India (now part of Madhya Pradesh), is watered by many rivers and streams, rising from the Vindhya ranges and draining its slopes and valleys. Malwa's landscapes streaked by its many rivers and streams with glades and pleasure-gardens on their banks; dotted with groves and meadows and woodlands stretching along the slopes of the hills; its holy spots and long low hills containing caves overgrown with bushes,[13] stir the poet's imagination and evoke in us the beauty that once was. It may well be that the poet belonged to this region and that Ujjayinī was his place of birth.

Ujjayinī was one of the great cities of ancient India with a continuous history of centuries as the capital of powerful kingdoms such as few cities possessed; it was during most of its history a cultural and commercial centre. Among its many names were: Viśālā, the wide and gracious city; Puṣkaraṇdini, the city of flowers; Mahākāla-purī, the city of Mahākāla (Śiva). Lying at the junction of the two great trade routes of ancient India, the east-west and north-south routes with their network of branches, Ujjayinī grew wealthy and prosperous. The trade routes connected the imperial capital of Pātalīputra (Patna) at the confluence of the Gangā[14] and the Son to various regions within the country; to the Arabian Sea ports such as Broach and Pātāla that carried the extensive overseas trade to Alexandria and Rome; and to the caravan routes extending west through the Kabul valley to the Mediterranean. Ujjayinī was the emporium of its time. The city was long a centre of learning and intellectual activity; an observatory had been built fairly early in its history and the prime meridian passed through the city, making Ujjayinī the Greenwich of ancient India. It was one of the earliest centres of importance for Buddhism, with some of Buddha's first disciples belonging to Ujjayinī; Jainism was well established.

Judging from the antiquity and great sanctity of the Mahākāla shrine, it is conceivable that the worship of Śiva was predominant.

Ujjayinī's splendour and opulence are reflected in Kālidāsa's writings. Its mansions and groves, its palaces and pleasure-gardens are described in vivid detail in the two poems in this volume. The glowing descriptions of the palaces and gardens in the dream-city of Alakā in *Meghadūtam*, as well as those of King Duhṣanta in *Śakuntalā*, who is a monarch of the mythic past, might have been drawn from those that made Ujjayinī splendid and beautiful in the poet's own times. But it is also likely that the poet was drawing on his literary reminiscences of the epics; some of the details of his descriptions, e.g., of the Yakṣa's mansion and gardens in Alakā and of the Vindhyan landscapes in *Ṛtusamhāram* are self-consciously allusive, but with the jewelled perfection that is all the poet's own.

> And Maya built in the Assembly Hall, a lotus pool peerless in beauty paved with priceless gems and studded with pearl-drops; therein bloomed lotuses with leaves of beryl and stalks of gems; a flight of crystal steps led down to brimming waters translucent in all seasons, stirred by lotus-scented breezes; abounding in many kinds of water-birds, turtles and fishes. . . . Surrounding the Hall were thick groves, beautiful, dark-blue, providing cool shade with many kinds of great trees ever blooming, redolent of flower-fragrances; and dotted all around with pools of blue waters haunted by wild geese, teals and red geese.
>
> (*Mbh.*: 2:3:23–26)

There are also verbal echoes of passages in the *Rāmāyana*, describing the palaces and gardens of Ravana's capital, Lankā.[15]

However, Kālidāsa celebrates the glory of Ujjayinī not only for its beauty and wealth, but also because it is a place of hierophany. It is one of the twelve hierophanic spots in the country, where Śiva, the Absolute, descended into Time and Space to abide as a terrestrial presence for the 'salvation of the godly'. Such a city, wealthy and cosmopolitan, possesss-ing a rich culture and a cultivated audience belonging to a leisured class and with a splendid court and merchant-guilds to provide patronage for the arts, would have been the ideal centre for the flowering of drama. Legends speak of the brilliant court of King Vikramāditya, learned, wise and generous, patron of poets and scholars. Some of the great dramas are laid in Ujjayinī; others build their plots round the life of the beautiful princess, Vāsava-dattā of Ujjayinī, daughter of the ruler of Avanti in the time of Buddha.

Though it cannot be stated with any certainty, Sanskrit drama probably developed in Ujjayinī under the patronage of the kings and merchant princes of that region. There is an interesting piece of information in Bāṇa's *Life of Harṣa*[16] where he mentions that Sumitra, the son of Agnimitra, who took great delight in drama, was attacked 'in the midst of actors', by one Mitradeva and had his head 'shorn off with a scimitar as if it were a lotus-stalk'. Sumitra is called Vasumitra in Kālidāsa's first play (*Mālavikāgnimitram*) and is the fourth Śunga emperor of the first century BC at which time it is highly probable that the capital had been shifted from Pātalīputra in the east to Ujjayinī. We can imagine that an emperor who was an enthusiastic patron of drama might have been present at a rehearsal or might even have been trying out a role himself. Kālidāsa's play, *Mālavikāgnimitram*, opens with a scene in the theatre attached to the palace, where the King and Queen are watching a dance performance by the heroine, Mālavikā, complete with music and other accompaniments. The theatre with its easily accessible costumes and props would certainly have been a most convenient place to plan and effect an assassination of a monarch who would otherwise have been heavily guarded.

This little anecdote in Bāṇa's work provides a possible date for the classical drama as we have it now. Fragments of plays written on palm leaves in the Kushan script, discovered in Turfan, Central Asia, and attributed to Aśvaghoṣa, the Buddhist philosopher and poet, show that the form of classical drama was well established by that time. Aśvaghoṣa's dates have been fixed in the period of the first century BC to the first century AD. The relative chronology of Aśvaghoṣa and Kālidāsa is disputed; but it is not unlikely that Kālidāsa is earlier than Aśvaghoṣa.

III

The origins of drama in India are shrouded in antiquity. Space does not permit a detailed discussion of the problem here, but some of the influences that directed its evolution might be outlined briefly. Three avenues may be explored: the Vedas, the epics and the dance.

The *Nāṭyaśāstra* (*The Treatise on Drama*) of Bharata, the oldest surviving text of the theory of drama and dramatics, claims a divine origin for itself. It styles itself as a fifth Veda, accessible to all, including those who were precluded from the study of the four Vedas,[17] like women and Śūdras; and sets out to instruct through pleasure. Brahmā, the creator, took elements out of the existing four Vedas to create this new fifth Veda known as *Nāṭyaveda.* Among its aims, as set out in the first chapter, are: to represent the ways of the world, both good and bad; to give good advice and provide enlightenment through entertainment; to bring peace of mind to those afflicted with the ills of the world and its many problems. Drama represents a generalized view of the world and the actions of persons divested of particularities of character; it does not deal with individuals and their specific situations and emotions. The chief goal of drama is to produce *rasa*, the aesthetic emotion, evoked by the appropriate mood built cumulatively through not only words, but also by mime and gesture, music and dance, costume and jewellery. *Rasa* is not raw emotion but emotion depersonalized, divested of all the accidents of circumstance; it is emotion re-presented, distilled by art. Sanskrit drama is therefore a blend of many elements: verse and prose, dance, music and spectacle. The *Nāṭyaśāstra* treats poetry, music and dance as one art. The words *naṭa* (actor, dancer, mime), *nāṭya* (dancing, dramatic art) and *nāṭaka* (play) all derive from one root, *naṭ*, to act or represent.

The *Nāṭyaśāstra* is obviously either a compilation of texts that existed prior to it in one form or another, or a systematic arrangement and organization of a body of floating theories and practices. In its present form it might well be later than Kālidāsa, depending on which century we choose to place the poet in. It is possible that the author of the *Nāṭyaśāstra* sat down to compose his treatise with Kālidāsa's plays before him. That a creative writer of Kālidāsa's genius and accomplishment would write according to the book is not very likely; it seems more plausible that a critic and theorist would draw upon the work of a great writer to formulate his theories.

Though we might be grappling with uncertainties because there is no concrete evidence to draw a clear line of descent from one to the other, the origins of drama could be traced back to the Vedas. In the *Ṛgveda* we find a number of poems with dramatic elements in them: dialogues such as the lively debate between Saramā, the hound of heaven and the Paṇis[18]—traders or demons of darkness—over wealth or tribute, where promises of friendship and veiled threats of hostilities are traded; the dialogue between Urvaśī, a celestial nymph, and the mythic king Purūravas,[19] which is the distant source of Kālidāsa's second play, *Vikramorvaśīyam*; monologues like the declamation of *Vāc* proclaiming her role in the creation of the universe;[20] soliloquies like Vasiṣṭa's,[21] a cry of despair rising out of a profound sense of alienation from the divine presence. In some of the poems in this group there are three or more voices speaking; and a few contain the germ of a story or a cryptic reference to an event, that could develop into a plot in the hands of a great dramatist—this is what did happen to the Urvaśī-Purūravas dialogue when Kālidāsa fleshed out the bare bones of the legend (or myth) into a delightful, lyrical play.

The Vedic hymns were chanted and sung by several voices and the presence of a refrain[22] in some suggests a choral element. The rituals themselves of the great sacrifices—and there were many of them extending over days and even longer periods—have a dramatic character because the complex round of ceremonies that accompanied the chanting contained an element of dramatic representation. The rituals are a re-enactment of cosmic events; the re-enactment is the essence of the Vedic sacrifice (*yajna*). It is conceivable that the priests officiating at the sacrifices played the roles of gods (*devas*) and seers (*sādhyas*) in re-enacting the cosmic events. There is mention in Vedic literature of maidens, beautifully dressed and jewelled, singing and dancing and circling the sacred altars with jars of holy water in their hands. A chariot race is mentioned, as well as a contest between a fair Vaiśya and a dark Śūdra for the possession of a round white skin symbolizing the sun (Light). These imply a certain amount of action that must have accompanied the chanting of the sacred verses and the performance of the rituals; a notion of conflict or contest is also implied—an essential element in drama.

It is suggested that the Urvaśī-Purūravas poem was a 'staged dialogue . . . a dramatic substitute for what had originally been the sacrifice of a male in a fertility rite after a sacred ritual wedding',[23] and that the theme of separated lovers derives from this. But it seems that the theme of separation and reunion of lovers also belongs to folk and fairy tale. However, the first part of the suggestion points to the possibility that the vegetation and fertility cults of the ancient world are among the contributing factors in the evolution of classical drama. It is interesting to note in this connection that the medieval and modern religious drama relating to Kṛṣṇa's nativity and exploits, culminating in the slaying of the cruel Kamsa by Kṛṣṇa, displays a ritual aspect that connects it to ancient vegetation cults. *The Binding of Bali* and *Kamsa's Slaying* are two plays referred to in the literature of the second century BC; it appears that in the staging of these early religious plays the colours black and red have been used symbolically in the make-up of the actors to represent dark winter and bright summer.[24]

The *mudras* (*hastas*) or hand-gestures used and the stances adopted during the performance of Vedic rituals (they continue in use even now), were incorporated later into classical drama. Often, the stage-directions in a play indicate miming, and call for a specific *mudra*, as for instance, in *Sak.*: 6:3, the *kapota-hastaka*, the dove-shaped hand-gesture that conveys adoration or supplication, where the hands are folded together with the palms slightly hollowed and not touching but with the tips of the fingers and the base touching, so as to form the shape of a dove. However, *mudras* and stances are not only part of the ceremonies accompanying Vedic liturgy, but also of priestly rituals in temples; for instance, the waving of lights before the deity goes through an intricate sequence of movements. They also belong to the grammar and vocabulary of the dance, which is closely associated with temple-worship and with Śiva who is imaged in stone and metal as Natarāja, the Lord of Dance.

The *Nātyaśāstra* assumes the close association of Śiva with the performing arts. For Bharata, in his dialogue with Brahmā, the Creator, speaks of having witnessed the dance of Śiva (Nīla-Kaṇṭta, the blue-throated god), 'full of feeling' and expressive of the sentiments of *sṛṇgāra* (love) conveyed through graceful sequences of movement and gesture.[25] And Śiva, highly pleased with the performance of the two plays, *The Churning of the Ocean* (*Amṛtamanthana*) and *The Burning of the Triple City* (*Tripura-Daha* or *Tripura-Vijaya*)—the latter play is mentioned in *Meghadūtam* (58)—composed by Brahmā himself and performed by Bharata and his troupe on the Himalayas against the natural scenery of its 'beautiful caves and waterfalls',[26] instructs his disciple Taṇdu to teach Bharata certain dance-sequences that formed part of the 'preliminaries'[27] in the staging of a play. This statement in the *NS* suggests the coming together of two traditions in the performing arts or the influence of one upon the other.

The 'preliminaries' (*pūrva-ranga*) consist of a series of religious ceremonies with prayers and offerings of flowers to the deities, performed with specific gestures and sequences of movements to the accompaniment of music. It serves a dual purpose—framing drama in a religious setting and providing the audience with some entertainment. Sanskrit drama is secular, but there is a religious and ritual dimension to it; the association with Śiva also provides the quality of prayer to what is basically secular drama, as evidenced by the invocation at the beginning and the benediction or *Bharatavākya*, the stanza spoken by the actor at the end of a play.

Bharata is obviously an assumed name. The Bharatas were originally the rhapsodes or bards[28] of the powerful Bharata tribe celebrated in the *Ṛgveda*. A bardic ancestry is therefore implied and presupposed in the name. Later, the word came to signify an actor. The bardic tradition of the epics had a strong influence on the development of drama. In the *Mahābhārata*, bards recite the story of the Great War and the events that led up to it, to Janamejaya, the great-grandson of Arjuna, the foremost warrior in that war. And the recital takes place at the performance of a great sacrifice. The story of Rāma and Sītā is recited by their sons Kuśa and Lava (*kuśi-lava*),[29] at their father's court before they are recognized and acknowledged. Recitations of stories may have taken the form of several voices delivering different parts of the narrative or of speaking the parts of the different characters and accompanying their recitals with appropriate gestures and facial expressions. Recitations of the epics continued to be popular forms of entertainment (and instruction) for centuries and have continued right to this day in temples and village squares.[30] The epics stand solidly behind classical literature in both drama and the long poem (*mahākāvya*). The plots of several plays and poems are taken from them.

Dancing figures found at Mohenjo-Daro[31] point to the antiquity of the dance as an art-form in India. The flexion of the torso of the male dancer, and the stance, the pert look and the hint of a smile worn by the little metal statuette of a dancing-girl, right arm on the hip, left arm loaded with bracelets, legs slightly bent at the knees, resemble stances and facial expressions that are still part of the language of the classical dance. The dance is an art-form that blends the lyrical and narrative modes, conveying them through mime and gesture articulated within the metrical pattern of the footwork. The dance also provides the elements of ritual and stylization to drama.

It would appear then that many of the elements of drama were already in place at a very early time, perhaps by the middle of the first millenium BC, at the time of Panini, the great grammarian who was also a poet. With various traditions converging around this time: the literary tradition of the Vedas and epics, the popular and folk play traditions centering perhaps round vegetation rites and festivals such as sowing and harvesting, the ritual drama and the dance with its story-line, it was inevitable that drama as we understand it should have been evolving into its final form. The moment was ripe for the emergence of a new art-form—the drama. All that was needed was the man of genius who could weld the different elements at hand to create the *nātaka* as we know it (a term loosely translated into English as drama or a play).[32] In the prologue to *Malavikāgnimitram*, Kālidāsa names his predecessors Bhāsa, Saumilla, Kaviputra 'and others'. While we shall never know whether one of these named or one of 'the others' who might have come earlier, was the author of the first play, we can be certain that in Kālidāsa's hands, drama reached a high peak of achievement.

The *Nātyaśāstra* is a compendious treatise on practically all the literary aspects of drama and all matters relating to the theatre, from the construction of the playhouse or *nātyamandapa* to audience-response.

Chapter 2 of the text gives us a general idea of the ancient Sanskrit theatre but we cannot claim to have a clear and accurate picture of it in all its details, because some passages are not very clear in their meaning and certain technical terms are variously interpreted by scholars.

> The *nātyamandapa* (playhouse) should be designed in the shape of a mountain cave, have two ground-levels, small windows, and be free from gusts of wind (drafts), so that the voices of the actors and singers as well as the sound of the musical instruments will be resonant.
>
> (*Natyaśastra*: 2:80–82)

The 'shape of a mountain cave' is an interesting detail, because not only does it reveal an awareness of the acoustical properties of structures but it also suggests that originally shows and spectacles and even plays might have been presented in cave-theatres.

The playhouse was built of close-set bricks of fine quality, on level ground, and faced east. The walls were plastered and then whitewashed; the inner walls were covered with beautiful paintings of sinuous, meandering vines and of men and women enjoying themselves. It is clear that Bharata intended the playhouse to be not merely a place of entertainment but one with aesthetic appeal. Carved figures of elephants, tigers and snakes and statues (on pedestals?) were required to be placed at different spots in the theatre. Architectural features and details were both functional and decorative: mouldings and supports in decorative woodwork are mentioned; ornamental turrets, balconies, railings, roundels and pedestals, niches, brackets, lattices, ornamental windows (*gavākṣa*: shaped like the eye of a cow) that were mechanically operated are some of the details of interior decoration mentioned.[33] Pillars are described as raised at different levels and beautifully carved with figures of women by the side of trees;[34] these remind us of the carvings and sculptured figures of *yakṣīs* and *vṛkṣakas* (tree-divinities) at Bhārhut and Sāncī and Mathura.

The text mentions three shapes of playhouses: oblong, square, triangular, and some verses suggest that a type of thrust-stage might have been in use. Three sizes are also mentioned. But Bharata strongly recommends that the medium-sized playhouse of 96 feet by 48 feet is the most suitable, because: 'in a larger playhouse, the voice will not carry far; it will lose its quality of tone and become weak and indistinct'; and due to its large size the subtle play of expressions on the face that are the means to convey the emotions and produce the *rasas* will not be seen clearly by the spectators sitting towards the back (*NS*: 2:28–20).

The playhouse was divided into two equal halves, the auditorium and the stage with the greenroom behind it, each 48 feet by 48 feet, if we take the medium-sized playhouse as the model. The auditorium had seats of brick and wood arranged in rising tiers 'like a staircase'.

The stage was raised 27 inches off the floor of the auditorium and demarcated into the front stage which was the acting area for the most part and the back stage where the musicians and drummers were seated. Jewels and precious gems were placed underneath the stage during the building of the playhouse according to prescriptions based on their auspiciousness. A wall with two doors, one for the entry and the other for the exit of actors, separated the stage from the greenroom. A curtain of rich material hung before the doors; off-stage effects might have been produced either in the space behind the curtain or in the greenroom itself: e.g., Hamsavatī's song and the bards' praise-songs in Act 5 of *Śakuntalā*; the mystic voice in Act 4 that announces to sage Kaṇva that his daughter is pregnant with Duhṣanta's son.

There was little or no scenery, and a minimum of props made of light materials were used. Language, therefore, became very important as in the Elizabethan theatre; the imagery painted the scenes and much was left to the imagination of the spectator. We see instances of this use of language in Act I of *Śakuntalā*, where the King as soon as he enters describes the fleeing deer and a little later he describes in detail the outskirts of the hermitage (1:12,13).

Sanskrit drama clearly reveals its dance-origins; miming is often indicated by the stage-directions. Dance is very much a part of it; the whole of the fourth act in *Urvaśī*, in the Bengal recension, comprises song and dance interspersed with snatches of prose as the King wanders around demented. Even where there is no formal dancing as such, it is clear that Sanskrit drama leans heavily on dance-technique: the stances adopted by the various characters, their gestures, facial expressions, their very gait and style of walking, belong to the grammar and vocabulary of the dance. There is little that is naturalistic about the dramatic art of the Sanskrit theatre.

Dramatic performances were usually held on special occasions: coronations and other royal events, great weddings, religious festivals and fairs. Private theatres, beautifully decorated, would have existed in the royal palace, mansions of nobles and merchants and perhaps in guild halls. The audience would have been select, comprising the few and fit. Open-air performances are also known, which were probably staged in front of temples or in their quadrangles, with large, mixed audiences. There might have been open-air theatres also. Bhavabhūti's play *Mālati-Mādhava* was performed for the festival of Kāla-priya-nātha (Śiva). But we do not know whether it was staged in an open-air theatre or in the temple-square.

Women played the female roles. Bharata is mentioned as putting it to Brahmā that drama could not be presented successfully without actresses and Brahmā, seeing the point made, created *apsarās* (celestial nymphs) for this purpose. But we find that in *Mālatī-Mādhava* the director (*sūtradhāra*) and his assistant take on female roles.

Certain stage-directions are conventional: 'enter with a toss of the curtain' indicates hurry, excitement, agitation; 'walk around' and 'turn around' indicate changes of location.

Costuming, jewellery and hair-styles were important, serving as the means of ethnic, regional and hierarchical signification; they also represented emotional states: for instance, 'Enter the King *costumed* as suffering from remorse' in *Śak.*: 6:5, and 'Enter Śakuntalā with her hair done in a single braid' to signify the grief of a woman separated from her husband (7:21).

Colour was used symbolically, both in the costumes and the make-up. Faces may have been painted, as is still done in the Kathakali and Chhau dance-forms. Four main colours, blue, red, yellow, black and four combinations of these, grey, gold, green and pink, appear to have been in use; other colours are also mentioned as blends of these.

Masks may have also been in use. The use of masks that rightly belongs to ritual drama, is significant, because the mask covers and transforms. It signifies the de-personalization of the actor and his transformation into a fictive character. The actor steps into the role assigned to him the moment the mask or make-up and the costume are put on, to *become* the character. All these external trappings of a character immediately convey a great deal about the play and the story to the least educated and unsophisticated among the audience.

Stylization in speech and acting, the symbolic use of colour, the use of masks (made up of paint and also of materials) and of dance and miming, all serve to distance the play-world of drama and separate it from the everyday world. The classical drama of India uses Prākrits or regional dialects as well as Sanskrit, which is spoken by Brahmins, kings and high officials. Women (even queens), children and the court-jester (*vidūṣaka*) speak Prākrit; low characters like the fishermen and policemen in Act 6 of *Śakuntalā* also speak in dialect. This provides Sanskrit plays with a rich variety in speech, but it is not possible to make the differentiation between the classical language and the dialects and between the dialects themselves in translation.

To what extent classical drama was a form of popular entertainment is hard to say. The relatively small size of the playhouse, whose seating capacity could hardly have exceeded 400, makes the Sanskrit theatre an intimate one with a small, select audience. The open-air theatres would have drawn a much larger and mixed audience but nothing definite can be said on this point.

IV

Turning to lyric poetry, the line of descent seems somewhat clearer than in drama. The *Rgveda* contains a few true lyrics of which *Rātri* (*Night*)[35] and *Aranyānī* (*The Spirit of the Woods*)[36] are notable. The hymns to *Uṣas* (*Dawn*) and the lovely marriage hymn, *Suryā's Bridal*,[37] are lyrical in tone. The *Atharvaveda* contains the beautiful *Pṛthvīsūkta* (*Ode to Earth*).[38]

Kālidāsa's poetry forms a kind of watershed in the vast terrain of classical literature, within which his finest poem, *Meghadūtam*, has a special place, standing as it does at the end of a long tradition of the narrative-dramatic poetry of the first millennium BC and at the head of a new tradition of lyric poetry.[39] His earlier poem, the epic, *Raghuvamśam*, brings to a close the great epic-saga tradition of the *Rāmāyana* and the *Mahābhārata*, with its emphasis on action, its exalted and heroic theme, its alternating narrative and dramatic styles and its story-within-story structure. But it also differs from that tradition. The poet places his own unique stamp on this new epic. The epic *Raghuvamśam* (*Raghu's Dynasty*), has the exalted theme: the rise and fall of an empire, the greatest of the solar dynasty; the lives and exploits of heroes, chiefly of Raghu, the most exalted of these heroes. He is portrayed as the ideal blend of a conquering warrior and a just and compassionate King. The epic lays out the ideal of kingship and holds the mirror up to princes. But it is more in the nature of a chronicle; character is not pitted against character; there is no play of opposing forces. Built on righteousness and the heroic valour of warrior-kings, the dynasty goes through a series of rulers of little note and no achievement and comes to an ignoble end with the reign of the last ruler, Agni-varṇa, a hedonist with no ideals, unmindful of his glorious heritage and of the interests of his subjects (he puts his foot out of the window of the royal balcony of audience for his subjects to pay homage to), a dissolute monarch who spends his brief life in a whirl of dissipation until it peters out in the silence of death. Secretly consigning his body to the flames, the council of ministers carry on, having consecrated the pregnant Queen and placed her on the throne. The last stanzas of canto 19 are filled with a quiet bitterness and the epic ends abruptly, incomplete and inconclusive.

The *Mahābhārata* and the *Rāmāyana* have lyrical passages interspersed in the narrative; however, these are not integral but peripheral concerns in the main thrust of the work. *Meghadūtam* (and to a lesser extent *Ṛtusamhāram*) announces a new poetic movement: a lyrical mode laying emphasis on exhibiting subtle emotional nuances rather than on weaving the story-line. As the mind turns inward, the imagination does not engage itself with the clash of external events of feuds and wars and the intricacies of power struggles that lead up to them, as the epics do, but plays delicately on the surface of the inner drama. Action is internalized. *Sṛṇgāra* (love) becomes the dominant emotional mode; the single stanza comes into its own to possess its autonomy. Though the stanzas are units in a long poem, each stanza is exquisitely crafted round one image, one feeling, one instant of experience.

V

The poet has left us seven works: three long lyrical poems, three plays and an incomplete epic. Their chronology is uncertain.

Poems	*Ṛtusamhāram*	*The Gathering of the Seasons*
	Kumārasambhavam	*The Birth of Kumāra* or *The Birth of the Son*
	Meghadūtam	*The Cloud Messenger*
Plays	*Mālavikāgnimitram*	*Mālavikā and Agnimitra*
	Vikramorvaśiyam	*Urvaśī Won by Valour*
	Abhijnānaśākuntalam	*The Recognition of Śakuntalā*
Epic	*Raghuvamśam*	*Raghu's Dynasty*

Ṛtusamhāram is an early effort, perhaps the poet's first that looks forward to the greater work to come; but it is by no means to be read as an apprentice effort. It is an accomplished poem, brilliant in parts. What strikes the reader immediately is the extraordinary particularity with which the world of nature is observed in all its variousness in the changing seasons: parched under the burning sun and devastating drought, revived and renewed in the rains with brilliant colours splashed all around; mellow in autumn's golden plenitude; shivering and pale under the wintry moon's icy glitter. Each season leaves on the landscape its impress of beauty caught in the glowing imagery.

The poem is both naturalistic and stylized. What the poet's eye notes with such loving precision is expressed in highly stylized imagery and diction that anticipate the more sophisticated and richly textured poetry of *Meghadūtam* and the intricate harmonies of *Śakuntalā*. The vision deepens and ambivalences render the structure and meaning of the later works more complex, but the keenness of observation of nature and the rich detail with which it is rendered is not excelled in any of them.

The poem is not simply a description of nature; it is an interweaving of the beauty of nature and woman, with the emotional response to both.

Dotting the woodlands are charming glades besides streams
haunted by timorous gazelles easily alarmed
—tremulous eyes like deep-blue water lilies enchanting—
and the heart is twisted with sudden longing.
(2:9)

An interesting point to note here and in other places in the poem, e.g., 6:18, is the direct address to the beloved in the second half of the stanza; the speaker turns to her from the scene they are both watching, to *tell* her of nature's beauty that images her own. It is in the nature of an 'aside', a comment bringing together the beloved and the gazelle, both shy and timid and possessing liquid, lustrous eyes, and the blue lily trembling in the pool; all three objects compared have one thing in common, the tremulous petal-eyes.

Whereas the beauty of nature magically heightens the loveliness of woman, transforming her into an enchantress, she in turn serves as an ornament for it. Beautifully dressed and jewelled, she provides the colour, glow and fragrance absent from nature when the cool seasons (cantos 4 and 5) etch the landscape in muted tones. Nature and woman complement each other, each enhancing the other's charm.

Analogies are drawn constantly between the natural and human worlds: men who have to travel far from home mourn desolate.

Seeing the glow of the beloved's dark eyes
in the blue-lotuses;
hearing the tones of her gold girdle bells

in the love-mad murmur of wild geese;
recalling the rich red of her lower lip
in the Bandhūka's flame-clusters . . . .
(3:24)

The two worlds interact. The flower-scented breezes and the enchanting twilights jewelled by the moon and stars kindle passion in man; the breezes *consort* with lotuses and wipe away their tears of dew-drops; clouds lean over to kiss the hills. The season steps in to deck lovely women with the prettiest and freshest flowers as a lover does and the wild forest-fire leaps up, 'smitten with longing', to clasp the greenery of the woodlands in a passionate and consuming embrace. The winter of separation makes the young girl and the slender vine grow pale and wither. Man and nature together celebrate a joyous festival of love and grieve together in sorrow. In Indian thought, a sharp line is not drawn between the worlds of man and nature. The universe is one ordered *Whole* of which man is a part. Imbued with the Spirit that is transcendent and immanent, the same life-giving essence that is in man[40] circulates in every part of it. The propelling force, therefore, in Kālidāsa's poetry, is to see nature not as a setting for man and a backdrop to the human drama, but to perceive it as possessing a life of its own and as related to the human world in many complex ways.

Both woman and nature with its teeming energies are the vehicles that carry the procreative energies of *Śakti*, Śiva's inherent power. When the poet says:

Conferring the radiance of the moon
on the faces of lovely women,
the entrancing tones of wild geese
on their gem-filled anklets,
the Bandhūka's vibrant redness
on their luscious lower lip,
the splendour of bountiful Autumn
is now departing—to who knows where!
(3:25)

he is not indulging in a mere flight of poetic fancy; the philosophical assumptions of his culture are behind it. In *Ṛtusamhāram*, woman and nature borrow each other's attributes when they are not competing in a friendly manner. In *Meghadutam* woman and nature are one, the identification is complete, the landscape *is* the beloved.

Sṛṅgāra, Love, in its many aspects is a perennial theme of lyrical poetry. Love, secure and fulfilled, or thwarted, betrayed, angry and jealous, and above all, love in separation, are all given glowing and poignant expression in Kālidāsa's poetry. In *Meghadūtam*, the various moods that love displays itself in are delineated in single stanzes, each like a miniature painting (sts. 26, 30, 31, 33, 41, 42 and 43). The two poems in this volume, *Ṛtusamhāram* and *Meghadūtam*, each treats of love in its two conventional aspects, love-in-union and love-in-separation respectively, though the latter is much more than just a love-poem. However this does not in any way make the two contemporary; in fact they mark the beginning and end of Kālidāsa's poetic career. *Rtusamhāram* celebrates the fulfilment of love with hardly a trace of anguish; *Meghadūtam* is a poem of longing and separation. *Śakuntalā*, having delineated love's ecstasy and fulfilment as well as its anguish in the separation that follows the anger and bitterness of its cruel betrayal, finally gathers it all in the closing scene in an epiphanic moment of recognition, restoration and reunion. It also adds something that is not present in the other two works—the child, token of love and symbol of continuity of the family, and survival of the self.

Young in heart, as yet untroubled by the weight of thought of the later work and untouched by the pensive note present in the other two works in this volume, *Rtusamhāram* is the exuberant response of the poet in love with the world in all its beauty; and in love with love itself. Where *Meghadutam* is haunted by the loneliness of the human heart, even in the midst of the world's loveliness, *Rtusamhāram* breathes an air of pure joy. Longing—and the word occurs again and again—has lost its ache because the beloved is close at hand, seated next to the speaker of the poem. The ardent expression of love's longing and the restlessness it rouses is in fact the response of the lover to nature's beauty and the beauty of the beloved mirroring and evoking each other. Coming at the end of the stanza, it is phrased to suggest an invitation to love.

Glancing at the amaranth's blossoming sprays
glowing in exquisite loveliness just-revealed

—loveliness that rightly belongs to the beloved's face—
how can a responsive heart not flutter in pain
stung by proud Love's flying arrows, my love?

(6.18)

There is an element of hyperbole in this young lover's statements: an extravagance of emotion and gesture is displayed from time to time. We see it again in st. 20, where he indulges in a flamboyant gesture of despair to convince the beloved that he is destroyed and consumed, to die again and again for love of her.

The patterning of the poem is interesting and intricate, the complexity of which has not been noticed before. The poem has been treated mostly as showing a keen observation of nature expressed in vivid descriptions. A canto is given to each season and the moods it creates in the natural and human worlds. Each canto is a self-contained unit, opening with the traditional announcement of theme and closing with a benediction. The title, *Rtusamharam*, or *Gathering of the Seasons*, unifies the poem. Kālidasa's titles hold a significance that unfolds in the course of the work.

The new year begins with Spring around the vernal equinox. But the poem begins with Summer so as to end with Spring: an auspicious ending, for Spring is renewal. The old year is dead and the advent of Spring is welcomed with song and dance and religious ceremonies. In ancient India this was known as the Spring Festival or The Festival of Love and it was celebrated with uninhibited revelry in a carnival atmosphere.[41] New plays were written and staged as part of the festivities. The prologue to Kālidāsa's first play *Mālavikāgnimitram* mentions it as the new play presented at the Spring Festival. We know from literary references that works were commissioned for special occasions: a royal wedding, or the birth of an heir to the throne, a royal victory, or possibly celebrations in great houses. It is likely that *Ṛtusamhāram* was just such an 'occasional poem', composed for and presented at the Spring Festival, in which case it is eminently fitting that it should end with Spring and bring the celebrations to a memorable close. The closing stanza is a prayer to the god of Love, the presiding deity naturally, of the festivities, attended by his companion Spring, asking him to bestow his blessings on the beloved in the poem, and on the audience.

The opening stanzas of Summer serve as a framework for the poem, visualizing a pair of lovers, seated perhaps on a balcony or terrace, as pictured in miniature paintings centuries later. (It is important to note that the love the poet describes so ardently and in such glowing terms is married love.) This parallel should not come as a surprise because miniatures were often painted either to illustrate love-poetry or were inspired by it. Once the scene is set, the refrain is dropped so as not to constitute an intrusive element in the flow of the poem, which then moves out of the small world of the lovers into the larger world outside: to the woodlands and fields and cities, and into the worlds of other lovers. But the poem always comes back to where it started, to the lovers and the audience. In the closing stanza the speaker sums up the beauties and virtues of the season and calls down blessings on the audience and the beloved. The movement is circular. The form of each canto and the poem as a whole is also circular; circles wheeling within a circle imaging the circling year into which the seasons are *gathered.* As Time is cyclic in Indian thought, it is rewarding to see the poem and *read* it as a celebration of Time itself in its endless circling procession of nights and days, of seasons, of worlds born, dissolved and born again, until the end of time. The rhythms of the human and natural worlds image the cosmic rhythms presided over by Mahākāla,[42] the terrestrial presence of Śiva enshrined in Ujjayinī, the poet's own city.

The word *samhāram* (gathering in, or collection) in the title of the poem has a specific metaphysical meaning, of universal destruction when all creation is *drawn in* at the end of time into Śiva, its ground and source. The mystery of Śiva and his presence is never far from any of Kālidāsa's works. In them the poet is revealed as a devotee of Śiva and Devī (Śaktī). This does not imply, however, that the poet is sectarian and narrow in his religious views. Śiva is the poet's chosen form for the adoration and worship of divinity (*iṣṭa-devatā*). Hindu praxis recognizes the propensity of the human mind *to image* and provides for it in the concept of the *iṣṭa-devatā.* A form iconic or aniconic, a mental image or sound visualized, as in the word *Om* (Omkāranātha is one of Śiva's names), is chosen as the object for rites of worship and as the focus for that single-minded meditation upon the transcendent which is the first step in the path of enlightenment (*jnāna*) and release (*mōkṣa*). The form chosen is one that the devotee (or his *guru*) perceives as eminently suited to his spiritual temperament and needs.

The invocations in the plays and the epic are made to the unitive godhead, *Śiva-Śaktī*: in *Śakuntalā* and *Mālavikāgnimitram* to Śiva's eightfold form perceptible to human consciousness; in *Vikramōrvaśiyam,* to Śiva as the Primal Being spoken of in the *Upaniśads;* and in the epic the indivisible Whole is invoked as the *Word. Kumārasambhavam* is all about Śiva, the yogi and ascetic, and about the sacred marriage of Śiva and Umā[43] (Śaktī), which in Śaiva mythology and metaphysics initiates the process of creation. *Meghadūtam* reverberates with Śiva's presence.

As the chronology of Kālidāsa's works is uncertain, it is only the sense of a developing pattern in the poet's *oeuvre* that places them in a certain, tentative order. That *Mālavikāgnimitram* is an early play and that it followed *Ṛtusamhāram* is fairly certain. It was probably followed by *Vikramōrvaśiyam,* the incomplete epic *Raghuvamśam* and *Kumārasambhavam,* also incomplete. *Meghadūtam* and *Śakuntalā* are clearly the last works of the poet. In these, Kālidāsa's vision has mellowed and deepened and the language responds like a finely-tuned instrument to every touch. The unerring choice of 'the word' that expresses perfectly and precisely the intended nuance of meaning,[44] and that *oneness* of language and thought that the poet prays for in the invocation to the epic, are fully realized in these last two works.

VI

These two works, *Meghadūtam* and *Śakuntalā,* which I have placed last in order in the poet's *oeuvre,* have certain features in common: they move in several worlds and touch upon different planes of consciousness; the poetic vision they project is similar and they share a pensive and reflective tone; a fairy tale element is present in both.

In *Meghadūtam* three worlds are laid out. At the world's summit, on holy Kailāsa, instinct with Śiva's divine presence, is Alakā, the Earthly Paradise; here below, are the worlds of nature and of human experience; suspended in between as it were, is situated the elemental world of the rain cloud which mediates between the natural and the divine worlds. For the rain cloud belongs both to the natural world and the divine order that sustains it, as the poem makes clear.

Alakā is a world created by our dreams and desires where Time stands still and whose ways are untrodden by the unimaginative; where 'sensual music' fills the nights to overflowing under the moonlight (*Megh.*: 7, 68, 72). No other work of the poet reveals more clearly the blend of the erotic and spiritual that characterizes Śiva-mythology and is reflected in Kālidāsa's work; a mystic feeling for the transcendental combines with a sensuous feeling for beauty in Woman and Nature to give his poetry its distinctive quality.

The action of the play *Śakuntalā* moves out of the 'green world' of Nature, set apart and centering round the heroine who is presented as the Lady of Nature, into the gilded world of Duhṣanta's palace and pleasure-gardens, and finds its resolution in yet another world—a higher world that is inaccessible to ordinary mortals and which partakes of the quality of timelessness because it is presided over by Mārīca and Aditi, whose origins *are* before the world ever *was*; a world that is the creation of art to be held against the insistent, pushing realities and pressures of the actual world.

The movement out of the green world is accomplished with much reluctance on the heroine's part. When she disappears from view behind a line of great forest trees, the green world, magical, vanishes too. I use the word 'magical' advisedly because a magico-sacral aura surrounds the deer that 'lures' Duhṣanta into the depths of the forest. The blackbuck is a sacred animal in the Vedas. The image in 1:6 of Pinākī (Śiva) is resonant with mythical allusiveness. The myth alluded to refers to the destruction of the Sacrifice of the gods by Śiva who was enraged at being denied his share in it. The Sacrifice (*Yajna*), out of fear of Śiva's arrow, flew up into the sky in the form of a deer; Śiva, aiming his arrow at the fleeing deer, decapitated it and its head became the star *Mṛga-Śiras* (Deer's head).

When Śakuntalā leaves the hermitage and the green world vanishes, what remains is 'an empty desert', for she is the Lady of Nature. Attempts made in Act 6 to restore this world and all the 'happenings' of the initial meeting of Duhṣanta and Śakuntala that led to their love and union, fail. The re-enactment of the events turns into a 'mirage'. The image of the mirage (6:16) ought to be linked with that of 'the empty desert'. The representation of that magical world with all its details, the blossoming trees and vines, 'the full-flowing' river, the mating deer and pairs of geese on the river-bank, rendered with dead accuracy by the amateur painter and praised by a pair of art-critics belonging obviously to the school of realism, remains just that—lifeless. The illusion that Duhṣanta strives to transform into the living presence of the beloved whom he has spurned is shattered by Mādhavya's caustic wit to which nothing is sacred.

No overt comment is made about the relative merits of these several worlds, nor is a stark contrast drawn between one and the other, for it is not characteristic of Kālidāsa's poetic vision to see experience in simple black-and-white terms.

Different planes of consciousness are touched upon in these two works: dream and awakening; delusion and loss of memory; disorientation where the mind whirls around unfocussed (*bhrama*); recollection and re-cognition. Interesting observations are made about a state of mind where recollection stands on the pre-conscious threshold, inhibited from stepping over the thin line drawn by the conscious mind acting as censor for whatever reason, to produce uneasiness and perplexity, until some incontrovertible, tangible fact breaks the barrier down. We refer to such passages as the following: the beloved, distraught, forgetting the melody no sooner had she composed it; hovering uncertain 'between waking and dreaming / a day-lily on a cloudy day neither open nor shut'; and nervously pushing back her tangled braid 'off the curve of her cheek' (85, 89, 91). In *Śakuntalā*, at the beginning of Act 5, we see Duhṣanta restless and disturbed after listening to the song in the background, but not knowing why. He does not relate the 'sadness ineffable' that falls all of a sudden like a shadow over his heart, to the memory of an event in his present life—the marriage to Śakuntalā—but to one in some former life, whose memory lies buried in the unconscious. The stage-direction at this point directs the actor to portray a state of bewilderment, disorientation—*paryākula* (*Śak.*: 5.9). At the close of the act, Duhṣanta again expresses the nagging doubts that cloud his mind and we leave him in a state of brooding uncertainty.

In both works, at certain points, the line between the real and the imagined or visionary worlds is hazy and wavering. In the play, in the portrait-episode (*Śak.*: 6. i 15-24), the real and the imagined fuse. It needs the caustic comment of the realist, Mādhavya, to break them apart and demarcate them into separate areas. To him, the line between the real and the illusory (not the imagined) is hard and clear and on its farther side lies madness, to which the King is perilously close, as he, Mādhavya, views the situation.

This is especially true in *Meghadūtam*. Perceptions of reality and illusion fuse as the actual world and the imagined worlds are interfused. The poem, cast in the form of dream vision teases us into thought, into asking what the real theme of the poem is. Is it only the exteriorization of a *yakṣa's* dream of love and longing? Or is it also the realization in language, of the poet's vision of Beauty (that is also Truth) which he seeks and sees everywhere, but only in fragments, not in that perfect *wholeness* which he seeks?

> But alas! O cruel one! I see not
> your whole *likeness* anywhere in any one thing
>
> (*Megh.*: 103)

It is the poet's passionate cry that the *whole* is cruelly denied to him even as a *likeness*, an image, a reflection. Is the poet not anguishing over the barriers that confront human vision and limit the imagination?

VII

Meghadūtam is a many-layered poem of great complexity and it will be my endeavour to unravel some of this complexity and point to the several levels of discourse that operate in it shaping an intricate pattern of meaning.

The poem's sources probably lie embedded in an extensive body of popular tales, much of which has been lost.[45] The legend of the Yakṣa who was banished under a curse for neglecting the duties entrusted to him by his overlord, Kubera, might have been familiar to the poet's audience. But we do not know this for a fact.

The old Sanskrit commentaries provide the barest outline of the legend in two versions that vary slightly in detail. In one version, the Yakṣa is put in charge of Kubera's beautiful groves and gardens, especially the sacred pool of golden lotuses, the holy lake Mānasa. But being away from his post of warder for a long time, the celestial elephant Airāvata comes in one day, ravages the gardens and rooting around in the lake, as elephants tend to do, destroys the golden lotuses. This incident is reflected in st. 64 as one of the Yakṣa's many poignant memories of home. In the other version, he is entrusted with the duty of gathering fresh lotuses from this same holy pool at dawn and bringing them to Kubera to offer in worship to Śiva (see sts. 7 and 73). Reluctant to leave his wife's side so early in the morning, the

Yakṣa once picks the buds late in the evening and keeps them ready for the following morning's worship. When Kubera takes the flowers up to offer to the Lord, a bee that had been trapped in one of the shut buds flies out and bites his finger. That morning happens to be a specially sacred one, the morning of the Awakening of Viṣṇu—*Hari-Prabodhinī*—after the long *yoganidrā* (sleep) of four months (110), which makes the Yakṣa's dereliction of duty more serious. The poem does not rehearse this story; it plunges straight into the heart of the matter, the central situation where the Yakṣa, fallen from greatness, is seen pining on a far hilltop, separated from his beloved.

Yakṣas and *yakṣīs* are ancient divinities belonging to the cults and cultures of the oldest inhabitants of the land. Envisaged as centres of powers in Nature out of which flowed all the rich blessings of life, they were personified and worshipped as deities of groves and waters that they guarded (see Glossary). Temples as well as small village shrines were built for their worship (*Megh.*: 25). Divinities of the sacred grove and indwelling spirits of the great forest trees are invoked in the play to bless Śakuntalā on the eve of her departure for her royal husband's home; and they bestow rich gifts on her and pronounce their blessings for her safe and pleasant journey (*Śak.*: 4.7, 13). In *Meghadūtam*, tree-goddesses are described as sharing the grief of the speaker (106).

As forces of Nature associated with life and fertility and guardians of sacred groves and pools, *yakṣas* and *yakṣīs* would have probably figured in folk and fairy tales. In the *Mahābhārata* saga, which is a vast amalgam of many elements which include popular tale, folklore, and fairy tale and legend, there are episodes where the Pāndava heroes encounter *yakṣas* guarding pools, one of which relates to Kubera's pool of golden lotuses. Men of great stature, power and valour, and women of uncommon beauty and grace met by the heroes of epic and romance are often asked with admiring wonder if they are beings of divine origin: *yakṣa, gandharva, apsarā.*

Apsarās, 'born of the Waters', the waters of creation (see note 8), are, like *yakṣa-yakṣīs*, associated with life and fertility and seen as beneficent powers. In the earliest mention of Śakuntalā in Vedic literature, she is described as an *apsarā* who conceived and bore the great Bharata at a place called Nāḍapit.[46] In the epic, which is the direct source for the play (see

Appendix III), Śakuntalā is not an *apsarā* herself but the daughter of one and she is presented as such in the play. Kālidasa does not let us forget that the heroine is not wholly of this mortal world of ours. She belongs to two worlds, sharing in the qualities of her parents who belonged to two different worlds, invested with Nature's beauty and spontaneous creative energies as well as its holiness, and inheriting the ability for ascetic control that makes her a striking presence in the last act though she speaks few words.

Abandoned at birth, Śakuntalā is looked after by birds (*śakunta*) that encircle her protectively so that she remains unharmed until the sage Kaṇva finds her and names her Śakuntalā because she was first adopted in a sense by the birds who cared for her. She is portrayed as the Child of Nature, or the Lady of Nature, kin to all forms of life in the sacred grove. Says Śārṅgarava, hearing the cuckoo's song:

> Kin to her during her woodland sojourn
> the trees now give her leave to go
>
> (*Śak.*: 4.12)

This aspect of Śakuntalā's personality ought to be kept in mind. She brings to the King something of significance that is lacking in his life. Duhṣanta's childlessness, referred to indirectly in Act 1 in the blessings pronounced by the anchorite, and emphasized in Act 2, is a metaphor for barrenness of more than one sort. I might venture to characterize it as spiritual barrenness. Duhṣanta is led by the deer into Śakuntalā's world, the green world of nature possessing plenitude, fertility, beauty and grace, and holiness. Later, he is led into yet another world, the golden world of Mārīca and Aditi which appears to be the world of nature *perfected.* Duhṣanta's narrow and enclosed world of the gilded court, circumscribed by the round of royal ceremonies and pleasures, is thus expanded by virtue of his encounter with Śakuntalā, who is of this world, and yet not wholly of this world.

Fairy-tale elements are present in the poem as well as the play. The sacred pool of golden lotuses guarded by a Genius with specific instructions to follow, the failure to carry them out, the curse and consequent loss of love, status and superhuman powers are characteristic of folklore and fairy tale. The frame story of the lost *Bṛhat-Kathā*[47] as retold in the extant *Kathāsaritsāgara* (*The Ocean of Story-Streams*) is one such, where the speaker, an attendant of Śiva, is banished from the Divine Presence for wrongdoing and cursed to fall into the human condition. Release from the curse and restoration is promised at the expiry of a term and when certain conditions have been fulfilled.

In the play, to the curse–fall–restoration motif, certain other elements are added: the loss and discovery of the child and heir to the throne and the loss and recovery of the token of identity; a pattern of dream–illusion and of forgetfulness–recollection–re-cognition, all of which are intricately interwoven.

Folk and fairy tale contain irrational elements; they are far from being realistic and are frequently amoral in the attitudes they display. The curses in them are prime examples of this irrationality, for the punishment meted out is invariably far in excess of the wrongdoing; often punishment strikes sudden and swift even in the case of an error committed unwittingly.

These factors should be kept in mind in our approach to and interpretation of the events in the poem and the play: the Yakṣa's exile, Durvāsā's curse and Śakuntalā's repudiation by the forgetful Duhṣanta. The proneness to indulge in strictly realistic, moralistic responses, seen often in critical evaluations of our literature ought to be played down and contained in an overall view which takes into account the several elements from different cultural-literary sources that come together to shape the world of a play or a poem.

The curse itself does not lend itself to any simple explanation. It represents a whole complex of ideas, one of which would be to perceive it as the exteriorization of a state of mind where some exclusive and obsessive preoccupation results in a psychological imbalance. This is the simplistic view held by the sage Durvāsā, who is himself obsessed with a sense of his own holiness and ascetic powers. Some critics adopt an ethical view. Tagore speaks of Śakuntalā's 'Fall'[48] and her redemption through penitence; S.K. De[49] describes the curse of Durvāsā as playing 'the part of a stern but beneficient providence'. But a curse is also a metaphor for the arbitrariness of life; it points to that inexplicable, even absurd element that is of the very essence of life and which is not only beyond explanations and justifications, but beyond all comprehension. Wherever a curse operates the human failing is trivial compared to the enormity of suffering entailed. It concretizes that troubling question which faces every human being at one time or another: Why did this happen? Why does it have to be so? The curse also shapes the answer to that question in the form of that uncertain certitude with which man has to shore up his crumbling faith in order to survive, call it Fate or *Karma* or 'the absurd', or simple acceptance—'This is how things are; this is life.' Śakuntalā herself blames her own actions in a former life for her unhappiness in the present: the Yakṣa's response is acceptance, with the faith that things have to change for the better. Kālidāsa does not preach; he does not moralize. He shows us life as it is in all its beauty and splendour as well as its inexplicable vagaries which bring misfortunes deservedly or undeservedly. It is significant that the poet does not underline the Yakṣa's wrongdoing in the poem. The poem does not describe it; it merely speaks of the curse as a consequence of 'neglect of a *special charge*', a failure to perform the duties belonging to *one's own office*; the phrases italicized are the two meanings of the phrase *svādhikāra-pramādah.* (The phrase in the text—*svādhikāra-pramattah*—is the adjectival form.) In both versions of the legend provided in the old commentaries, the duties assigned to the Yakṣa appear to be a privilege and an honour bestowed on him and his failure to carry them out seems to indicate that he was insufficiently sensible of the high regard and esteem in which he was held by Kubera, his overlord. The golden lotuses are one of Kubera's 'nine treasures'—the sacred pool itself is one of the 'treasures' carefully guarded; among Kubera's many attendant-lords, it is our erring Yakṣa who is *chosen* to bring fresh lotuses each dawn to offer to the Supreme (Śiva). In this connection it is interesting to note the comment made by the King when he conveys his own awareness of the esteem in which Indra held him and which spurs him to do 'momentous deeds' (*Śak.*: 7:4). The neglect of duty under the stress of an obsessive love (or passion) that bears within itself the seeds of its own unhappiness and leads to near-tragic consequences seems to have engaged the profound concern of the poet. For we see him returning repeatedly to a consideration of it in varying situations to explore it in slightly different ways: in *Meghadūtam*, in *Śakuntalā* and in *Vikramorvaśiyam.* He touches upon it lightly in the epic.

In the poem, the reason for the curse is not explicitly stated, but we infer from the form it takes—separation from the beloved—that it was related to the Yakṣa's passionate love for her. The words used in the poem to characterize the Yakṣa are significant: *kāmī* (passionate), *kāmārta* (sick with passion); one who whispered in her ear words of no special import, only to touch her cheek with his lips (102). A curse usually deprives the person of the object that was responsible, directly or indirectly, for his or her wrongdoing. But in *Śakuntalā*, Durvāsā's curse neatly phrases the failure of duty (wrongdoing in his eyes), in balanced clauses. The punishment is far in excess of the negligence of which Śakuntalā was guilty; there were extenuating circumstances in her case. What makes the Yakṣa's dereliction of duty more serious is that it happened on a specially sacred day known and celebrated as The Awakening of Viṣṇu—*Hari-Prabodhinī* (110). However, the point that is subtly made in the play is, that Śakuntalā was also not sufficiently appreciative of the esteem in which her father held her and which prompted him to *entrust her*, rather than one of his pupils, with the important duties of welcoming guests and offering them hospitality during his absence from the Hermitage (*Śak*.: 1.12.+2,3). The word used in the text means 'put in charge' or 'appointed to'. Anasūyā has to remind her more than once of her obligations to perform the duties of hospitality and in fact, it is she and not Śakuntalā who actually performs them when the King arrives at the Hermitage as a guest. A traditional interpretation would treat the disregard to appointed duties in the cases of both the Yakṣa and Śakuntalā as a betrayal of trust.

In the other play, *Vikramorvaśīyam*, a double curse is seen operating, both called down on Urvaśī on account of the errors she commits when she is disoriented by her obsessive passion for the King. The initial curse exiles her from heaven, but out of pity, it is commuted to a limited period on earth as the wife of the King whom she loves so passionately. To celestial beings, life on earth as a mortal is tantamount to dire punishment. But here the poet balances the loss against the gain—the loss to Urvaśī of her great status in heaven and the bliss of a paradisal way of life, against fulfilment on earth of her love for the King. The second curse takes effect as a consequence of the first when Urvaśī, whose love for the King is intolerantly possessive, is seized by jealousy and rushing blindly in anger into the sacred grove of Kumāra, forbidden to women, she is at once transformed into a vine. The King himself dotes so much on Urvaśī that, leaving the governing of his kingdom to his ministers, he passes his life in a round of pleasures with her, valuing what he describes as 'desirable servitude'[50] to her more than the glory he had gained through his conquering prowess. And when he loses her he is plunged into madness.

In the epic,[51] Aja is devastated by the untimely and sudden death of his Queen, Indumatī, whom he loved to distraction. Drowned in inconsolable grief, he cannot come to terms with it despite the wise counsel of the Royal Preceptor, the sage Vasiṣṭa and he barely manages to survive to carry on as king till his son grows up to shoulder the yoke of sovereignty, at which point Aja abandons his body to rejoin his wife in the other world.

The exile theme is found in both the *Mahābhārata* and the *Rāmāyana*, but considering how frequently the motif of a curse–exile–penance following the breaking of a command is present in Sanskrit literature (the Purānas or old chronicles have many such examples, and the Purānas contain a great deal of folklore and fairy tale), I would hazard the guess that it was a motif deeply embedded in the popular imagination and used in different ways in the floating body of popular tales. But the parallel with Rāma's exile is noteworthy if only because the poet refers to it so pointedly in the opening stanza.

VIII

Meghadūtam is a *dūta-kāvyam* or messenger-poem, the first of its kind, giving rise to a spate of imitations over the centuries.[52] To call it a *dūta-kāvyam* is only to place it in a definable genre. The poem is much more than just a messenger-poem, as I shall try to indicate later on. The *Nāṭyaśāstra*[53] lists the *dūtī* or female messenger among the dramatis personae, as a character. The device is therefore well known in literature. The *Ṛgveda*, the earliest Indian text, mentions one.[54] However, while noting that in the *Ṛgveda*, the *devas* send Saramā, the hound of heaven as a messenger to the Paṇis to negotiate what would now be described as a trade deal (and a very one-sided one at that), and that in the *Mahābhārata*[55] a golden swan carries love-messages between Nala and Damayantī, it must be stressed that these parallels have little relevance in the serious consideration of our poem. In the land where the beast-fable had its origin, the idea of using a non-human messenger must have been a very old one. It was probably the most commonly used device in story-telling, and story-telling was indeed a very ancient art in India. More to the point is the parallel with Hanumān's journey from another hill not far from Rāmagiri, taking Rāma's message and his signet-ring to Sītā sorrowing in distant Lankā. The poet himself draws attention to Hanumān's meeting with Sītā in stanza 99. Further, in this *Rāmāyana*[56] episode, there is some description of the landscape and the events that happen during Hanumān's aerial flight, whereas in the Nala-Damayantī story in the *Mahābhārata*, the bird-messenger is a mere mechanical device; it is not central and integral as the cloud messenger is in our poem.

Further, the similarities between *Meghadūtam* and the *Rāmāyana* which some Sanskrit commentators point out, can be more fruitfully viewed from another standpoint, as indicative of a fundamental factor—the poem's filiation. Kālidāsa places himself firmly in the *kāvya* tradition which begins with the *Rāmāyana.* The continuity of literary tradition is proclaimed here as it is in his other works. But a great writer uses his literary inheritance in many different ways, often relating himself to it by differences rather than by similarities. Kālidāsa's poem is one of a kind, owing little to what went before and leaving nothing for what came after, having exhausted all the possibilities of the form.

In ancient cultures, non-human forms of life, birds, beasts and even trees, were believed to possess superhuman abilities and powers; to have a special kind of wisdom and bear a special relationship to sacred forces.[57] Such beliefs were part of the thought of the early Paleolithic culture of the Eurasian landmass. But to cast a rain cloud, an inanimate, elemental thing (as the poet himself reminds us in st. 5) as a messenger, is to have made a literary choice of extraordinary imaginative power and poetic sensibility. The poet dismisses the Yakṣa, it is true, at the very beginning of the poem (5) with a cavalier gesture, as one love-sick, pining on a hilltop, clouded in mind and unable to discriminate between the intelligent and the inanimate forms of life. A double purpose is served by this. The light-hearted, almost flippant gesture of dismissal is made by the poet to distance himself from his fictive creation; the authorial voice is no longer heard after this point. This is significant because in the absence of the authorial voice, we are given the option of a *reading* that is not strictly bound to the frame of reference provided by the poet's contemporary world, and are therefore able to pursue lines of interpretation and understanding of the poem which are not defined by the norms and ideals of its culture. But it is necessary to point out that an interpretation conforming to the values of that world could and ought to be held in tension with any other adopted.

Any work of art of sufficient depth does contain within itself hints of self-questioning. While it reflects its own time and landscape, it often adopts a stance that can only be defined as questioning, if not critical. A great writer does not passively accept the social mores and moral values of his world in their totality, though he may not push his implicit questioning of these to a position of articulate dissent. More about this later when assessing where and how the weight of the poetry falls. Secondly, the seeming lack of discrimination in the speaker of the poem makes the poem what it is; and the cloud, an elemental thing blended of the four elements (as all forms of life are in ancient cosmogony) becomes not only a unifying symbol in the poem, but transformed by poetic power, also a central character—the Yakṣa's 'other self'. There is a deliberate irony here which makes the conception of the cloud's role in the poem unique.

Meghadūtam is more than a poem of longing and separation with glowing descriptions of nature. Myth and legend, dream-vision and literary reminiscences are blended with topographical and conversational[58] dimensions to give a love poem depth and a multi-layered texture. Further, the lover-beloved (*nāyaka-nāyikā*) framework of the dramatic tradition in which the poem can be seen as placed in its own times is raised to another level where it is the landscape that figures as the beloved of the cloud-lover which is itself the *alter ego* of the real lover who is the speaker in the poem. The natural and physical characteristics of a rain cloud as well as its mythic associations (which we shall come to presently) are brought into play during its long course over a vast stretch of land, and constantly and consistently related through some of the most richly-textured imagery in the poet's work, to legendary and semi-historical places and personages. Many of these places are holy spots of pilgrimage; places of atonement and purification associated with persons guilty of wrong-doing of one kind or another. The poem is a totally new genre in the lyric mode.

We realize at the end, when we have completed our *reading* of the poem, that the relationships between the human and natural worlds which are explored in the way they are and the objectives set out in the poem could only have been undertaken and articulated so effectively by making a rain cloud the messenger. The appropriateness of the choice is clear when we trace the distant source for the kinship of cloud and hill which functions as a key metaphor. A Vedic text[59] tells of the myth of the ancient winged mountains, first-born of the Creator, that flew around creating hazards in mid-air, until Indra, sustainer and protector of the universe, severed their wings and fixed them to the earth like pegs; the severed wings floated free transformed into 'thunder clouds'.

Hence, they ever float over mountains; this is their origin.

The poet is able to make use of this mythic association of cloud and mountain to set up a relationship between them and by extension between the cloud and the landscape, which is a crucial one in the poem. Behind this specific and organic relationship lies the general and symbolic one of the marriage of heaven and earth, on which the well-being of the world depends. In st. 19, a lover-beloved relationship is implied between earth and her cloud-lover; the cloud, as we note in st. 6, is the power of Indra, lord of heaven.

The cloud is introduced at the opening of the poem by the key-phrase, 'embracing the crest of the hill'. What was once sundered and placed in two separate planes, aerial and terrestrial, is united. This parallels the situation of the lovers in the poem and their spatial separation. Alakā, the dream-city where the beloved lives, is the abode, high up in the Himalayas, of *yakṣas*, semi-divine beings who move freely in the air and through space like the cloud. The hilltop of Rama's Hill, on the other hand, is of the earth, earthy, where the lover, shorn of all his powers, is fixed, earth-bound. He is unable to move freely, like the primeval mountains which had also transgressed the cosmic law *Ṛta* that relates and binds all forms of being in a harmonious pattern of behaviour so that order may be maintained in the universe. The separation and reunion of cloud and hill is a metaphor for the *yakṣa's* own parting from his beloved and the reunion which he so keenly longs for and finds vicariously in the coming together of cloud with hill and stream. Human love and union (for all practical purposes the Yakṣa and his beloved are human) are placed in the larger frame of the cosmic union of heaven and earth. This is one among many metaphors that builds the totality of meaning of this multi-layered poem; and it constitutes the initial step in the shaping of the central role of the cloud. A silent cloud which at first glance seemed to be no more than a captive audience to a love-sick *yakṣa*, turns out on closer scrutiny to be an actor playing a unique role and fulfilling a number of functions that are instrumental in realizing the objectives that the poem has set out for itself. But before the cloud can accomplish all this, it has to be endowed with a special status above and beyond what the bare Vedic myth has provided. It has to be invested with the powers and responsibilities which are part of that status.

Cast right at the beginning in the role of a lover, of hill (2,27) and stream (26, 30, 31, 42, 43) and of the whole landscape (19), the cloud is invested with qualities moral and physical through a series of images and comparisons that serve to magnify and glorify it. But first, a personality is created for it round a few phrases from Puranic accounts of *Origins.* The Purānas[60] not only provide descriptions of the origins and genealogies of gods, anti-gods and demons, of kings, seers and sages, but also of inanimate forms like rivers, mountains and *clouds.* The *Puskaravartaka* clouds in the poem (6) are described as 'possessing deep resonant voices and the power to assume various shapes at will'; as 'brimful of water, raining down beneficial rains'; and, as appearing as agents of destruction at the end of an epoch to preside over the dissolution of the universe. Thus they are envisaged as participating in the creative-destructive cycle of the cosmic process, being finally subsumed in the primordial *waters* in which the creative principle lies hidden, resting, until it is time to recreate the universe. Our cloud is born of this lofty lineage. It is the instrument of Indra, lord of heaven and bountiful giver of riches. A cluster of images delineate the cloud as the fertilizing force in the worlds of nature and man: trees and shrubs burst into luxuriant bloom (25, 27, 28); cranes and wild geese rejoice at its arrival knowing that it is mating time and form its retinue as it moves north majestically to Kailāsa and Lake Mānasa which is also the breeding place for the birds (9, 11). The onset of rains is that magical time in a tropical country, of the greening of the earth after the burning summer and devastating drought; of hope springing up in the hearts of grieving women waiting anxiously for the return of their husbands who have to travel to far places on business of various kinds (8, 49). The rainy season in Indian literature is like springtime and all that it suggests in western literature. But it is also the time of unendurable anguish for those separated from their loved ones, as the Yakṣa and his beloved are.

As the poem progresses, the rain cloud, nobly-descended, as we have seen, is gradually elevated in status through the attribution of qualities and virtues enumerated as pertaining to the character of a hero: splendour and grace, courage and compassion, poise, steadfastness of purpose, self-respect that will not tolerate an insult, high breeding, courtesy, gentle speech, charm and beauty of form. It is to be presumed that the Yakṣa invests the cloud with the qualities and virtues that rightly belong to himself as a hero.

By various comparisons with the deities in the pantheon—Balarāma, Kṛṣṇa, Viṣṇu—the cloud is touched by the light of divinity and is provided with its own epithets, as all forms of divinity possess and ought to possess: *jala-da* and *jala-dhara* (giver and bearer of water), *jīmūta* (containing the precious water that sustains life). It is addressed as brother and friend, a refuge, and implored for help in distress. The cloud assumes different shapes to perform its several functions as a benefactor to nature and man: as a lover, desirable, welcomed by the rivers; as a stern judge who punishes the presumption of the *Śarabhas* puffed up with vanity and in the form of Viṣṇu's dark-blue foot extended, curbs the arrogance of Bāli. Balarāma was not only a form of divinity, being the elder brother of Kṛṣṇa and a part of the Supreme incarnated on earth, but also a cult-hero, as is clear from the epithet Plough-Bearer; a cult-hero who harnessed the waters of the river Yamunā for irrigation to benefit his people and therefore a benefactor of humanity. He was also a personage guilty of wrongdoing, like the Yakṣa who atoned for it as he did through the instrumentality of the cloud (as we shall see later). Thus this particular comparison serves more than one purpose.

The cloud's other awesome aspect as described in the Purānas is also brought in at various points in the poem. As it sweeps along the sky, soaring up like the uprooted peak of a great mountain, it displays its size and power. It hurls down thunder and hail like missiles to scatter the *Śarabhas* and break their overblown pride (56). In the Mahākāla passage (34–38), which constitutes a high point in the poem, the cloud takes on the aura of divinity by virtue of its resemblance to the blue-black throat of Śiva and is therefore viewed with awe and admiration by the celestial attendants of the Lord. The image suggests that the cloud is part of the Supreme, and a little later it does become a part, merging into the 'forest of uplifted arms' of the god who *dances* the universe into existence. At this point the cloud attains its apotheosis, performing the role of the drum in the Cosmic Dance. The imagery in this passage should be carefully noted; there is an undertone of subdued violence. A wild energy is conveyed in images that combine power and beauty which is of the essence of the Śaiva conception of creation. The tremendous power of cosmic energy, *Śakti*, flows into time and space, shaped by the guiding principle, Śiva, into the pattern of dance. The images of the dark forest of uplifted arms and the blood-red glow of dawn and sunset (the word *Sandhyā*,[61] evening, signifies both dawn and sundown), splashing a tropical sky and reflected on the dark cloud thundering, point to both the dawn of creation and its destruction, at the beginning and end of Time. And the cloud-drum image occurs again (58) in connection with the destruction of the triple-city. Tripura or the triple city symbolizes the triple darkness of ignorance, evil and illusion and is linked with the demonic elephant (38) which in Śiva-mythology was the illusory form created by the heretic sages to attack manifest deity (Śiva). Śiva's cosmic dance is a continuing re-enactment[62] of cosmic events and the places on earth where they occur are the cosmic centres for the millions of devotees. The shrine of Mahākāla is one such; it is also an important stop on the journey of the cloud which is a pilgrimage for the Yakṣa, as we shall see presently.

That the cloud does the bidding of a higher power in helping to sustain the world and preserve order is made clear by several of the comparisons which serve to set it up as a foil to the hero (*nāyaka*) of the poem, the Yakṣa; in fact it is presented as an *ideal*, which the hero does not appear to be. The cloud is a wanderer-at-will (*kāma-cārī*), moving freely as a benefactor to nature and man; it asssumes whatever shape it *wills* (*kāmarūpī*) because it is the instrument of a higher will. The Yakṣa, on the other hand, is subjected 'to an alien will' (8), because he is self-willed and his will is directed by obsessive passion to the exclusion of other duties and responsibilities; he is described as *kāmī* and *kāmārta*, passion-ridden and sickened by passion. In the traditional framework of meaning, the cloud is a *dharmic* hero and the Yakṣa has swerved from the path of *Dharma*.

The Yakṣa, shorn of his powers, the eight *Siddhis* which all semi-divine beings and perfected seers possessed, is confined in the human existential condition and tied by the terms of the curse to his place of expiation, Rāma's Hill. The only action he is left with is purely verbal which takes the form of a long lyrical monologue, and action by proxy which can only be undertaken by the cloud:

Far off, his way barred by an adverse decree
(101)

. . . he, gone beyond range of your hearing,
not seen by your eyes, speaks
through my mouth to you, . . .
(102)

is the preamble of the Yakṣa's message to his wife. The cloud is already perfect in the role of lover to the landscape; it now has to take on another role, that of the lover in the poem, the hero, and become his 'other self'. To effect this, the landscape has to be identified with the beloved—*kāntā.* And this is what the poem does next.

The beloved, the third person in the poem, is the unseen lady, seen only through the eyes of her husband and occasionally overheard, but whose presence is dominant and pervasive in the poem. The Yakṣa sees her everywhere.

In the śyāma-vine I see your slender limbs;
your glance in the gazelle's startled eye:
the cool radiance of the moon in your face,
your tresses in the peacock's luxuriant train:
your eyebrow's graceful curve in the stream's small waves:
but alas! O cruel one, I see not
your whole likeness anywhere in any one thing.
(103)

He hears the tones of her voice, seductive, loving, half-inviting, half-reluctant, in Vetravati's waters purling along her banks with 'knitted eyebrows of tremulous wavelets'. Wherever he turns he sees only her; every detail in the landscape is but a small part of her. Only the whole landscape can hold out the possibility of yielding that 'whole likeness' which he complains of being cruelly denied.

The natural world and the human world both participate in the divine. They both share in the cosmic creative energy, *Śakti.* And in so far as they are vehicles for this cosmic energy, they reflect each other. The creative forces in nature and in woman both flow from the same source and reservoir. There is an interchangeability, then, of the roles of nature and woman; symbolically each part, each limb of the feminine form has its corresponding form in nature. This is already made clear in *Ṛtusamhāram* (see section 5 of introduction).

In the great reliefs of Bharhut and Sanci, the sculptor has seen this vision of an all-embracing cosmic energy manifesting itself in the beauty of form of nature and woman. The teeming energies of nature blossom in flower and tree; the sensuous forms of *yakṣīs* and *vṛkṣikās* (tree-spirits) twine round blossoming vines and trees, clasping them.

The imagery invests the landscape with a personality. When the Yakṣa tells the cloud of the river Gambhīrā with her clear waters, 'a tranquil pool of consciousness', and 'those dazzling upward leaps of glittering fishes bright as water lilies' which are her welcoming glances, what he is seeing and talking about is not the landscape, but the beloved. In Kālidāsa's poetry landscapes are specific, yet symbolic. As the poet caresses the landscape with his language, it takes on the form and identity of the beloved in the Yakṣa's imagination. On reaching Vidiśā, the speaker says to the cloud:

. . . you shall at once obtain
the unalloyed fulfilment of a lover's desire
tasting Vetravatī's sweet waters, as a lover his beloved's lips,
with sonorous thunder passing along her banks
as she flows with knitted brows of tremulous wavelets.
(26)

and on meeting Nirvindhyā:

wearing a girdle strung of chiming bells
—a row of water-birds plashing on her undulating waves—
weaving her sinuous course with charming unsteady gait
to reveal eddies forming her navel
—such coy gestures are women's first statements of love.
(30)

The speaker tells the cloud:

be sure to be filled with love's fine flavour.
(30)

and again, in another tone of voice, the speaker remembering the sorrow of the beloved, envies the cloud the happiness he himself cannot have:

Crossing that river, O fortunate lover!
Yours will be the happy task to induce Sindhu
visibly grieving at your absence,
her waters shrunk to a thin braid and pale
with the paleness of dry leaves
fallen from trees rooted on her banks,
to cast off the sorrow withering her.

(31)

The rivers are the *nāyikās* (heroines) listed in the *Nātyaśāstra*,[63] and they express the many moods of the beloved that the Yakṣa knew so well during their brief life together: feigning anger and displeasure, coy, playing hard to get, proud and noble (*gambhīrā*) but loving.

The cloud as the Yakṣa's proxy and alter-ego, and the landscape as the substitute for the beloved are consolations which the poem constructs for the speaker but which can only be offered to him as the poem progresses. We begin inevitably in a world without consolations, with nothing to hold on to: the Yakṣa has only the agonizing sense of the loss of every thing of value in his life and the haunting memory of 'her' who had to be left behind 'unsupported' (*abalā*). The word *a-balā*, without strength, does not imply weakness but the absence of 'supportive-ness'; the centre of a woman's world was the husband and children and the beloved is left without either. The poem begins on a note of sorrow and despair; the passionate cry, '. . . banished / from wife and kinsman by divine decree, I entreat you' (6), rings out, pointed by a sharp sense of alienation brought about by the violation of hierarchical order. A world is fractured.

There are certain poetic qualities that are difficult to convey in a translation without some explanation. The first stanza conveys so much and with such economy, through suggestion, allusion and by its cadences that an analysis of the four lines is necessary to give some idea of the dense texture and feel of the original poetry.

kascit kāntā-viraha-guruṇā svādhikāra-pramattah
śāpenāstam-gamita-mahimā varṣa-bhōgyēna bhartuh
yakṣas cakre janaka-tanayā-snāna-punyōdakeṣu
snigdha-chāyā-taruṣu vasatim rāmagiryāsrameṣu

Sanskrit metres are quantitative; short syllables have the value of one *mātra* (an instant), long syllables of two. In addition, conjunct consonants and consonants that immediately precede them are counted as long: e.g., both the consonants in the very first word *kas-cit*, are counted as long. The compound words are hyphenated for readers who do not have any Sanskrit, to read more easily; in the original it runs as follows: *Kascitkāntāvirahaguruṇa svādhikārapramattah. . . .* The metre used is the stately Mandākrānta which is defined as appropriate for love poetry. Each line is 17-syllabled with a pause after the tenth. The lines have a measured cadence in an intricate pattern of 3-syllable units: - - -, - u u, u u u, - - u, - - u, - - (- is long and u is short). The compound words in the first line move heavily, as if the weight of sorrow bears down on each syllable: *kā ntā-vi ra ha gu-ru ṇa, svā dhi kā ra pra ma ttah;* they do not come tripping on the tongue. Taking the second line apart to show how the metrical pattern 'suggests' (*dhvani*), setting the tone and mood: *Śāpēna* (by the curse) *astam-gamita-mahimā* (gone or *set*, the glory); here the two words are combined by rules of euphony to become *śāpenāstamgamitamahimā*; we have here four long syllables suggesting how time drags on (*śā pe nā stam*), followed by five short ones (*ga mi ta ma hi*) to show how quickly glory flies away, then a long syllable (*mā*) and a pause (caesura). There is almost an echo of a sigh at this point because a quick breath has to be taken before continuing. Again the second half of the line has five long syllables; 'the harshness of the 'r', 'sh' and aspirated 'b' suggest the unendurable harshness of the separation; *bhogya*—what is *eaten* or *enjoyed*, is *sorrow*; the word *bhartuh* (the Lord's) from *bharta*, one who 'bears, protects, sustains', implies a certain feudal relationship of lord and vassal with rights and obligations on both sides. The second word of the first line—'heedless of duty'—is balanced against the second word in the third line—'waters hallowed by Janaka's daughter's baths', suggesting in the first place that the Yakṣa's disregard of his Lord Kubera's command resulting in his neglect of duty is to be seen in contrast to Sītā's perfect fulfilment of duty; and in the second, that the waters hallowed by her touch would purify the erring Yakṣa. It is in the rightness of things that his transgression be expiated by the performance of penance in the place where Rāma and Sītā spent part of their exile following *dharmic* ideals while carrying out the parental command after voluntarily renouncing the throne.

The word *varṣa* in the opening stanza, signifies a 'year' as well as a 'holy spot'. Both time and place are set out by the use of a single word. The first image in the poem, of the setting sun—*astam-gamita-mahimā* (literally, the sun of his glory having set)—conveys both the sense of loss of powers and their restoration at the end of a specific period, a year, just as the sun's glory is restored at sunrise the next day.

The metre chosen by the poet, Mandākrantā, with its long lines and intricate pattern serves two purposes. The long line is able to present a scene or a moment of experience in significant detail within its compass. For example, the first line in st. 30 is one long compound word made up of seven units each describing one detail in the scene being viewed:

vīcikṣobhastanitavihagaśreṇikāñcīguṇāyāḥ

vīci—kṣobha—stanita—vihaga—śreṇi—kāñcī—guṇāyāḥ
wavelets—agitated—sounding—birds—rows—pearl—girdle-strings

The compound word takes in the scene as the eye sees it and expresses it with striking immediacy: the river (metaphor for the beloved), its girdle formed by white water-birds splashing and calling as they sway on the wavelets (an element of turbulence is indicated by the word *kṣobha*), gliding along like a woman wearing a girdle edged with tinkling little gold bells; it evokes a poignant memory of the beloved.

The intricate patterning of alliterative syllables provides the verse with a formal structure that serves to contain the emotion which is intense at times, the emotion which threatens to disrupt the tone and structure of the poem. The emotion is contained within the strict metrical pattern and the stanzas attain to a sculptured, contemplative beauty, of the kind displayed in the superb art of Bharhut and Sanci.

The highly self-conscious manner in which the language of the poem shapes itself also contributes to this containment; st. 101 is a good example; I quote the first two lines of the text :

angenāngam pratanu tanuna gāḍhataptena taptam
sāśreṇāśrudrutam aviratotkaṇṭham utkaṇṭhitena

angena angam pratanu tanuna gādha-taptena taptam
sāsreṇa asrudrutam avirata-utkaṇtham utkaṇthitena

(The second set of lines are split for easy reading.)

We see here, a repetitive pairing of words, with one word in the instrumental case—*angena, taptena, sāśreṇa*, etc. referring to the Yakṣa and the other in the accusative—*angam, taptam, aśrudrutam*, etc. to the beloved. The deliberate wordplay imposes a formal pattern that contains the stark emotion at this point. Such effects are possible only in a highly inflected language like Sanskrit and poses problems of translation into uninflected languages like English.

Mandākrānta, as already noted, is a very intricate metre and to sustain it over a hundred and more stanzas in a long poem with such depth of feeling and complexity of thought superbly articulated, without a moment of monotony to mar its total effect, is indeed a brilliant *tour de force.*

A tone of uncertainty marks the opening. A *certain yakṣa* passed *some* months on the hill top of Rāmagiri, which is the only thing particularized to furnish the allusion to the *Rāmāyana*, separated from his beloved. He is given no name because he is Everyman; any man suddenly and unexpectedly torn from his newly-wed wife[64] whom he loves passionately. The poet makes a point of stressing this fact in describing the Yakṣa as *kāmī* (2)—passion-filled—and *kāmārta*—passion-ridden. Towards the end of the poem, a distinction is made between passion or craving for pleasure, *bhoga*, and love, *prema* (112).

The beloved has no name either; apart from the word *kāntā*, or beloved, she is referred to as 'brother's wife', the Yakṣa being the cloud's brother, and 'your friend', where the cloud is addressed. Naming bestows identity and the poet refrains from doing so.

The nature of the wrongdoing that brought such swift and bitter punishment on the Yakṣa is also left unspecified. That he violated his Lord's command is seen as sufficient reason. What matters is that *Dharma*, the Law, is inviolable; the precise form the violation might take in any given situation is beside the point.

It is not sufficient to translate the word *dharma* by one word into English; it means the Law, duty, right action, moral and social order, virtue, or the inherent property of a thing. All these several meanings are included in the concept of *dharma*. The word is derived from the root *'dhṛ'*, 'to support'; *dharma* is the reflection or earthly copy of *Ṛtā*, the Cosmic Law on which universal order depends. As such it is a coordinating concept in a world-view where these several meanings are brought together, and the ethical, social and religious life of man is integrated. *Dharma* is the firm base and support of the existential condition, the frame on which all relationships are woven and through observing which life takes on meaning and gains fulfilment. Failing to perform 'appointed duties' is an infringement of the Law, which in turn upsets the delicate balance of the network of relationships, and endangers *Order.* In this connection it is interesting to note the comment made by the Royal Chamberlain in Act 5 of the play, *Śakuntalā* (4), about the operation of the Cosmic Law which binds the Sun and Wind and the serpent that holds up the Earth, and the king. Order is thus maintained.

Even though there are dramatic elements in *Meghadūtam*, there is no attempt at characterization. No story is provided; the slender narrative is contained in just the first five stanzas; the nature of the speaker's wrongdoing remains unspecified. All this unspecificity is deliberate; there is deep poetic logic behind it, indicating that the poet's concerns that direct the main thrust of the poem lie elsewhere—in the journey and its significance.

Rāma's Hill and Alakā are the two halves of the fractured world we spoke of. The wrongdoing which led to the breaking apart of the world of the Yakṣa and his beloved has to be expiated. The fractured world has to be made whole again through penance, through suffering. All this can only be effected through the instrumentality of the cloud which, as we have seen, has been presented as embodying *dharmic* ideals and realizing them through its conduct and actions; and which has further been presented as the Yakṣa's 'other self'. The journey is a bridge connecting the two halves. At the same time we should note that the poem offers us only the hope of restoration; the end is deferred.

In the texts established by the old commentators, Mallinātha and others, the poem is divided into two parts: *Poorva* and *Uttara Megham*, the former comprising the journey, sts. 1–65, and the latter, the Alakā-part, sts. 66 to the end. Many printed editions still observe this division which indicates an implicit recognition on the part of the commentators of the past of the structural and tonal differences between the two parts, though the poem is a unified whole—unified by the presence of the cloud, the speaker's voice and the continuity of the journey.

Rāmagiri in the Vindhyas and Alakā on the Kailāsa mountain are not simply two points on the map of India, nor the journey from one geographical point to the other the path traversed by a passing rain cloud during the monsoon. It is also an inner journey, through an interior landscape contoured by literary reminiscences and peopled by bitter-sweet memories. Rāmagiri and Alakā are the beginning and end of this *journey* too. At one level of discourse, the poem feeds on memories and in turn feeds them, until the whole landscape, inner and outer, is meshed in a network of memories. The cloud's journey through the actual, physical landscape stretching between the two mountain ranges, both sacred to Śiva and Śaktī (Pārvatī, who is invoked as Vindhya-*vāsinī*, the dweller on the Vindhya), functions as a metaphor for the inner journey. For, through reverie, dream-vision, the 'waking dream' of st. 106, the speaker travels every step of the way with his 'other self' and by means of it, to Alakā, to his home and to his beloved. The intense longing roused by the cloud's appearance, the 'brooding' (*antar-bāṣpah*, pent-up grief), and the poignantly imagined return, are verbalized. Sorrow shared is sorrow lightened and becomes easier to bear, says Priyamvadā in the play (*Śak.*:3.13.–1). At another level, the speaker treads devoutly the path of pilgrimage.

Two kinds of *tīrthas* (fords), sacred bathing places on rivers, streams and pools, like Apsarā's Pool, holy Saci's Pool and Indra's Landing mentioned in Act 5 of *Śakuntalā*, are described in the *Mahābhārata:* those that are accessible and those that are inaccessible. Both are places of pilgrimage that bestow spiritual merit and lead to *mokṣa* (release from rebirth). One should 'go in thought' to the holy spots that are inaccessible, says the *Mahābhārata.* On account of the curse, all the sacred places that the cloud and we see and pause at during the journey are inaccessible to the Yakṣa. He has to 'go in thought', which is what he does. The actual start of the pilgrimage for the Yakṣa and the cloud, his alter-ego, is Mahākāla, heading north to Kailāsa, both places being sacred to Śiva and Śaktī and hallowed by their temporal presence. The north, in cosmography, is the place of light and life; and the south, the abode of Yama, God of Death, is the place of darkness and death.

The inner and outer journeys have a parallel movement as they pass through their respective landscapes and they are related by the literary reminiscences that the poem draws heavily on. The inner journey progresses through memories re-lived vicariously through the cloud-landscape relationship and it passes from the recognition of wrongdoing in the form of a violation of order, to an understanding hammered out of the mind's dialogue with itself. The recognition, however, of wrongdoing and the violation of hierarchical order for one thing, is not made explicit at any point. It is implicit in the manner in which the cloud is portrayed and held up as an i*deal*; the awakening in nature under the beneficent touch of the rain-bearing cloud is also suggestive of renewal, which in turn implies restoration and a new life.

Those images in the poem that serve to magnify and glorify the rain-cloud are also images bodying forth the ideas of transgression, punishment and penance followed by purification. Balarāma, for instance, to whom the cloud is compared, resorts to the holy waters of the Sarasvatī to expiate his sin of Brahmanicide; Bali, who is subdued by the ever-extending triple stride of Viṣṇu, to which the cloud is also compared, is a case of overweening pride as the story-tellers of the Purānas see him. In all these examples, the cloud is asked to pause over these spots where the events of the myths and legends occurred and offer worship as a devotee on behalf of the Yakṣa, though it is itself not guilty of any form of transgression.

The acts of penance and purification are emphasized. The cloud is promised a pure inner being, even if its exterior remains dark, just as Balarāma and Bali were purified. It is constantly praised as a benefactor, intent on service to others, especially to the weak and helpless and those struck by adversity, and is linked to other hallowed personages who have also been benefactors in the past such as Ganga, the celestial river that descended to the mundane world, not only to provide salvation to the sinful sons of Sagara, but to become the greatest benefactor of the land and the people as well. Images of salvation are interspersed in the description of the landscape, even where there is no wrongdoing involved: for instance, in the Mahākāla passage, which we have already noted and again at the peak still known as Śiva's Sacred Foot (57) on the way to Kailāsa, the cloud is promised the eternal station of the Lord's attendant (*Śiva-padam*). As the cloud is the alter-ego of the speaker, it is reasonable to conclude that these acts of adoration and worship lead the Yakṣa from a fallen state upwards to a state of blessedness.

Much of the imagery surrounding the cloud, either through comparison, identification or association, as when the cloud is asked to *transform* himself into a flower-cloud and rain blossoms that have been freshened and sanctified by being sprinkled with the waters of the heavenly Ganga (before her descent into this world) on Skanda, the emanation of Śiva's effulgence to battle the dark forces threatening the world, serves the purpose of providing a way to redress the alienation from the divine. We should again refer this back to the Yakṣa, for the cloud is itself sinless, dedicated to the happiness of others and not its own. This is brought out most clearly in st. 60, where a sharp contrast is drawn between the self-abnegating cloud which is welcomed as a guest by Kailāsa and Rāvaṇa who is punished for his sublime egotism. Rāvaṇa wished to uproot the peak of Kailāsa and carry it to his palace with Śiva and Devī on it, so as to have the sacred presence of the Primal Parents always with him and for himself alone.

This geographical part of the poem as Wilson terms it,[65] is therefore a pilgrimage for the cloud, as it is to millions of Indians; more so, it is a pilgrimage for the speaker of the poem. Mental worship and adoration of the divine (*mānasa-pūja*), with offerings made mentally when circumstances did not permit of their actual performance, and the 'going in thought' on a pilgrimage when it was not physically possible to undertake one, is very much a part of Hindu thought and praxis. An example of this is seen in the poem itself, when at the beginning, the Yakṣa welcomes the rain cloud with a few wild flowers and affectionate words.

In st. 109, the Yakṣa speaks words of significance, having, as it appears, come to a conclusion after reflecting deeply: *bahu* meaning many times or greatly and *viganayan*, pondering over, deliberating.

> But no more of me; reflecting deeply
> I bear up drawing on my own inner strength.
> You too, lady most blessed,
> should resist falling into utter dejection.
> Whom does happiness always attend
> or misery always befall?
> Man's state on earth like the rim of a wheel
> goes down and comes up again.

I interpret this stanza as conveying a sense of the speaker having attained to some measure of wisdom; I suggest that the poet intends us to read it this way. In support of this suggestion I might point out that the tone of the poem and with it the tone of the speaker's words, changes sharply from this point on, to lead to the benediction (*Bharatavākya*), which is instinct with peace, 'all passion spent'. Peace enters the mind when the inner being is purified in the fire of *tapasyā* (penance, penitence, contemplation—the Sanskrit word cannot be translated by a single English word). The Yakṣa's words constitute more than a statement of resignation by a man shoring up his grief. It ought to be read as a positive utterance of understanding, even of faith.

As the tone of the poem changes, we sense that the speaker has extricated himself from that brooding passion of sorrow for his fate and the fate of his beloved, the sorrow that we saw pouring out in rising anguish (sts. 82–92), reaching a peak of intensity (sts. 101–108), until it is reined in, in the first half of st.109. In this stanza, a measure of objectivity is revealed in the generalization phrased in the second half. We get a sense that the Yakṣa's mind is no longer clouded as it was when we first met him (5). He is now able to provide consolation to his 'second self' left behind in Alakā, 'unsupported'. It goes further. The objectivity gained is sufficient to enable him to express the wish for general happiness which is characteristic of the *Bharatavākya* spoken at the close of all literary works in Sanskrit.

Several poems in the *Ṛgveda* end with a prayer addressed to the deity invoked in the poem to grant blessings; the speaker, or seer of the poem presumably acts as the spokesperson for the congregation and therefore the community as a whole. I venture to suggest that the tradition of speaking the *Bharatavākya* derives from this. At which point in the evolution of *mahā-kāvyas* (long poems) and dramas, this became established as a convention is perhaps not easy to determine. But even if the convention *had* become established by Kālidāsa's time, we ought not to overlook the fact that a great poet *uses* conventions to serve his own purposes. The *Bharatavākyas* in *Meghadūtam* as well as *Śakuntalā* seem to have a special significance.

In *Meghadūtam*, the last stanza marks a point of *return*. Like the wheel (a water-wheel, known also as a Persian wheel), the poem comes full circle to close on a note of quiet acceptance and a subdued feeling of hope. The pronoun 'you' includes the audience and the world-at-large with the cloud;

the speaker also includes himself, because the cloud is his alter-ago. As he wishes the cloud 'greater glory' in all the lands it would roam over, we notice that the phrase harks back to the opening of the poem where the Yakṣa is presented to us as fallen from *great glory* (*astam-gamita-mahimā*).

Both Rāma's Hill and Alakā are sacred spots. But to the Yakṣa, the former is a place of suffering and torment, a place of deprivation. To divine beings like *yakṣas* and *apsarās* (celestial nymphs), to be earth-bound and lead the life of mortals, is a torment. The Yakṣa's anguish is amply apparent, being verbalized at length. Its intensity is indicated by the use of the plural 'hermitages' in the opening verse, suggesting that he moved around restlessly from one hermitage to another seeking peace. There is irony here. It underlines the contradiction in the situation, between a hermitage, a place of passion-free tranquillity, and the tormented soul of the passion-ridden lover (*kamī*, *kāmārta*). Alakā, on the other hand, is a place of joy, love, plenitude, where there are no changes of seasons; all flowers bloom at all times. In our mundane and flawed world, the *kadamba* bursts into bloom at the first rains; the *lodhra* and the jasmine (*kunda*) bloom in winter, the *kurabaka* in spring and the *śirīṣa* in summer (67). Not so in Alakā. For Alakā is not burned by the sun but illuminated by the radiance of the moon on Śiva's forehead. It is the Earthly Paradise. That is the Yakṣa's simplistic way of seeing the world, clouded as his mind is by passion and anguish. He is a man unable to come to grips with the present, his mind forever dwelling in the past that is lost to him and which he idealizes. We dimly hear the authorial voice that pointed this out at the beginning of the poem before it retired into a decorous silence. But as the poem makes amply clear, Alakā is not simply a hedonist's paradise; there is sorrow at its core and a human heart grieving in anguished separation.

The beloved, with her husband in exile, banished, and without a child, lives, or what is truer, *exists* in a world that holds no real meaning for her. Eschewing all entertainment and all personal adornment—fine clothes, jewels, flowers, fragrances—she has no thought other than her husband's safe return. The imagery used to describe the beloved and her situation is one of privation and deprivation, of disorientation, of fading and waning and wasting away, cut off from life's deepest springs. She is compared to a day-lily on a cloudy day, uncertain whether to open or to close, a lotus deprived of sunshine or blighted by hoar frost, the waning moon in its very last phase, a sliver, before it is swallowed up by darkness. The lotus-sun is a key image in Sanskrit literature, and here the sun is the husband (79). A whole set of stanzas, sixteen to be exact, from 81 to 96, is devoted to the description of the beloved, grief-struck and leading the life of a woman parted from her husband (*proṣita-bhartṛkā*).[66] In *Śakuntalā*, one stage-direction and a stanza suffice to describe the heroine sorrowing in separation. This is accounted for mainly by the difference in treatment of the idea in the lyric and the dramatic modes.

Alakā is therefore a place where life's fullness is not truly realized in its totality; something is lacking. It is a place of *innocence*. And Rāma's Hill is more than a place of deprivation and torment as the Yakṣa perceives it to be. Framed as it is in the opening stanza in an epic allusion, it can and ought to be seen as a place of penitence and purification. Sanctified by Rāma's enduring presence (12), by his steadfast adherence to duty and by Sītā's purity and constancy (the beloved is compared to her in sts. 10, 99), it is a place of *experience* where love is tried and tested; it corresponds to Mārīca's Hermitage in the play (*Śak*.: Act 7). We might add that not only love but also strength of character is tried and tested, as it is in *Śakuntalā*. One of the prime virtues of a hero is resilience and the courage to endure. In a certain kind of ethic, suffering and penance (*tapasyā*), is a part of learning and growing up; sometimes it is the only way to gain that maturity which is at bottom the ability to see life steadily and as a whole. A harsh ethic but not exclusively Indian in conception. The speaker of the poem, as we saw earlier, attains to some measure of understanding that is more than resignation or sheer acceptance of the inevitable. For acceptance of the situation is already in place at the very beginning of the poem: 'the wrath of the Lord of Treasures' and the resulting banishment has been accepted as the 'divine decree'. This is one view which we shall typify as the ethical-hierarchic that might be adopted in interpreting the poem. But as indicated earlier, it is not the only possible approach; it compasses only part of the poem's meaning and the vision it embodies. The poem itself directs the reader to another set of responses.

There are two worlds in the poem: the world of the mythic and epic past, and the world of the present of the speaker, the poet and *his* reader. Again, by shifting our point of view slightly and translating the terms, we can see the two worlds as the world of the imagination framed in dream and memory, and the real, every-day world. A sharp line is not drawn between the two; the two worlds are continuous and phase into one another as the poem moves constantly between them. Alakā is a presence in the distant background in the first section (which I shall label as the Mahākāla section), clinging to Kailāsa's slopes beside the holy Mānasa lake, and the beloved's presence is pervasive (7, 8, 10, 11). The splendour of Ujjayinī is reflected in the Alakā-world; the same flowers bloom though in a different and more perfect setting. But the Mahākāla and Alakā sections differ in mood and tone. The fomer is celebratory in tone, joyous and reverential. Beginning on an elegiac note the poem swings into a joyous celebration of love and the beauty of nature blossoming under the beneficent influence of the rain cloud. The effect of the poetry is to create the impression that the curse and the exile provide the opportunity for this celebration. The poet uses them for this purpose. There is an expansion of consciousness for the reader as several landscapes unfold before him. Each stop on the cloud's journey and the speaker's pilgrimage is related to some memorable event in the past and sometimes a poignant memory, intensely personal, of the speaker is evoked; st. 51 is a beautiful example. The amber coloured eyes of Revatī, Balarāma's beloved wife, reflected in the wine, evoke memories of the Yakṣa's own beloved wife as she sat with him drinking the wine that reflected the colour of *her* eyes. And this poignant memory is interwoven with the literary memories of the fratricidal war of the epic and all the wrongdoing that was part of it, and of Balarāma's own transgression purified by the waters of the river most celebrated in the Vedas, the holy Sarasvatī on whose banks the ancient civilization first arose.

It has been suggested that some personal experience of the poet underlies the longing and the grief of parting that the poem voices so eloquently. But one has to be careful in bringing a writer's biography into his work, especially with one so reticent and self-effacing as Kālidāsa. It is misleading to treat literature as a transcript of life as it is actually lived.

The Yakṣa when we first meet him is shorn of his powers and earth-bound like one of us mortals; he is humanized to elicit our sympathy fully. But his 'other self' (and we with it), soars, floats in the air, roams freely in space as in his pre-lapsarian state, providing a double-perspective of the world: one, close and detailed, the human perspective that sees the beads of sweat collecting on the temples of the flower-gatherers and the bee hovering over a swaying spray of white jasmine; the other, a panoramic view of the whole landscape in a larger and all-inclusive perspective of the earth itself like a beautiful woman wearing the broad river with its gleaming white waters like a single strand of pearls. We have an overview not only of the planet we live on, but get to see vast spaces where the colossal elephants that guard the quarters roam, and the laughter of the Primal One towers up into space as eternal snows gathering from the beginning of Time. The experience provided by even a cursory reading of the poem is an explosion of the imagination bodied forth in bold conceits such as the one here of Śiva's tumultuous laughter and the striking conceits which occur earlier (sts. 19, 42, 49, 52, 62). With a careful *reading*, we find ourselves exploring the poem's ever-expanding world of meanings, as images open up whole vistas extending back into time (38, 45), or through the play of several ideas as in the image of Ganga on Śiva's head, an image in which we are not only taken back into mythic Time when Ganga descended on earth from heaven, but taste the delicious sense of humour in the rivalry that is part of the relationship of the sisters whom myth makes co-wives—Ganga and Gaurī—the one proud and exultant, having found a permanent place on the head of the Supreme, the other angry and jealous. (Sitting on someone's head is a colloquial way, in many Indian languages, of expressing the dominance of a much-spoilt person over another.)

The two views are not mutally exclusive, for there is an ambivalence at the heart of the poem. An ideal—a *dharmic* ideal—is set up; but the radiance of the love of the Yakṣa and his beloved glows so strongly in the poem that the beauty of the poetry dulls the edge of whatever wrongdoing it was on the part of the Yakṣa that brought such dire and swift punishment in its wake. Further, the nature of the transgression not only remains unspecified; it is not stressed and underlined either. The quiet acceptance by the lovers of the pain of separation of such an intense love induces the feeling in the reader that such love has to have a place in the accepted scheme of things. The two views *should* be held in tension against each other.

The celebratory tone of the first part of the poem continues into the Alakā section which begins on a paradisal note and continues in that mood till st. 80, at which point the elegiac tone with which the poem began takes over, making doubts surface about the poem's conclusion. Does it have a 'happy ending'? As we contemplate the poem as a whole, we are filled with doubts and misgivings. The weight of woe carried by the poetry in the Alaka section is too overwhelming to be ignored. *There* she sits as he pictures her in his grief, in the midst of Alaka's loveliness, a 'young girl', sorrowing, 'alone, speaking little', 'the Creator's masterwork':

> How beautiful, if sorrow had not made
> Sorrow more beautiful than Beauty's self.[67]

We should not forget that the beloved is a young girl of sixteen years—bālā. Kālidāsa uses this word again in the play referring to Śakuntalā (3:2). These two heroines are in the first flush of youth and experience love for the first time in all its freshness and ardour; it is a love that takes over their whole being as an all-enveloping experience embracing every moment of their young lives. In the play, the feeling of the heroine's youth is strengthened by the use of the word *mugdhā*—innocent and inexperienced (*Śak*.: 1:24; 2:3). And then tragedy strikes, unexpectedly. A strong sense of the pity of it all is inescapable.

A series of stanzas, each picturing the grieving beloved in vivid detail like a miniature painting (82–92), carefully delineates her in gradual decline: pale and wasted, distraught and disoriented, unmindful of her personal appearance, praying for her husband's return with no thought but of him. She is presented as desolated, at death's door:

> Seeming like the last sliver
> of the waning moon on the eastern horizon
> (88)

before it is swallowed up in the total darkness of the new moon. This stanza harks back to the Yakṣa's fears for his beloved at the opening of the poem (4). Will she survive? The poet, by stopping short of the last two stages of grief—withdrawal and death—of the ten mentioned in the *NS*,[68] leaves the outcome uncertain. However, this image is itself ambivalent, because the disappearance of the moon is only *apparent*; the moon waxes in *time* and is restored to its glory.

This description of the beloved is by no means a conventional picture of a wife mourning the absence of her husband.[69] It might have become conventional later and it probably did and classical dance continues to portray the grieving heroine (*prosita-bhatṛkā*) in this stylized and conventional manner. However, Kālidasa's poetry conveys the beloved's emotions of love and anguish in such a manner as to make the reader feel not simply that *this was the way* she felt and acted but that there is *no other way* she could have felt or acted, the images are so totally infused with the emotion they embody. And this serves as a prime example of the point made earlier in the introduction (page 24) with reference to drama and to *Śakuntala*. Kalidasa's accomplishment lies in the manner in which his poetry escapes the constraints of the poetics of his time even while it acknowledges those poetics, if indeed there existed a *poetics* at that time that directed his genius.[70]

The elegiac tone of the poem continues to make doubts surface repeatedly in our minds. Will the cloud reach its destination in time? Will it reach it at all? The cloud has already been characterized as inanimate, 'blended of mists and light, winds and water' (5) that could dissipate any time into its constituent elements. Its life is enmeshed in the life of all things in nature, animate and inanimate. Will it get lost in the clear waters of the river Gambhīrā, lost in love for her? (42, 43). We are also reminded more than once that it suffers from a proclivity for delay and loitering around when it should be steadily going north towards Alakā (24, 28, 40). It has to be asked not to pause too long dallying on the hill where *kadamba* groves burst into bloom at its touch and peacocks welcome it with joy, and not to spend too much time on terraces watching pretty girls. At one point, we encounter the suggestion that the cloud may have melted into the presence of Mahākalā (Śiva as Great Time), and at another that its devotion is to be rewarded by obtaining the eternal station (*Śiva-padam*) of the *gaṇas* or attendants who stand round the Supreme in their allotted places (38, 57). The poet has carefully placed such sign posts here and there on the path of the cloud to alert the reader to the possibility that mishaps may occur on the way, that the journey might not have a 'happy ending', and more, that it might not have an ending at all. The outcome is uncertain.

This is not to stack the cards against a happy ending, but to draw attention to the strategy of the poem, to the manner in which it deploys the imagery and lays out several possibilities of viewing the poem that results in a fuller understanding of its meaning. There are other images in the poem that prefigure the reunion of the parted lovers and a happy outcome. The authorial voice does not dictate any view as preferable, having erased itself from the text right at the beginning. We see the beloved placed beside the jasmine that is revived by a fresh shower of rain drops (97); like Sītā she lifts her face up to hear the 'glad tidings', 'her heart opening like a flower in eager expectation' (99). Two significant images argue for a happy ending: one we have already noted as ambivalent—the image of the last sliver of the waning moon on the eastern horizon; also ambivalent is the other image of the Persian wheel which comes up, returning like the rising sun (109). It symbolizes the year, which is the period of the curse. But the wheel *re-turns*; ever-turning, endless, it is a symbol of *time*. Waning and waxing, the turning wheel, everything is part of the *Play* of *Time* (Mahakala) presented on the cosmic stage in the dance-drama referred to in st. 58.

Further, the beliefs that formed part of the ethos in the poet's own time ought not to be overlooked. Penance, purity of love and constancy found their own rewards. The beloved and the speaker in the poem suffered and richly deserved the reward of reunion and the restoration of their original happy state. The touching belief that the chastity of a loving and loyal wife had the power to overcome all obstacles and accomplish her heart's desire, which was none other than her husband's well-being and happiness, and her own, the two being identical, would have directed the responses of audience and reader in the past. Did not Sāvitrī encounter Death, conquer it and restore her dead husband to life? But the comparison with Sītā is of doubtful value on this point, because though Sītā was restored to her husband and to her rightful position as queen at Ayodhyā, she did not 'live happily ever after' with Rāma.

In the poem the journey has no end because we do not know what *happened* at the end; we are not told. The poem is open-ended, leaving us with the hope that the lovers will be re-united; no more than that. And while there *is* hope, hope is but a 'slender thread'. Otherwise, we move in an area of suppositions: that the cloud could and did reach its destination and delivered its message of hope; that the beloved survived to receive it; and that the speaker was able to return to her at the end of the curse. The cloud, an elemental thing, bound by the laws of nature, makes its annual, recurrent journey, endlessly. We are sure of only one thing, that the journey continues, 'ever keeping to the north', which is the place of life and light and the temporal presence of Śiva with his Śakti. The effect that the totality of meaning of the poem's structure and language sets out to create and succeeds in doing *is*, that the end is not important, the going is; and the *going* is an exploration. It is an ongoing exploration; it was for the poet in his *oeuvre*, and it is for the reader.

IX

The poem deploys its resources on a large scale. The canvas is the vast stretch of land from the Vindhyas to the Himālayas, crisscrossed by great rivers and innumerable streams, dotted by sacred fords and places of pilgrimage associated with myth, legend and hierophany. From a solitary hermitage the poem moves out into vast spaces and into different planes of consciousness. The landscape unfolds gradually as the speaker describes it *introspectively* in sorrow and the *recollected* emotion of joy; it is presented from several points of view. The lonely 'voice' sounds in the background while the foreground is filled with the busy hum of great cities and the myriad sounds of nature celebrating the advent of the season of love and renewal ushered in by the rain cloud.

The cloud sweeps along, brimming with life-giving water the thin trickles of rivers, thin as the single braids of grieving women looking out anxiously for their husband's return; driving women of pleasure to their midnight trysts in an exuberance of passion; making the landscape bloom, and renewing the earth. As the poem's canvas expands in range and sweep, the rain cloud gains in physical magnitude and attains an extra-ordinary status. It is transfigured by the light of divinity into something strange and unfamiliar, into something marvellous. Having gathered on its long course the sacral aura of the hallowed places it has passed through and paused over—Mahākāla, Skanda's Hill, the holy rivers and their sources—it finally arrives, sanctified, fit to enter the holiest of places, Kailasa, temporal abode of the Supreme. And it arrives like an honoured guest, prefiguring the speaker's own return home.

The landscape is drawn in a definite pattern to form a backdrop. Starting at a point on a remote and lonely hilltop where the speaker of the poem is visualized as seated watching a rain cloud curling round the crest of the hill, the canvas expands in range and sweep until it is *drawn in* to a point on another remote and lonely hilltop—a gem-studded pleasure-hill—opposite the casement where the beloved is presented, restless and anguished. As the landscape starts to expand from a small space and then narrows down to another small space, the rain cloud goes through a corresponding process of magnification followed by a diminution and descent, scaled down to the ordinary and familiar. It settles down on the jewelled crest of a miniature hill, transformed to the size of an elephant cub, small enough for the beloved to feel comfortable with.

Within this large and inclusive pattern of symmetry several minor symmetries are fitted in carefully. We see the obvious symmetries immediately, the two hilltops with the lonely figures on them and all that vast space of land in between, symbolizing spatially the love-in-separation of lover and beloved in the *nāyaka-nāyakī* tradition. Then we note the less obvious: she is his 'second self', the moon shorn of its glory to his sun whose lustre is dimmed, the fading lotus that waits for his 'ray-fingers' to wipe off its dew-tears and make it bloom again. The Yakṣa's armlet slipping off his 'wasted forearm' parallels the beloved divesting herself of all ornaments, casting them aside and lying pale and emaciated (2, 92). He wakes up suddenly out of a 'waking dream', cooled by Himālayan breezes scented by the fragrance of her body, imagining he was holding her in his arms; she is woken up out of a dream in which she fancies she was in his arms, by the breeze cooled by fresh rain drops and scented by the jasmines (106, 96). Coming out of his reverie, he sees a rain cloud on the hill, resembling a playful elephant; and she sees a small elephant cub on the jewelled pleasure-hill outside her window. Words, phrases and images echo one another and form links. Many such verbal and other symmetries provide the detail that shapes the world of the poem.

At the close of the poem we become sharply aware that we are still on Rāmagiri and the rain cloud is still clinging to the crest of the hill. Nothing seems to have changed—or has it? The voice is still echoing within us. The poem has come back to where it started; its form is circular, as in *Ṛtusaṃhāram*. But we have travelled far and wide in space and time. Time takes several forms in this poem: the past, present and future; the mythic, epic and cosmic; days, seasons, the year and aeons. The beloved counts days out laying a flower for each day that has gone by and reckons the hours by her sleepless anguish. The period of the curse is a year, one revolution of the sun; the symbol for this in the poem is the *water-wheel* (109). The remaining period of separation is four months or one season, the season of the rains, when Viṣṇu is immersed in contemplation. (The year was originally divided into three seasons of four months each.) Time is measured out by the steps of temple dancers, reflecting the great dance of creation. Time stands still in Alakā where the seasons do not change and all flowers bloom at all times and the *yakṣas* who live in a world of order experience only love and happiness. We have seen that uncertain time in the future when the parted lovers hope to enjoy on nights bright with the autumn moon, all the pleasures imagined during the long separation. We have even glimpsed Time, beyond aeons, at its very beginning, when the Dance began; when Śiva's laughter started to pile up into the eternal snows of the Lord of Mountains and Viṣṇu's triple-stride measured out the Universe. We return finally to our short span of time in the theatre or the temple at Mahākāla, to the time it took for the poem to be chanted, initially perhaps by the poet himself. And we have not moved except in our imagination.

X

The play *Śakuntaḷā* is a beautiful blend of romance and fairy tale with elements of comedy. In the last sections of the *Śatapatha Brāhmaṇa* that are devoted wholly to a description of the rituals of the Horse-Sacrifice (*Aśva Medha Yajna*), where the names of some of the Kings who performed them are mentioned, we come across this line: 'In Nāḍapit, the Apsarā Śakuntalā conceived (bore) Bharata.' This is the earliest literary reference to Śakuntalā and her son (the little boy Sarva-damana in the play) who performed many horse-sacrifices on the banks of the river Yamunā after he had conquered the world, thus fulfilling the prophecy of the mystic personage, Mārīca, in the play (7:33). Nāḍapit is glossed by the commentator[71] as Kaṇva's hermitage. But that identification has obviously been made on the basis of the Śakuntalā-Duhṣanta story in the *Mahābhārata*,[72] where, however, the name Nāḍapit does *not* occur. The original story of Śakuntalā referred to in the *SB* is lost to us; we have only a very long and earthy version of it is the epic (*Mbh.*:1: chs. 62–69). It must be our guess then, that Nāḍapit was some place of enchantment, a pool of *apsarās* perhaps, where strange things could happen and mortals meet and fall in love with celestial nymphs.

With the very first lines of the play we are transported to a world of enchantment. A handsome, young, king, out hunting, is lured far out into 'another world'; and the inevitable happens. The song of the actress (*naṭī*) has already lured the waiting audience into this world. Music is used skilfully to make this transition. A point to note here is that the word used for the fleet deer that has drawn King Duhṣanta far away, is '*sāranga*' which is also the name of a *raga* or musical mode. The *raga*, *sāranga*, is defined as one that through the 'attractive arrangement of notes, *colours* the mind of the hearer.' (*Ranga* signifies colour, paint and also the stage.) Music projects the appropriate mood.

The play is located in the mythic past in a world where mortals still moved with gods; the human and divine intermingled. In this world, the gods were not distant but friends of heroes like Duhṣanta who participated with them to keep order in the universe. By removing the action of the play into the world of the past, distant in time, a poetic and dramatic purpose is served; it inhibits a realistic approach to the play. It clearly marks the line that separates the fictive world of the play from our every day world. In the Sanskrit text the two words '*Atha*' (now) and '*Iti*' (thus) at the beginning and end of a play enclose it as it were; literally, it would read as follows: *Now* begins the play, entitled *Abhijnānaśākuntalam*; and *thus* ends the play, etc.

The play-world thus created contains another world—the world of the deep and dark forests near the river Mālinī, the 'green world' into which we are lured by the deer and where we meet Śakuntalā, the Child of Nature, who as noted earlier on, is also envisaged as the guardian deity of the woodland.

As already noted, *apsarās*—born of the *Waters*, i.e., the creative waters where life originated—are powers of Nature, associated with fertility and plenitude as *yakṣa-yakṣīs* are. In the ancient myth of the Churning of the Ocean by gods and anti-gods to obtain ambrosia, the cup of immortality, the *apsarās* rose out of the waters, together with many other wondrous things, including Beauty (*Srī*) herself (see under Myths, Appendix II).

In the Vedic myth referred to, Śakuntalā is an *apsarā*, and the daughter of an *apsarā* in the epic tale which is the immediate source of the play. This is an aspect of her origin that is important to keep in mind, because in the play she is seen as the Lady of Nature, one who lives in the 'green world', into whom has flowed 'the beauty born of murmuring sound'; she possesses the beauty of nature as well as its holiness. In her, 'nature' and 'nurture' blend without being in opposition to each other, for her 'green world' is also an *āśrama*, a hermitage, a *tapo-vana*, or penance-grove, where tranquillity prevails ordered by discipline. She is an 'ornament' of the Hermitage (an image out of the gilded world of the royal court), as well as a creature of the woodlands; both phrases are the King's. Not only are a number of flower-images other than the conventional one of the lotus-petalled eyes and slender vine-like arms used to describe her; she is also *seen* as a flower—the jasmine. She and the jasmine are constantly brought together (like the beloved in *Meghadūtam*); they are sisters, born of the same mother—Nature. Can this flower, this 'sensitive plant' survive in the 'other world'—the glittering gilded world of the Paurava monarch? It cannot, it seems. Śakuntalā herself poses this question: 'Rent from my dear father's lap like the sapling of the sandal tree uprooted from the side of the Malaya mountain, how can I survive ever in an alien soil!' (4.22.-2,3). This image of the sandal tree will recur in a later, very significant context in Act 7, to which we shall refer presently. Act 5 is clear proof that she is trampled on, stripped and mutilated (figuratively) and is at the point of death when she is rapt from the astonished gaze of the beholders by a shaft of light (5.33b). In this connection it is very important to note two facts made clear in the play. Firstly, Śakuntalā is never seen as actually living in the gilded world of the court and being a part of it. The fact is only talked about in various ways by different people at different times; but it is not part of the play. She is never brought into direct contact with the Queen, or the Queen Mother or any of the ladies of Duhṣanta's palace, as the heroine of *Vikramorvaśiyam* (*Urvaśi Won By Valour),* also an *apsarā,* is. Śakuntalā is a heroine different from the others: Mālavikā and Urvaśī, the noble Dhārinī[73] and Ausīnarī,[74] Sudaksinā and Indumatī.[75] She is special, in a class by herself with the beloved (the Yakṣī) of the poem, *Meghadūtam.*

Secondly, the benediction is not spoken in this play in the world of the court, in the King's world. It is spoken in a world beyond this, which is the *perfected* world of the Primal Parents, Mārīca and Aditi. There is talk certainly of a return to this world. But the play comes to its end in Mārīca's Hermitage, on Hema-Kūta (Kailāsa) which mortals cannot reach. 'But mortals cannot come to these regions on their own, noble lady.' (7.20.+1)

Before the king can enter this world he has to be purified. First he proves his worth by battling the forces of darkness and disorder that threaten the order of the universe. For this he has to be roused from the state of utter despondency into which he had fallen, weighed down by an overwhelming sense of guilt. He had become disoriented, nerveless and swooned away (6:28). It is significant that it is deep concern for someone close to him, Mādhavya, that pulls him out of this depression, lacking the will to live. Duhṣanta's path to Mārīca's Hermitage and the finding of what has been lost is essentially similar to that of the Yakṣa's in the poem, though they are framed differently because of the differences in the two literary modes—drama and lyric. The images of sanctity and purification are repeated: Viṣṇu's triple-stride, Ganga's celestial stream, the sacred pool of golden lotuses.

The whole of Act 7 is placed in the world of Mārīca's Hermitage, where the 'highest penances are wrought' in the penance groves of the Perfected Seers; it is a world which ascetics perform the severest austerities to attain. Here Mārīca (the luminous) born of the Self-Existent Light, himself performs penance with his consort, Aditi. The last stage direction that brings the play to a close is: *Exit all.* No distinction is made between the characters belonging to the Hermitage and the mortals who have to descend to Duhṣanta's capital.

In *Vikramorvaśiyam*, whose theme is also the marriage of a mortal, King Purūravas, descended from the moon, to a celestial nymph, and their parting and re-union, the benediction is spoken on earth, at the King's court after Nārada who has come down to earth with a message of goodwill from Indra, has consecrated the little prince Āyus (from whom Duhṣanta is directly descended) as the heir-apparent.

Another significant point to note in the last stanza of *Śakuntalā* (the benediction) is the tone and quality of the final words of the poet and dramatist:

May the Self-Existent Lord who unites in Himself
the Dark and the Light,
Whose Infinite Power pervades the Universe,
annihilate forever the round of my births.

(7 : 35)

Nīla-lohita is the epithet used for Śiva; *nīla*, suggesting the dark-blue of the poison the Lord swallowed at the Beginning to save the newly created world, and *lohita* (*rohita* is a variant), the brightness of Gaurī or Śaktī. The diads and triads in Indian thought are richly multivalent and their meanings and symbolism can be endlessly explored and defined: day–night; light–dark; beauty–power; end–endless, and so on. The tendency of the human mind is to see the world as constituted of categories of polarities; the bent of the Indian mind leads it to see these as *balanced,* and to attempt to reconcile them in a *one-ness* in which the opposites are perceived as aspects of one and the same. The duality is reconciled in the Trinity, as in the classic *Trimūrti* (the three-aspected) image of Śiva at Elephanta near Bombay. Mārīca is described as the offspring of the *Self-Existent Energy* (7:27); this should be read in juxtaposition with the benediction.

There is one further point to consider in relation to the benediction. *Abhijnānaśākuntalam* is Kālidāsa's last work and the words spoken last are therefore eminently fitting as the final utterance of the great poet and dramatist; it is his farewell to his work, and to the world in an ultimate sense. Kālidāsa has arrived at that point in his life and career where 'every third thought' is of the other shore. But the words have a deeper poetic significance in the dramatic structure of the play. The two worlds of the play, the green world of the woods and the gilded world of the Royal Court, are too far apart (as we shall see presently), and the reconciliation, re-union and *restoration* cannot be celebrated in either of them. Whereas the two worlds in the poem, *Meghadūtam,* are continuous and even interfused, there is a sharp break made in the play between the two worlds at the close of Act 4. Therefore, that moment of epiphany has to *happen* elsewhere, in another world which I shall call the 'golden world' of the Imagination, a phrase suggested by the word *Hema-Kūta* (Golden Peak) (7.8+6–8), which is a mystic region that the Purānas place beyond the Himālayas, in the vicinity of the mythical Mt Meru or Sumeru. It is not the initial world of enchantment we stepped into, the green world of the deep and dark forests; it is, as we saw earlier, a place coveted by ascetics who perform the severest penance to gain it; the place where the highest forms of penances are wrought in the penance groves of the Perfected Seers and is filled by the luminous presence of the Primal Parents of the universe. Here, the

common bird or petal
And all complexities of mire . . . .

are miraculously transformed into the 'glory of changeless metal', into 'the artifice of eternity'.

The difference in tone and character of the two worlds—the initial green world and this golden world which is the *artifice* of eternity—is seen clearly in the kind of imagery that shapes them. (The two worlds of Acts 1 and 7 reflect each other in many respects, as we shall see.) The world of Act 1 is the world of *nature*, with flowers blooming, honey-bees hovering over them, of green foliage and tender young shoots and buds being prised open, of clear waters flowing in channels to lave the roots of trees and the fresh cool spray of Mālinī's snow-fed waters wafted by the breeze. The colour-words present in the descriptions are those of the fresh colours of the woodlands and of budding youth. In Act 7, on the other hand, the colour-words are drawn mostly from a world of gold and gems and jewels (but of an elemental world, and not words describing the glitter of the Royal Court): the *golden sheen* of the waters, the glitter of rain drops, the gleam of the flickering lightning and the liquid gold of the mountain itself reflecting the red and gold of sunsets. Here, the lotuses are golden as in Alakā; the places of meditation are not green meadows where deer roam or the roots of trees under the green shade of leafy trees, but jewelled caves with celestial nymphs, gorgeously dressed and jewelled and seductive, walking about. It is a world of austere beauty, luminous with the light of the spirit; it is not a world of Nature, spontaneous, informed by instinct, but of nature *perfected* by restraint and discipline. In the last act, time past, present and future are brought together in Mārīca's blessings, to be contained within the golden round of Time; the world in the text, *yuga-śata-parivartanaih* is literally 'the revolutions of hundreds of epochs' (aeons) (7:34).

Certain prophecies are made in this golden world about the future, after Duhṣanta's time. The interest in this act is focussed on the little prince, the future Bharata (Bearer of the earth) who is to inherit the future. Mārīca's prophecies (7. 33. 33.-1) echo the incorporeal voice of the Mystic Fire that has already spoken (4:4). The little boy, flanked by two hermit women is the centre of the last Act, as Śakuntalā, his mother, accompanied by her two friends, is of the first. The two acts reflect each other in many respects. The scene where the King, after dismounting from the chariot, is about to enter the grove of Mārīca's Hermitage and has his first glimpse of his son, is a replica of the scene in Act 1 where also the King, dismounting from his chariot at the fringes of the grove of Kaṇva's Hermitage, enters and sees the boy's mother for the first time. The *finding* of the lost son and heir precedes and leads to the *re-cognition* of the mother. An interesting parallel is provided in the last scene of Shakespeare's *The Winter's Tale.*

Words are keys to open doors for the imagination on its journey of exploration into the fictive world. The title—*Abhijnānaśākuntalam*—underlines the central issue in the play. Śakuntalā is *recognized* by virtue of a *token* of love, not by love itself. In the absence of concrete, tangible 'proof of love' and marriage, she is lost; she is nothing. Again, there is an interesting parallel with Shakespeare. In *Othello,* proof of the heroine's chastity and love is demanded. Desdemona's chastity hangs on a handkerchief; Śakuntalā's on a ring. Both heroines are blissfully unaware of the importance of the *token.* To them love is its own proof and a witness to their chastity. It is in Acts 5 and 6 that Kālidāsa probes most deeply into the heart of his society's accepted norms and values. He makes Miśrakeśī ask a highly significant question (6.13, + 10, 11): '. . . . does a love like this need a token of recognition? How can this be?'

The probing is accompanied by another equally significant question—the question of *knowing,* which is related to the *re-cognition* of Śakuntalā at the close of the play. How does one know? Is 'the truest *inner prompting',* its own unassailable authority' to the noble and virtuous? This is the way of knowing that the King claims for himself; but the claim is subjected to ironic scrutiny and found to be not well-founded.

What is *knowing*? The King at first knew Śakuntalā carnally, as an object; and frankly as an object of pleasure. She is a flower to smell, a gem to hold and an ornament to wear. She is hardly a person to him. It is only at the close of the play that he sees her as a person and *knows* her truly. Something has to be added to *his view of her* to make him see her as a 'person' of intrinsic beauty and not merely a beautiful object. In *Meghadūtam* the idea of outward lustre being the *semblance* of inner glow (of powers) is introduced in the opening stanza. Priyamvadā (4: lines 9–10) is able to correlate outer beauty with the inner. But Duhṣanta seems to be unable to do this until the long separation and grief at losing her and his son and an intense sense of guilt, give him eyes to see deeply. When Śakuntalā stands before him, pale with suffering, the flesh mortified to let the spirit glow forth, the King truly *sees* her and knows her 'Aha! Here is the Lady Śakuntalā; it is *she* :

Dressed in dusky garments,
her face fined thin . . .
(7:21)

It almost appears as if her exquisite beauty had been a barrier to his understanding of her. All he saw then was the glow of passion and youth and beauty which he described in images of blooming flowers and tender shoots. Initially, Duhṣanta had known Śakuntalā only carnally; she was an object of pleasure to be enjoyed. The imagery of Acts 1 and 3 convey this quite clearly. He is the 'bee circling at day break over the "jasmine's cup"'. Even while he is setting himself up as the noble and self-restrained man shying away from the touch of another man's wife, his appreciative eye, the trained eye of a connoisseur of feminine beauty sees the sweetness beneath the enveloping veil, 'barely-revealed', as she stands 'like a bud / not burst into bloom . . . / a tender sprout among yellowing leaves'.

The play examines accepted ideals and the relation of what *seems,* to what *is,* of *semblance* to truth, through the comments of Mādhavya and by means of ironies built into the structure and language of the play. A fine example of the ironies that convey a critical point of view is in Act 1. Duhṣanta is passing himself off as the Paurava monarch's Minister for Religious Affairs, visiting the penance-groves that are specified as Groves of Righteousness (*Dharma-Araṇya*), to see that they are free of impediments to the performances of all sacred rites. Yet, by ceaselessly hunting and creating terror and confusion in the woods, he is responsible for the wild tusker 'crazed with fear' charging into the sacred grove like the 'very embodiment of hindrance to penance'. Recklessly charging towards Kaṇva's Hermitage chasing a blackbuck, he stops short of killing the sacred animal only when an anchorite stands barring his way. Again, there is unconscious irony in Duhṣanta's words, when he admonishes the little boy teasing a lion cub in Mārīca's Hermitage and describes him as 'the young of a black serpent that spoils / for other creatures the pleasant sanctuary / that is the fragrant sandal tree' (7.18). In this image, Duhṣanta is the black serpent which initially trespassed into the sanctuary (Kaṇva's Hermitage); the sandal tree should be linked with Śakuntalā's description of herself as 'the sapling of the sandal' rent from the side of the Malaya mountain—its sanctuary (4.21.+8–10). When this image is seen in the context of the trial-scene in Act 5 and placed beside the images the King uses to characterize Śakuntalā's conduct—the turbulent river sullying its own 'crystal stream' and uprooting the trees growing on its banks and the cuckoo stealthily creeping into another's nest and leaving its offspring there—the irony is devastating.

The whole of Act 5 is disturbing, full of ironies; questioning is implicit in its tone from beginning to end. The question of truth-speaking and dissimulation is raised; wearing the mantle of virtue while practising deception is characterized as the art that princes are taught. A reference to manuals on statecraft such as Kautilya's *Arthaśāstra* may be seen here. But Kālidāsa alerts the reader to another view. A king who gains or inherits sovereignty has to keep it, guard it presumably, by whatever means are deemed necessary. What then is the ideal of kingship? More important, what does the word *rāja-ṛṣi*, royal sage, mean? How is a king a sage? Is the word a mere 'praise-word' as the young hermit says in unconscious irony? A public image as different from or opposed to a private image? The play raises many questions but by no means in a strident manner. Further, Kālidāsa does not leave us without an idea of what a royal sage should be. In the verses spoken by the two young hermits who see the King for the first time, we have a sketch of a monarch who is a great warrior and a good ruler, a complete king or royal sage (2.14,15). Dilīpa, the founder of the illustrious solar dynasty in Kālidāsa's epic, *Raghuvamśam*, is this ideal monarch, a royal sage. But is Duhṣanta one? Verse 14 is interesting on account of its use of certain words in their double meanings: *āśrama*[76] is a hermitage and also one of the four stages in a man's life; *yoga* is contemplation, but it also means 'through' or 'by means of'; *vaśin* is one who has his senses (passions) under perfect control and a king who has his subjects under perfect control, that is to say, the kingdom is well-ruled. Each of the two meanings refers to one of the two parts of the compound word, *rājā* (ruler) and *ṛṣi* (sage). It strikes us as something of an etymological exercise, true to the letter; the young hermit who is also a student is displaying his knowledge. I leave it to the reader to judge whether it is true to the spirit.

The play subjects not only the ideal of kingship but also the character of Duhṣanta as King and man to an ironic scrutiny. In the process, Duhṣanta's personality is seen as far more complex and interesting than it would be if we were to perceive him as the ideal hero (*dhīrodātta nāyaka*) of the ancient texts on drama, and as a *rāja-ṛṣi.* He is presented as the great King he undoubtedly was in the popular imagination fed on story and legend. His personal appearance is described in images that convey majesty and strength as well as uncommon beauty and grace of manner. His frame is likened to that of a magnificent tusker roaming the mountains and as being spare and instinct with energy; his beauty of face and form dazzle like a priceless gem cut and polished by the exquisite art of a master craftsman. Even the rather cantankerous Śārṇgarava grudgingly admits that the kingdom is well-ruled. A number of images glorify him as a godlike hero; the very first image compares him to Śiva himself. But we have to keep in mind that the *sūta* (charioteer) who makes this comparison is also a bard and bards are given to praising highly the monarch they serve. However, an ironic point of view is adopted to show this great King as more human and fallible and less godlike and ideal. A 'public image' of Duhṣanta is built up by the 'praise-words' of hermits and bards alike; the latter are the public relations officers in the bureaucracies of the past. But, there is the 'private image' of the King too, the face other than the 'royal face' that we see from our privileged position as readers and audience. We see this when the King is in the company of the friend and close companion, Mādhavya, who is probably a childhood companion of Duhṣanta's, judging from his words in Act 2: 'Mādhavya, my friend, you have always been accepted as a son by our mother.' It is also sharply revealed in the many 'asides' given to the King in the play, mostly in Acts 1 and 3, as he watches Śakuntalā from where he is concealed behind bushes and thickets of vines. The two together, the 'asides' and the familiar and relaxed conversation with Mādhavya, complete the characterization which cannot be accomplished in all its fullness by the ceremonious verse alone used to project the royal and public image. Often the 'two faces' are dialoguing, commenting on each other through carefully arranged juxtapositions as in Act 2.

Another device used to project the two images of the King, is symbolic gesture. Act 1 furnishes a striking example of how symbolic gesture is manipulated to achieve several ends. On entering the sage Kaṇva's penance-groves, after some distance, Duhṣanta dismounts, takes off the regalia, his crown and jewels, and hands them over with his bow and arrows to the charioteer. This gesture (and I suspect that on the stage it would have been done deliberately and elaborately like a ritual by the actor), is symbolic in two ways: it represents the reverence the King feels in the sacred grove and all that it stands for and for the great sage who presides over it; it also signifies the act of 'putting off' of the royal image. The 'public image' of a king is a *mask* which he puts on like an actor putting on theatrical make-up and the costume to suit the role he is about to play. It goes with the regalia and the pomp and panoply which serve to impress and dazzle the world and through that to control it. Duhṣanta now enters the Hermitage simply dressed, like an ordinary person, a visitor. Further, in putting off his 'royal face', Duhṣanta is released from certain expectations and inhibitions on the part of others as well as his own. He enters another world, far removed from the court and its pressures in more senses than one—Śakuntalā's world. Śakuntalā does not see him in his awesome majesty and splendour. She and her friends see Duhṣanta simply as a noble from the court, an officer of the King which is how he introduces himself. And we too begin to see him, not as the great monarch bearing the heavy burden of his dynasty's fame and surrounded by the aura of Puru's idealism and exemplary conduct, but as just a young and handsome courtier, well-spoken, with an eye for pretty girls. The effect of the 'unmasking' is to put Śakuntalā's friends at ease; and a lively conversation ensues. However, this too is a mask, for Duhṣanta is the King only pretending that he is not the King. Priyamvadā and Anasūyā soon see through his threadbare disguise and the mask is quietly dropped, though the girls play along and keep up the pretence. But the action has already been initiated; Śakuntalā has fallen deeply in love and the plot must now move under its own impetus.

A good deal of good-humoured irony is also pointed at the ascetics in the Hermitage; those 'hermits rich in holiness' who have blazing energy hidden deep within like sun-crystals that can suddenly kindle into flames if provoked, are in fact as tame as the deer they love and care for. It is an outsider, Durvāsā, who blazes into a furious passion at being disregarded, and the object of his fury is a guileless and innocent young girl. The ideal of asceticism is being questioned here and a contrast drawn a few lines later between Durvāsā, self-important and arrogant, and Kaṇva. The patriarch Kaṇva is the ideal of a sage put forward, self-restrained and noble, gentle and warm and understanding.

Ascetic claims are also subjected to ironic scrutiny in Act 5. Kaṇva's disciples do not come off very well. Śārṇgarava is an angry man, arrogant and tactless; we can see him develop into a Durvāsā in time. We are surprised to see that he does not convey the message of Kaṇva (his guru) to the King in the sage's own words. Śāradvata, is a cold, harsh and uncharitable ascetic, somewhat obsessed by the idea of cleanliness. Neither seems to exemplify the popular idea of ascetics and of ascetic ideals. In contrast, the high priest for whom Śārṇgarava and Śāradvata show some contempt is the only one in the trial-scene who makes a kind and humane gesture towards the suffering Śakuntalā. And it is he who sees the miracle—Śakuntalā transported to another world.

Foreshadowing as a device is used a great deal in the play and skilfully. Śakuntalā's adverse fate is mentioned right at the beginning. (The sign given to Kaṇva at the cave of fire at Prabhāsa strikes one, however, as being cryptic.) Hints of future events are strewn around in the conversation of Śakuntalā and her friends. But the most important examples are in Act 5. The theme of failing memory, 'wakeful one moment / shrouded in darkness the next' and 'the dying flame', in the chamberlain's speech have subtle overtones. Then comes the song of betrayed love, sung in the background and we see the strange effect it has on Duhṣanta. Music makes a portent more ominous.

O, you honey-pilfering bee!
Greedy as ever for fresh honey,
once, you lovingly kissed
the mango's fresh spray of flowers—
and forgotten her—so quickly—?

This little scene takes us back to the beginning of the play, to the first little scene where Duhṣanta stands concealed behind the trees envying the bee that is hovering round Śakuntalā's face. The same word *'madhu-kara'* is used for the bee and used quite consciously. Sanskrit is a language rich in synonyms and the different roots from which the words are formed account for subtle nuances in meaning. The question that comes to the mind is—what is in store for Śakuntalā? We do not know that the Ring has been lost. And Kālidāsa's audience would not have known it either, because the Ring and the curse are not part of the Śakuntalā-Duhṣanta story in the epic that the audience would have been familiar with.

We already know about the King's many amorous adventures and his proneness to philandering from his conversation with Mādhavya in Act 2:

KING: Until you see her, you will continue to hold forth like this.

MĀDHAVYA: If that is so, she must indeed be a miracle of beauty to arouse such breathless admiration in *you*.

Mādhavya's remark immediately before this exchange of comments, about the King's jaded appetite seeking fresh interests is reinforced by the second line of the song. What is different, however, is the streak of callousness underlying the King's comment on Hamsavatī's song—'Yes, I once loved her deeply . . . .'—a callousness that turns into cruelty in the trial-scene that follows immediately.

Śakuntalā, a young girl—*bālā*, the word the King refers to her by, is a girl of sixteen—is out of the sheltered hermitage where she has grown up as her father's 'life-breath' for the very first time when she stands trial in the enclosure surrounding the royal Fire Sanctuary. The King's words are barbed with venom and unworthy of a great king who is the protector of the sacred groves in his realm. An example of the insults Duhṣanta flings at her is the comparison with the cuckoo that *flies* away, *abandoning* its offspring in the care of another bird. The reference is not only to her mother, Menakā, one of the Apsarās (who *fly* in the air), who abandoned her child, Śakuntalā, but to Śakuntalā herself who according to him is trying to pass off her offspring as his child. When Duhṣanta first met Śakuntalā, he found the strange circumstances of her birth an added attraction; she was the 'lightning's splendour', not of this earth. But that was in another world; it was Śakuntalā's, not his. In the world of the court, which she had characterized as 'alien soil' on which, like the sapling of the sandal tree rent from the parent mountain, she would not survive, Śakuntalā is unimaginably humiliated. Stripped of dignity and modesty, unveiled in public, an outrage in that society (as it is still in some societies), every word she speaks is twisted into a lie. Finally, she stands alone, abandoned by all. Such isolation is of the essence of a tragic situation in life. The play is poised on the edge of tragedy from which it must now be retrieved.

A point that should be noted is, that Śakuntalā is on trial in a very special place. It is not the King's hall of justice, where in other circumstances, the fisherman might have stood trial for having a valuable ring, the royal signet ring, in his possession. It is the 'raised enclosure of the Mystic Fire'—*Agni*, which witnesses men's deeds and words—which the King himself has selected as the place 'proper to receive ascetics'. The Mystic Fire has already announced Śakuntalā's marriage to Duhṣanta to Kaṇva, and prophecied the greatness of the son to be born of this union. The marriage is therefore a sanctified one.

Kaṇva is a revered sage, a *kulapati*, or head of a community of ascetics and the King has expressed his profound veneration for the sage in whom holy power (Brahmā) is vested as a result of his 'immense penance'. His people would have shared this view. Yet, his regard for the sage carries little weight in Duhṣanta's assessment of the situation at this juncture. It has no influence on his manner and conduct or the way he judges the sage's daughter. This might partly be the consequence of the manner in which the two disciples, especially Śārṇgarava, handle the situation. By putting the marriage of Śakuntalā to the King on a quasi-legal instead of a sanctified basis, as one would expect an ascetic to do, and by introducing public opinion as a factor into the situation, Śārṇgarava foregrounds the question of *proof* in the mind of someone responding defensively as the King does. Doubts about the legality of the marriage and the legitimacy of the unborn child would inevitably surface in the minds of the ministers, the court and the people. And these doubts have necessarily to form part of the King's reasoning as he faces an unexpected and difficult problem. (In the epic story, Duhṣanta clearly states these doubts as the reason for his repudiating Śakuntalā in the Hall of Assembly.) He poses a question to Śārṇgarava to which a clear answer cannot be given. The alternatives are, as Duhṣanta puts it, the desertion of a legally wed wife or adultery (or what seems to him to be adultery). Which is the lesser evil, he asks, since both are forbidden by the law and regarded as heinous sins. Śārṇgarava has no answer. It is a problem which the audience might have pondered over. Insensibly, the sanctuary of the Mystic Fire (*Agni-śaraṇa*), has been transformed into a court of law. Śakuntalā stands no chance of winning her case because she cannot produce the only concrete evidence of a secretly contracted marriage, the royal signet ring given to her by Duhṣanta. She is lost. In the last moments of her hour of sorrow and tribulation, when she flings her arms up to the indifferent skies and invites death as her last resort, a flash of light appears and carries her away. Śakuntalā vanishes, never to be seen again in this world. The reconciliation and reunion of Śakuntalā and Duhṣanta takes place in another world, the 'golden world' of the Primal Pair. The resolution of the plot is effected in this mythical world; therefore, one way of *reading* the play is to see it as having a fictive ending. By introducing the device of a *deus et machina*, the situation is saved, temporarily; the tragedy is averted, but the tragic tone remains.

The story of Śakuntalā and Duhṣanta in the *Mahābhārata* (recounted briefly in Appendix III) is the main source for the play. In it, Śakuntalā is portrayed as a fiery and spirited girl who fights tenaciously for her son's rights. She literally reads the Law to the King and when she finds him obdurate, gives him such a tongue lashing that we practically see him squirming on his jewelled throne and wishing he were elsewhere. The story as the epic tells it in the swinging narrative style, is powerful though rough hewn. It reflects the epic tone and the way of life of the heroic age. But to Kālidāsa, it provides the bare bones of a story which he has shaped into an intricate plot structure to produce a deeply moving play that probes and asks questions. Kālidāsa has drastically changed his sources to convey his own vision of life and his view of certain problems which seem to have deeply concerned him. The epic story has only two characters, Śakuntalā and Duhṣanta, with Kaṇva making a brief appearance. In the play, the conception of the two main characters are totally different, Kaṇva is an important figure and we have all the minor characters which are the dramatist's creations, for which there is not even a hint in the epic story. Kālidāsa has also introduced the curse and the King's loss of memory, and the Ring as the token of recognition. The story of the Ring might have been part of some old tale, folk or fairy tale, which is lost. The epic story has a happy ending. An incorporeal voice heard by everyone in the Hall of Assembly testifies to the truth of Śakuntalā's words and accepted as proof of marriage and the legitimacy of the son.

I venture to suggest that the characterization of the hero and heroine and the general mood of the play might be influenced by the old, lost tale of the Apsarā Śakuntalā, of which only a tantalizing hint remains embedded in the Vedic text referred to earlier. Śakuntalā's close association with nature, her kinship with tree-divinities (*yakṣīs*) and the reference to her as the 'guardian deity' of the Hermitage, point to this. The terms in which Duhṣanta talks of his meeting with her—'Was it a dream? a magical vision?. . . .'—and the frequent use of the word *moha* (and *sam-moha*) which has several meanings—wonder, illusion or delusion—to mention a few in this context, also point in this direction.

Other meanings of *moha* are: bewilderment, perplexity, the inability to discriminate. It is a state of mind hovering between different planes of consciousness, where the real and the imagined are interfused as in the portrait-episode in Act 6, which the pragmatist Mādhavya would characterize as being on the verge of madness. In fact it is one of the last stages in the progress of an unhappy lover which leads to death, as laid down in Bharata's *Nātyaśāstra*. The delusion under which the King labours is brought on by the curse, ostensibly. The operation of the curse is described in images of veiling, darkness, blindness and drunkenness with its unsettling consequences. We might single out as an example the comparison with a man who sees but does not *recognize* the object, who then infers its appearance and disappearance from traces (or a token) left behind (7.31). The curse and the manner in which it operates is related to the problem of recognition. It should therefore not be treated, as is often done, simply as a device to gloss over the unpleasant side of Duhṣanta's nature—his proneness to philandering, the streak of callousness in him verging on cruelty, his self-indulgence—or to exonerate him from the blame of harshly repudiating Śakuntalā and in so doing showing disrespect to a great sage. That might very well be one of the purposes of the curse. Kālidāsa's audience would have been as mixed as any audience at any time anywhere; and their responses would have varied, as in the case of audiences now. To see the image of a great monarch, a hero of the celebrated Puru dynasty which held a special place in story and therefore in the popular imagination, tarnished by ignoble behaviour without cause, was (and is still with some) bound to have been emotionally difficult to accept. To strip a people of cherished myths is not to be lightly undertaken. But as the curse can be seen and interpreted in more than one way, it ought to be considered as the means which Kālidāsa uses to explore different states of consciousness and to probe beneath the surface of Duhṣanta's personality.

While the loss of the Ring and the loss of memory resulting from the curse, provides the necessary complication in the plot structure, there is something else to which Kālidāsa alerts us. He directs us to question the whole idea of furnishing tangible proof for all those things in life we take on trust: love, constancy, fidelity. In Act 6, while the King and Mādhavya discuss the circumstances in which the Ring has been lost, Miśrakeśī makes a significant observation: 'Does a love like this need a token of recognition? How can that be?' I would take it that she refers to the love of both Śakuntalā and the King at this point. There are many instances in the literature of the world where this question needs to be asked: in the *Rāmāyana* when Sītā is asked to prove her chastity by undergoing the ordeal of fire a second time to allay the suspicions of the public: in Shakespeare's *Othello* and *King Lear* where proof of fidelity and of filial love is demanded, with tragic consequences. Śakuntalā is placed in a situation where she is unable to furnish proof of her marriage to the King who has in the meantime forgotten her. The royal signet ring which is the mark of authority and used to stamp documents to validate them (perhaps to stamp objects too, to prove the *legitimacy of ownership*) has gained an added importance and status: Śakuntalā is recognized or not recognized by virtue of its presence or its absence. As the play progresses, this Ring, an inanimate thing — 'a mindless thing' as the King describes it, becomes a *character* in the drama and plays a *role*. Its fall and loss goes hand in hand with the fall of Śakuntalā's fortunes and the loss of memory of the King and his fall into delusion and 'deep dejection'; its finding brings awakening and pain. The theme of *knowing* and *re-cognition* hinges on the presence or absence of the Ring.

XI

The *viduṣaka* or jester in Sanskrit drama is the friend and close companion of the hero. He performs two functions in the play which are related to the two meanings contained in the word: a figure of fun who excites laughter by his odd appearance and manner and his witty speech; and a 'detractor' or critic who deflates everyone around him through the exercise of a sharp and often caustic wit.

An ill-favoured hunchback, Mādhavya, the *viduṣaka* in our play, is the butt of ridicule for the world, which in turn is the target of his wit. And this includes him; for Mādhavya can laugh at himself. For example, at the opening of Act 2, we hear him talking to the King about the bent reed growing by the river bank, buffeted by the force of the current and tottering 'to and fro with the grace of a hunchback's gait'. Mādhavya's wry laughter is not without an element of pathos, a hallmark of most clowns and jesters who play the fool.

A relationship of deep affection exists between King and jester. It is reflected even in the tone of their conversation which has the easy familiarity of two friends who have grown up together from childhood. Mādhavya often addresses the King, in private, as *vayasya*—dear friend (literally 'one of the same age'). The King is able to put off his regalia and his public image, remove himself from the splendour and pressures of the court and relax in Mādhavya's company and be himself as he can with no one else.

As the friend and confidant of the King, Mādhavya is a privileged person and this fact taken together with the capacity to laugh at himself, makes him something of an ironic commentator in the play. His wit is no respecter of persons; even the Queen receives her share of his barbed comments and the King himself is not exempt. There are several examples in Act 2 where Mādhavya slips in some pointed criticism of the King, under the guise of affectionate banter. On entering, he first treats the audience to the sorry tale of his aching joints. His body is battered, galloping all day over rough paths following the King whose lust for the chase seems to be boundless. (Hunting is regarded as one of the eight vices that princes are warned against in manuals on ethics.) He misses the good life: good food, rest, sleep and 'sweet dumplings', needless to say. This is Mādhavya's *mask*; using it, he plays his role true to form, pretending to be slow on the uptake, but sharp and astute as he slips in his ironic comments smoothly and adroitly. He stands like a broken reed, supporting himself on his stick and when the King asks 'And what has paralysed your limbs?', knowing full well what Mādhavya's ploy is likely to be, the latter seizes the cue he has been waiting for. (King and jester understand each other well.)

MĀDHAVYA: A fine thing to ask; do you hit me in the eye—and then ask why it is watering?

KING: My dear friend, I do not follow; make your meaning clear.

MĀDHAVYA: If the bent reed by the river totters to and fro with the grace of a huncback's gait, does it do so on its own . . . hm . . . or, is the force of the current the cause?

KING: Why, in that case, the force of the current is the cause.

MĀDHAVYA: Yes, as you are, in mine.

KING: And how is that?

MĀDHAVYA (*as if angry*): Go on, you abandon the affairs of the kingdom . . .

This is how he puts it to the King. He, Mādhavya, the hunchback, is only an insignificant reed growing beside the river tottering and perhaps his well-being is not that important. (We have to link this with what the King says towards the end of the Act, that he is like a river which has to divide to go round a rock—an obstacle.) But, the affairs of the kingdom are a different matter; and the King is neglecting them to lead the primitive life of foresters, chasing wild animals (and a girl), unmindful of his duties. However, Mādhavya does not push the point too far; after all Duhṣanta is the King and kings could suddenly turn against the best of friends if provoked. But he has made his point to the King and to the audience, and lets it rest there. A little later in the Act he makes an oblique reference to the same point, when he tells the General, Bhadrasena, that the King is 'recovering his true nature' and asks the General not to fan the King's lust for the chase, but to go to hell himself.

Again, as he is leaving, rather put out, the King stops him to ask for help in 'a matter that will not cause you the least bit of exertion'. Mādhavya knows what the matter is but he pretends not to and asks rather ingenuously: 'Like tasting sweet dumplings, perhaps?'

Mādhavya's witty comments effectively deflate the King whenever the latter makes self-serving statements or holds forth on the theme of Śakuntalā's charms. When the jester remarks drily that there was little point in attempting to meet Śakuntalā once more since she was the daughter of a sage and therefore beyond the King's reach, Duhṣanta retorts with a flourish: 'You are a dull fellow, Mādhavya. Has Duhṣanta's heart ever been drawn to a forbidden object?' and proceeds to explain Śakuntalā's real parentage, to which Mādhavya's tart comment is: 'Oh! That's how it is, eh? Like one whose palate jaded by enjoying delicate candies made of the sweetest dates, hankers after a taste of the sour tamarind, you too, Sir, sated with the pleasures of the royal apartments . . . are consumed with a passion for this hermit-maiden.' Mādhavya deflates the King's craving for beautiful women by placing it on the same level as his own for sweet dumplings and candied dates; and further, sets against Duhṣanta's phrase describing Śakuntalā as 'the flower of the fragrant jasmine', his own of 'the sour tamarind'. Again, to the King's rapturous outburst regarding Śakuntalā's shy responses, that concludes with: 'Love neither shone radiant nor was it concealed', Mādhavya's quick retort is: 'What, Sir, did you then expect her to leap into your arms as soon as she set eyes on Your Honour?' And again, 'Go quickly, Sir, and rescue her before she falls into the hands of some forest-dwelling hermit with greasy head and hair plastered down with *ingudi* oil'.

Mādhavya provides the element of wit and humour so necessary to offset the element of romance in the play. His sharp comments serve as the tart tamarind to the cloying sweetness of Duhṣanta's declamation on love, its raptures and its pain. They also bring an ironic and critical perspective into a court where there is considerable adulation of the King; for Mādhavya serves as a foil to the court bards, whose duties are to compose and sing hymns of praise to the reigning monarch. His refreshing wit blows in some fresh air into the hothouse atmosphere of the court.

Though Mādhavya shoots off his witty barbs at the King whenever an opportunity presents itself, he is a loyal and true friend, supportive and not given to flattery. But this relationship of king and jester has to come to an end before the play proceeds to its conclusion. At the end of Act 6, Mādhavya is dismissed, not casually, or with disdain, but affectionately and with honour. He is entrusted with an important assignment, to inform the Chief Minister, Piśuna, about the momentous mission the King is setting out on and the circumstances leading up to it, and to instruct the minister to carry on the government in the meantime. Mādhavya accepts the royal command and leaves with quiet dignity. We never see him again; for he is no longer needed as the King's companion, to amuse and divert him. His witty comments, his homely wisdom spiced with time-worn proverbs containing sound practical sense are not needed either; not where Duhṣanta is headed for. And Mādhavya has no place in that 'other world', in the mythic world of Act 7; neither in the vanguard of Indra's battles against the dark forces nor in the 'golden world' of the Primal Pair, Mārīca and Aditi.

Duhṣanta is no longer the King he was. He has grown in understanding and has learnt compassion and caring for others. This is implied in the ruling he makes, which almost sounds like the setting up of a legal precedent, that the estate of the wealthy merchant who died in a shipwreck should not be confiscated by the state, but be inherited by his unborn child. This ruling has an extension in the form of a royal proclamation, that the King would be a friend and kinsman to all his subjects who follow the right path. Duhṣanta had to experience the grief of childlessness for himself and realize the dangers to an heirless kingdom before he is able to understand and feel for his subjects. He seems to have grown in another way too. After a long spell of penitential grief, he has gained the capacity to know and value true love, which is a matter of more than the delight of the eye and of pleasure. When he meets Śakuntalā again in Mārīca's Hermitage, he *sees* her, knowing her true worth; it is recognition, or *abhijnānam,* the highly suggestive word which forms the first part of the compound word that is the title of the play—*Abhijnānaśākuntalam.* The carnal knowledge he had of Śakuntalā which had carried him to dizzying heights of rapture only to plunge him into deep despair under the weight of an overwhelming guilt, is transformed. Mādhavya has no place in this changed world.

Initially, Mādhavya has no place in the 'green world' situated within deep forests. With the kind of opinion he expresses regarding ascetics—longbeards, with greasy heads and hair plastered down with *ingudi* oil, he cannot possibly feel at ease in Mārīca's Hermitage. In fact he would have been miserable in the 'golden world'. The jester has his feet firmly planted on the earth; we cannot imagine him sitting at the feet of Mārīca and Aditi, hymning their praises. In this connection Mādhavya's words to Duhṣanta when he is released by Mātali at the close of Act 6, are significant: 'He was about to slay me as if I were a *sacrificial beast,* and here . . . you welcome him. . . .' The denouement towards which the play is now leading, demands that Mādhavya be *sacrificed.*

The *viduṣaka* or jester of Sanskrit drama, belongs essentially to the world of the court, especially to the world of jealousies and intrigue of the royal harem. Apart from the aged chamberlain, he is the only male permitted entry into the inner and private apartments of the palace. This is the *viduṣaka's* world where he practises his cleverness, his talent for manipulation to bring the hero's many love affairs to a successful conclusion and to placate the other wives (or queens) or trick them into accepting the latest object of the hero's affections, as co-wife or queen, as the case may be. However, Mādhavya is not the typical *viduṣaka*; he is hardly involved in intrigue. As Śakuntalā is a different kind of heroine, Mādhavya is a different kind of jester and king's companion. The heroine and the jester never meet in this play. With exquisite poetic tact, Kālidāsa keeps them and their worlds apart. Mādhavya, as we noted earlier, never enters the 'green world'; he stands on its fringes complaining about his aching joints. At the end of Act 2, he is shunted off to the capital, ostensibly to take the King's place as a surrogate son in the Queen Mother's rites to ensure the succession. (That Duhṣanta is childless is made quite clear at the play's beginning.) He is absent in Act 3, where Duhṣanta courts Śakuntalā and their Gāndharva marriage takes place. In the trial scene in Act 5, Mādhavya is again not present when the ascetics and Gautamī arrive with Śakuntalā; he has been despatched immediately before this to pacify Queen Hamsavatī, smarting under Duhṣanta's neglect of her, the reason being that it would have been fatal to the plot to have had Mādhavya around at that point. In the two earlier plays of Kālidāsa, the *viduṣaka* is thrown into close contact with the heroine (*nāyikā*). But all Mādhavya knows about Śakuntalā is what the King tells him; he hears a great deal about her from Duhṣanta; he sees her in a portrait done by Duhṣanta. Śakuntalā is presented to the jester only through the eyes of the hero—*nāyaka*. And unlike the jesters in the other two plays, Mādhavya is bored by the whole matter of Śakuntalā.

No one from the court comes into close contact with the heroine of this play: in fact no one belonging to the court gains entry into her world—'the green world'. The King's retinue and companions only mill around its periphery, creating terror and confusion. And they leave with the jester at the close of Act 2, when he departs in state in the role of the King's younger brother—the heir apparent. When the play begins to gather all the threads—the *sutradhāra*, the director-producer, is the one who holds all the threads in his hands—and wind to its conclusion, the true heir apparent, Śakuntalā's son, Sarva-Damana, is in place, acknowledged as son and heir by the King.

In these and in many other respects, some of which have been discussed or touched upon, this play is totally different in tone, treatment of character and issues, from Kālidāsa's other plays. The moral and poetic vision that structures *Abhijnānaśākuntalam*, is unique as it is in *Meghadūtam* and it is somewhat similar. This seems tc suggest that they were written at about the same time and were the poet's last works. There is a gentle melancholy under the surface in both works, even in the happiest moments, an undercurrent of regret at the passing of the first flush of happiness of a newly-wed pair of lovers. In *Meghadūtam*, when the lovers are reunited, if ever they are, we sense that their love would be a chastened one; in st. 112, the poem draws a contrast between *bhoga* or sensual enjoyment and *prema* or deep affection; between passion and love. This contrast is more fully articulated in the play. At the end, the glow of youthful and exuberant love and happiness of the first and third Acts of the play has faded into the common light of duty; the focus and interest shifts to the son born of those first moments of intense passion. The last stanzas of the poem are coloured by a certain tentativeness of statement, and a hope for the reunion of the Yakṣa and his beloved wife. In the play, the long period of penance for Śakuntalā and repentance for Duhṣanta end in a reconciliation based on mutual respect and trust that brings some measure of happiness for both by finding a common ground in the child and his future.

There are moments of overhanging gloom, even darkness in *Abhijnānaśākuntalam*. There are moments too of bitter irony accompanied by flashes of pure good humour. But the play, though it has had its tragic moments, closes on a note of serenity, expressing the poet's vision of peace and harmony in a world where order has been restored. The little prince Sarva-Damana—All-Tamer—will grow up and be known as Bharata, he who bears, protects and sustains the world. It is after him that the country is called Bhārata Varṣa (modern Bhārat or India), the land of the Bhāratas who are the people of India.

All those born in this land before Bharata,
All those born after, are called after his name.

(*Mbh.*: I.69.49)

Ṛtusaṃhāram

(*The Gathering of the Seasons*)

A poem in six cantos

Canto I : Summer

1
The sun blazing fiercely,
the moon longed for eagerly,
deep waters inviting
to plunge in continually,
days drawing to a close in quiet beauty,
the tide of desire running low:
scorching Summer is now here, my love.

2
Night's indigo-masses rent by the moon,
wondrous mansions built on water,
cooled by fountains; various gems
cool to the touch; liquid sandal;
the world seeks relief in these
in Summer's scorching heat, my love.

3
Palace-terraces perfumed, luring the senses,
wine trembling beneath the beloved's breath,
sweet melodies on finely-tuned lutes:
lovers enjoy these passion-kindling things
at midnight in Summer, my love.

4
Curving hips, their beauty enhanced
by fine silks and jewelled belts;
sandal-scented breasts caressed by necklaces of pearls,
fragrant tresses bathed in perfumed water:

with these women soothe their lovers
        in burning Summer, my love.

5
Swaying hips; soles tinted deep rose;
anklets with tinkling bells
imitating at each step the cry of the wild goose:
        men's hearts are churned by desire.

6
Breasts rubbed smooth with liquid sandal,
crowned by strings of pearls lustrous as dewdrops,
hips encircled by gold girdles—
        whose heart will not yearn restless?

7
High-breasted women in the flush of youth,
limbs shining with beads of sweat, throw off
heavy garments and put on thin stoles
        right for the season to cover their breasts.

8
The breeze of moist sandal-scented fans,
the touch of flower-garlands on the beloved's breast,
the lute's exquisite murmuring sound:
        these now awaken sleeping Love.

9
Gazing all night longingly
on the faces of lovely women sleeping happy
on terraces of sparkling white mansions,
the moon pales[1] at dawn struck by guilty shame.

10
Hearts burning in the fire of separation,
men far from home can scarcely bear to see
the swirling clouds of dust tossed up
from the earth burnt by the sun's fierce heat.

11
Antelopes suffering from Summer's savage heat,
race with parched throats[2] towards the distant sky
the colour of smooth-blended kohl, thinking:
—there's water there in another forest.

12
As enchanting twilights jewelled by the moon
instantly kindle desire in pleasure-seekers' minds,
so do the graceful movements, subtle smiles
and wayward glances of amorous women.

13
In an agony of pain from the sun's fierce rays,
scorched by dust on his path, a snake with drooping hood
creeps on his tortuous course, repeatedly hissing,
to find shelter under a peacock's shade.

14
The king of beasts suffering intense thirst, pants
with wide open jaws, lolling tongue, quivering mane;
powerless to attack he does not kill
elephants though they are not beyond his reach.

15
Dry-throated, foaming at the mouth,
maddened by the sun's sizzling rays,
tuskers in an agony of growing thirst,
seeking water, do not fear even the lion.

16
Peacocks, exhausted by the flame-rays of the sun
blazing like numerous sacrificial fires,
lack the will to strike at the hooded snake
thrusting its head under their circle of plumes.

17
Tormented by the hot sun, a herd of wild boars
rooting with the round tips of their long snouts

in the caked mud of ponds with swamp-grass overgrown,
appear as if descending deep into the earth.

18
Burning under the sun's fiery wreath of rays,
a frog leaps up from the muddy pond
to sit under the parasol hood
of a deadly cobra that is thirsty and tired.

19
A whole host of fragile lotus plants uprooted,
fish lying dead, sarus cranes flown away in fear,
the lake is one thick mass of mire, pounded
by a packed elephant-herd pushing and shoving.

20
A cobra overcome by thirst darts his forked tongue out
to lick the breeze; the brilliance of his crest-jewel
flashes struck by brilliant sunbeams; burning
from Summer's heat and his own fiery poison
he does not attack the assemblage of frogs.

21
A herd of female buffaloes frenzied by thirst
emerges from the hill's caves, heads lifted up
sniffing for water, spittle overflowing from cavernous jaws
and frothing round their lips, pink tongues hanging out.

22
A raging forest fire burns tender shoots to a cinder;
cruel winds hurl shrivelled leaves high up with impetuous force;
all around waters shrink to the bottom in the sizzling heat;
O what a scene of horror the woodland's outskirts present!

23
Birds sit panting on trees shorn of leaves;
lean monkeys troop into caves overgrown with bushes;

wild bulls roam around looking for water;
elephant cubs diligently draw up water from a well.

24
Relentlessly driven by the force of violent winds,
the fire, brilliant as the vermilion petals
of the mallow rose unfolding,
speeds in every direction, smitten with longing to clasp
the tops of trees, bushes and creepers, and burns the earth.

25
Springing up at the skirts of the woodland,
the fire's glare tires the creatures of the woodland;
it blazes in the glens fanned by the winds,
crackles and bursts through dry bamboo thickets
and spreads in the grass, waxing each moment.

26
Incited by the winds, the wild fire roams
on all sides of the woodland, seeming to assume
multiple forms in the bright silk-cotton groves;
it glitters, burnished gold, in the hollows of trees
and springs up tall trees, to branches whose leaves are singed.

27
With their bodies burning in the fire's fierce heat,
elephants, wild bulls, lions, lay aside their enmity
and come quickly out of grasslands scorched by fire, together
like friends, to rest on the river's wide, sandy banks.

28
O lady, whose singing flows so sweet
in the night over the moonlit terraces,
may Summer waited upon by lovely women,
when pools are strewn thick with lotuses
and the air scented by Pātala flowers,
when waters are pleasant to laze in
and garlands of pearls cool with their touch,
pass in greatest delight and ease for you.

Canto II: Rains

1
With streaming clouds trumpeting like haughty tuskers,
with lightning-banners and drum beats of thunder claps,
in towering majesty, the season of rains
welcome to lovers, now comes like a king, my love.

2
Overcast on all sides with dense rain clouds, the sky
displays the deep glow of blue-lotus petals,
dark in places like heaped collyrium, smooth-blended,
glowing elsewhere like the breasts of a woman with child.

3
Implored by cātakas tormented by great thirst,
and hanging low weighed down by large loads of water,
massed clouds advance slowly, pouring many-streamed rain:
and the sound of their thunder is sweet to the ear.

4
Hurling thunderbolts that crash down to strike terror,
bending bows strung with lightning-streaks, letting loose
fierce sharp-shooting showers—cruel arrows fine-honed—
clouds, relentless, wound the hearts of men far from home.

5
The Earth covered by tender shoots of grass
brilliant as emeralds shivering into points of light,
by up-springing Kandalī leaf-buds and by ladybirds,
dazzles like a woman decked in gems, green and red.

6
A bevy of peacocks that sound ever-delightful,
eagerly watching out for this festive moment,
caught up in a flurry of billing and fondling,
now begin to dance, gorgeous plumage spread out wide.

7
Rivers swollen by a mass of turbid waters
rush with impetuous haste towards the seas,
felling trees all around on their banks
like unchaste women driven by passion-filled fancies.

8
Adorned with piles of tender tips of lush green grass
lying scattered, fallen from the jaws of browsing does,
and beautiful with burgeoning trees,
Vindhya's groves now captivate the onlooker's heart.

9
Dotting the woodlands are charming glades by streams,
haunted by timorous gazelles easily alarmed
—tremulous eyes like blue water lilies, enchanting—
and the heart is twisted with sudden longing.

10
Clouds loudly roar again and again:
nights are pitch-dark:
only the lightning's flashes light the way:
even so, amorous women driven by passion
are on their way to midnight trysts.

11
Clouds burst with terrifying peals of thunder;
lightnings flash. Women shrinking in fear
cling closely in bed to their loved husbands,
guilty though these men are of philandering.

12
Teardrops from eyes lovely as blue lotuses
rain down on soft lips red as ripe berries:
wives of men who travel far are desolate,
and toss aside their jewels, flowers and fragrances.

13
Thick with insects, dust and bits of grass,
a dirty-grey in colour, headed downward,
rain water snakes slowly on its tortuous way,
watched anxiously by a brood of nervous frogs.

14
Bees forsake pools where lotuses have shed their petals;
sweetly humming, the fools thirsting for honey
swarm round circlets on the plumes of dancing peacocks,
in the hope they are fresh-blossoming lotuses.

15
Infuriated by the thunder of the first rain clouds,
wild elephants trumpet again and again:
their temples spotless as bright blue-lilies are drenched
by the flow of rut with bees swarming over them.

16
Inlaid on all sides with sparkling waterfalls,
teeming with peacocks commencing their dance,
rocks kissed by low-hanging, rain-filled clouds—
the mountains kindle unbearable longing.

17
Blowing through groves of Kadambā and Sarja
and Ketakī and Arjuna, shaking the trees,
scented by the fragrance of their flowers,
consorting with clouds and cooled by rain drops—
whom do these breezes not fill with longing?

18

Hair cascading down to the hips,
fragrant flowers nestling behind the ears,
pearl strings fondling the breasts,
wine perfuming the breath—
women set the hearts of their lovers on fire.

19

Gleaming with rainbows,
filigreed with the lightning's glitter,
life-giving clouds, pendent, packed with water—
and women dazzling in gem-set earrings
and girdles festooned with bells—
both work together to steal
the hearts of men journeying abroad.

20

Women twine round their coiled hair
wreaths woven of fresh Kadambā flowers,
Kesara buds and Ketakī fronds,
and place the Arjuna's blossoming sprays
as pendants over the ears,
arranging them in many pleasing shapes.

21

With gorgeous mane of hair flower-scented
and limbs rubbed smooth with liquid sandal
and cream of black aloes,
hearing the thunder's voice
in the early hours of the night,
women slip at once away
from the apartments of their elders,
and quickly enter their own bed-chambers.

22

Lofty clouds deep-blue like blue-lotus petals,
stooping low, rain-laden, shot through with rainbow gleams,

move imperceptibly, waved on by gentle winds:
they seem to carry away the hearts of women,
grief-stricken, parted from husbands who travel far.

23
The first fresh showers break the drought,
the woodland seems to thrill with joy
as Kadambās burst into bloom;
it laughs displaying the Ketakī's bright leaf-buds
and dances; trees sway gesturing with wind-swept branches.

24
This season of massed rain clouds arranges
chaplets of Bakula blossoms twined with buds of Mālatī,
Yūthikā and other fresh-blooming flowers
on the heads of young wives as a fond husband would,
and fresh Kadambā sprays to fall over their ears.

25
Women adorn their beautiful breasts with nets of pearls,
and drape pale delicate silks round their shapely curving hips;
the fine line of down above the navel rises up
to meet the cool tingling touch of fresh raindrops:
how charming are the folds that furrow their waists!

26
Perfumed by the Ketakī's pollen-dust and
cooled by the fine spray of fresh raindrops,
the wind that instructs in dance
the trees bowed by loads of flowers
ravishes the hearts of men sojourning abroad.

27
'This noble mountain is our firm support
when we are bent double carrying loads of water'
thinking thus, rain clouds bow low to offer their gift of showers

and gladden Vindhya's hills grievously scorched
by the savaging flames of Summer's fierce forest fires.

28

A source of fascination to amorous women,
the constant friend to trees, shrubs and creepers,
the very life and breath of all living beings—
May this season of rains rich in these benedictions
fully grant all desires accordant with your well-being.

Canto III : Autumn

1
Robed in pale silk plumes of Kāśa blooms,
full-blown lotuses her beautiful face,
the calls of rapturous wild geese
the music of her anklet bells,
ripening grain, lightly bending, her lissome form:
Autumn has now arrived, enchanting as a bride.

2
The earth is bright with Kāśa blossoms,
nights with the cool rays of the moon;
streams are lively with flocks of wild geese
and pools are strewn with lotuses;
groves are lovely with flower-laden trees
and gardens white with fragrant jasmines.

3
Prettily girdled by glittering minnows darting about,
garlanded by rows of white birds on the margins,
with broad curving flanks of sandy banks,
rivers glide softly like young women rapt in love.

4
Squeezed dry of rain, a host of clouds
palest silver like delicate sea-shells,
float free in places, waved back and forth
by brisk winds with the utmost ease:
the sky appears like a great king
fanned by a hundred fleecy chowries.

5
The sky glows, a mass of glossy collyrium,
the earth dusted by Bandhūka pollen
is the colour of dawn;
mellow golden are river banks
and fields with ripening corn:
whose heart in the days of youth will not be seized with longing?

6
Its topmost twigs are tangled by a gentle breeze;
sprays of blossoms rise out of delicate leaf-crowns;
bees are whirling drunk on honey trickling down;
whose mind is not ripped by the beauty of this Kovidāra tree?

7
Splendidly jewelled by numberless star-clusters,
Night wraps herself in moonlight's shining robe
when the moon her face struggles free of obscuring clouds.
Day by day, she grows like a young girl
stepping gracefully into proud womanhood.[3]

8
Ringing with mournful belltones of wild geese,
waters dyed rose-red by lotus pollen
and ruffled by circling ripples where teals plunge in,
banks noisy with black ducks and sarus cranes jostling,
streams all around bring delight to watchers.

9
The moon, the eye's delight,
captivates all hearts with aureoles bright;
Bringer of Joy, showering beams cool as snowflakes,
it consumes the limbs of women
pierced by the poisoned arrows
of separation from their husbands.

10
A breeze sets the bending ears of corn swinging,
great trees bowed down by masses of flowers dancing,
pools thick with blossoming lotuses quivering;
and violently unsettles soft young minds.

11
The breathtaking beauty of rippling lakes
breathed on by a passing wind at daybreak,
where lotus and lily glow brilliantly
and pairs of love-drunk wild geese float entrancing,
suddenly grips the heart with longing.

12
Lost is Indra's bow in the bowels of the clouds;
lightning, the sky's banner, quivers no more;
egrets no longer beat the air with their wings;
peacocks do not watch the sky with upturned faces.

13
The dance-display ended, Love deserts the peacocks
to attend the honey-sweet concert of wild geese;
Beauty, Genius of Blossom-Time, forsaking
the Kadambā, Kutaja, and Kakubha,
the Sarja and Aśoka, now dwells, in the Sapta-parna.

14
Redolent of the fragrance of Śephālika blossoms,
resonant with bird-song in undisturbed quietness,
groves with lotus-eyed gazelles wandering in the glades
kindle restless longing in everyone's heart.

15
Playfully tossing lotuses, pink, white and red,
deliciously cooled moving fondly among them,
wiping away the dewdrops edging their petals
the breeze at daybreak rocks the heart with wild longing.

16
People rejoice to see the village-bounds
crowded with large herds of cows lying undisturbed,
where ripe grain lies spread in heaps on threshing floors
and the air rings with cries of wild geese and sarus cranes.

17
The gait of wild geese surpass the rare charm of women's steps,
full-blown lotuses the radiance of their moon-bright faces;
blue water lilies rival the lustre of passion-glowing eyes,
delicate wavelets the play of their eyebrows graceful.

18
Śyāma creepers curving with tender flower-filled twigs
usurp the brilliance of women's jewel-loaded arms;
fresh jasmines peeping through vibrant Aśoka flowers
rival the sparkle of smiles brilliant as moonlight

19
Young women fill with a wealth of jasmine buds
their thick midnight-blue hair curling at the ends;
they place varied blue-lotuses
behind ears decked with fine gold earrings.

20
Globed breasts adorned with pearls sandal-misted,
wide curving hips with girdles strung with bells,
precious anklets making music on their lotus feet,
lit with happiness deep within
women now enhance their beauty.

21
A cloudless sky inlaid with the moon and countless stars
wears the exquisite beauty of lakes glowing
with the sheen of emeralds, and strewn with moon-lotuses,
wide open; and a regal swan floats serene.[4]

22
Autumn skies are enchanting, star-sprinkled,
lit by a clear-rayed moon; serenely beautiful
are the directions of space, free of thronging rain clouds:
the earth is dry; waters sparkling clear;
breezes consorting with lotuses blow cool.

23
Wakened by the morning beams, the day-lotus
now expands to look like a lovely maiden's face;
but the moon-lotus droops with the setting moon
like the smiles of women whose husbands are far from home.

24
Seeing the glow of the beloved's dark eyes
in the blue-lotus,
hearing the tones of her gold girdle bells
in the love-mad murmur of wild geese,
recalling the rich red of her lower lip
in the Bandhūka's flame-clusters,
travellers, their thoughts whirling, lament.

25
Conferring the radiance of the moon
on the faces of women,
the melodious tones of wild geese
on their gem-filled anklets,
the Bandhūka-bloom's vibrant redness
on their luscious lower lips,
the splendour of bountiful Autumn
is now departing, to who knows where!

26
Full-blown lotuses, pale-pink, her face,
deep-blue lilies unfolding, her dark eyes,
fresh white Kāśa blooms, her bright robe,

glowing with the brilliance of moon-lotuses,
may this Autumn, like your beloved
lost in love for you,
fully grant your heart's highest happiness.

Canto IV : The Season of Frosts

1
The sudden burst of the barley's young shoots
shows delightful; Lodhras are in full bloom;
paddy golden ripe; lotuses all withered:
thick-falling dews usher this season of frosts.

2
Pearl-garlands pale, misted with liquid sandal,
lustrous as dew drops or jasmines or the moon,
do not enhance with their elegance
the orb-like breasts of graceful women.

3
Delicate bodices do not tenderly touch
the swelling breasts of young women moving
with exquisite grace;
fine new silks do not cling to their curving hips;
bracelets and armlets do not clasp their arms.

4
Women in their pride of beauty and youth
do not adorn their hips with gold girdles, gem-studded,
or their lotus-feet reflecting the glow of lotuses
with anklets that sound the bell-tones of wild geese.

5
Women now prepare for love's festival,
perfuming their hair with black-aloe smoke,

tracing leafy lines on their lotus-faces,
and rubbing their bodies with white-aloe salve.

6
With faces pale and drawn, from love's weariness,
young women whose lips smart from love-bites
are afraid to laugh out loud
even when a happy occasion arises.

7
Seeming sensible of the sensuous beauty
of women's breasts, sad to see them pressed so hard,
the frosty season cries out at dawn, letting fall
dew drops that cling to the tips of blades of grass.

8
Fields richly covered with ripening rice
where charming does roam in herds
are sonorous with the calls of damsel cranes.
Ah! What restlessness they arouse!

9
Where the chill waters of lakes shimmer
blue lotuses open wide in beauty;
mallards court in wild excitement:
all hearts are transported with boundless delight.

10
Languishing blanched in the chilling frost,
ever-shivering in the blowing wind,
like a sprightly girl parted from her love,
the Priyangu now grows pale, my love.

11
Mouths redolent of the fragrance of flower-wine,
limbs perfumed from mingled breaths—
men and women sleep, twined in one another's arms,
blended in the sweet poetry of love.

12
Sharp imprint of love-bites on bruised lips,
the lover's[5] fine nail-inscriptions on breasts—
these clearly reveal the passionate enjoyment,
relentless, of women in the first flush of youth.

13
A certain young woman, mirror in hand,
decorates her radiant lotus-face, basking
in the gentle warmth of the mild morning sun
and gazes with interest, pouting, at the love-bites
her beloved left when he drank his fill
of the nectar of her lower lip.

14
Yet another, her body limp
from toiling at passion's intense play,
her lotus-eyes painfully red
from the long night's long vigil,
—richly-flowing mane of hair waving
wildly over weary, drooping shoulders—
falls asleep,
warmed by a tender sun's gentle rays.

15
Other young women whose willowy frames
sway a little
bearing the burden of high, swelling breasts,
remove from foreheads framed by hair,
midnight-blue like dense rain clouds,
the faded chaplets worn at night
—the exquisite fragrance quite lost,
once enjoyed—and dress their hair again.

16
Another, with curving eyes, and
dark hair flowing down in playful curves,

the charm of her lower lip restored, radiant,
looks down at her body enjoyed by her lover,
notes carefully the nail-marks
and then glowing with joy, puts on her bodice.

17
Toiling long hours at love's passionate sport,
other lovely young women o'ercome with fatigue,
have their slender, languid bodies massaged with oils:
—the chilly air makes their breasts and thighs tingle.

18
May this season of glittering frosts, delightful
by virtue of its many excellences
that enthralls the hearts of women;
when the village-bournes are brimful
of bountiful harvests of golden grain;
when the dew falls thick
and the air is sweet with the curlew's notes,
fully grant you all happiness.

Canto V : Winter

1
Stacks of ripe rice and sugar-cane cover the earth;
the air rings with the hidden calls of curlews;
love grows exuberant: Dear to lovely women,
winter is now here; hear now, my love.

2
People close their windows tight, light fires,
keep warm in the sun and wear heavy garments:
men find the company of youthful women
pleasing at this time of the year.

3
Neither liquid sandal chilled by moonbeams
nor breezes cool with falling dew, nor terraces
of mansions bright with the autumnal moon,
delight the mind at this time of the year.

4
Cold, cold, with heavy dews falling thick,
and colder yet with the moonbeams' icy glitter,
lit with ethereal beauty by wan stars,
these nights give no comfort or joy to people.

5
Wives eager for love, their lotus-faces
fragrant with flower-wine, enter their bed-chambers
aromatic with the incense of black aloes,[6]
taking betel-rolls and garlands and hot perfumes.

6
Women whose husbands continue unfaithful
though bitterly chided again and again,
note them flustered, visibly shaken by guilt:
yet, yearning to be loved, they overlook these wrongs.

7
Enjoyed long through the long night in love-play
unceasing by their lusty young husbands
in an excess of passion, driving,
unrelenting, women just stepped into youth
move at the close of night slowly
reeling wrung-out with aching thighs.

8
With breasts held tight by pretty bodices,
thighs alluringly veiled by richly-dyed silks,
and flowers nestling in their hair, women serve
as adornments for this wintry season.

9
Lovers enjoying the warmth of budding youth,
pressed hard against breasts glowing golden,
saffron-rubbed, of lively women gleaming sensuous,
sleep, having put to flight the cold.

10
Young women in gay abandon drink at night
with their fond husbands, the choicest wine,
most delicious, exhilarating,
heightening passion to its pitch:
the lilies floating in the wine deliciously
tremble under their fragrant breath.

11
At dawn, when the rush of passion is spent,
one young woman whose tips of breasts are tight

from her husband's embrace, carefully views
her body fully enjoyed by him
and laughing gaily, she goes from the bed-chamber
to the living-apartments of the house.

12
Another loving wife leaves her bed at dawn:
elegant and graceful, slender-waisted,
with deep navel and ample hips;
the splendid mane of hair with curling ends
flowing loose, the wreath of flowers slips down.

13
With faces radiant as golden lotuses
and long, liquid eyes; with lustrous red lips
and hair playing enamoured round their shoulders,
women shine in their homes these frosty mornings,
bearing the semblance of the goddess of beauty.

14
Young women burdened by their ample loins,
and drooping a little at the waist,
wearied bearing their own breasts, move very slowly:
quickly casting off garments worn at night
for love's sweet rites,
they put on others suited to the day.

15
Staring at the curves of their breasts covered by nail marks,
touching gingerly the tender sprout of the lower lip
bruised by love-bites, young women rejoice to see
these coveted signs of love's fulfilment,
and decorate their faces as the sun rises.

16
This wintry season that abounds with sweet rice,
and sugar-cane,

and mounds of dark palm-sugar dainties:
when Love waxes proud
and love's sport is at fever-pitch;
when the anguish is intense of parted lovers:
May this season be to you ever auspicious.

Canto VI : Spring

1
Sprays of full blown mango blossoms—his sharp arrows,
honey-bees in rows—the humming bowstring;
Warrior-Spring set to break the hearts
of Love's devotees, is now approaching, my love.

2
Trees put forth flowers, waters abound in lotuses,
women's thoughts turn to love; the air is sweetly scented;
mornings are pleasant and days delightful:
all things are more alluring in springtime, my love.

3
The waters of pools, gem-studded girdles,
the moon's brilliance, women proud of their beauty,
mango trees bowing low with blossoms: on each
Spring pours its profusion of bounty and grace.

4
Fine woven silks dyed scarlet with mallow juice
swathe round hips; delicate silks saffron-dyed,
shining pale gold, veil the perfect orbs of breasts:
women now dress with light-hearted elegance.

5
Fresh Karṇikāras nestle at their ears,
Aśoka blooms and fragrant full-blown jasmines
dapple trembling blue-black curls—they gain brilliance
when chosen to enhance the sensuous beauty of women.

6
Garlands of pearls moist with white liquid sandal
caress the breasts; armlets and bracelets clasp the arms,
and girdles with golden bells embrace the hips
of lovely, love-tormented women.

7
Lines of petal and leaf are delicately traced
on the golden-lotus faces of graceful women;
beautiful, like pearls set in between gems,
amid the traceries spread beads of sweat.

8
Women whose limbs unknot and become limp
under the nagging ache of love, take heart
reviving from the nearness of the husbands they love;
they are now filled solely with impatient longing.

9
The Bodiless One makes women thin and pale
languid from desire, to stretch and yawn greatly
again and again; breathless and flustered
from the excitement of their own loveliness.

10
Without form, Love now shapes himself many ways:
in women's roving, wine-heavy eyes,
in their pale cheeks and in their hard breasts,
in their sunken middle, in their plump buttocks.

11
Love has now made the limbs of beautiful women
bewitching from langour, sleep-induced;
their speech somewhat slurred, drowsy from wine; their glances
awry from the arch play of arching eyebrows.

12
Young women languid with intense desire,
smear their fair breasts with liquid sandal

blended well with dark sandal and saffron,
musk and fragrant priyangu seed.

13
Struck by spring fever, to cool their bodies,
people quickly put off heavy garments
and wear thin ones instead, dyed red with lac-juice,
and perfumed by the incense of black aloes.

14
Drunk on the honey of mango blossoms,
the koel rapturously kisses his mate:
the bee, too, humming among the lotuses,
whispers sweet flatteries to his sweet love.

15
The hearts of women throb with deep yearning
watching mango trees swaying in the breeze
with low-hanging sprigs of coppery-red shoots,
and branches showing off their blossoming loveliness.

16
Gazing on Aśoka trees putting forth tender shoots
and covered down to the roots in a profusion of buds
coral-red and rich copper,
the hearts of maidens budding into youth
fill with ineffable sadness.[7]

17
Tender leaf-shoots on young Atimukta creepers
bend and wave in a gentle breeze; their lovely blossoms
ardently kissed by intoxicated honey bees:
intently watching, lovers experience sudden longing.

18
Glancing at the amaranth's blossoming sprays
glowing in exquisite loveliness, just-revealed,

—loveliness that rightly belongs to the beloved's face—
how can a sensitive heart not flutter in pain
stung by proud Love's flying arrows, my love?

19
All around Kimśuka groves blaze fiery red,
trees swaying in the breeze bend low flower-laden;
instantly transformed by Spring, the earth glows
like a radiant young bride in her robe of red silk.

20
Lost already to beautiful girls,
are not young men's hearts pounded to bits
by Kimśuka blossoms bright as parrots' beaks?
Are they not already burnt
by the golden champa's brilliant blooms?
And now, the cuckoo with its honey-sweet notes
sounds their death knell.

21
The liquid notes, indistinct, of koels enraptured,
the exulting hum of honey bees, intoxicated,
make the hearts of even decorous and bashful brides,
highbred, of noble houses, greatly perturbed.

22
Gently frolicking with the mango's flowering branches
carrying the koel's cooing, far, in all directions,
the balmy breeze, dew-free, blows most gracious,
captivating all our hearts now in springtime.

23
Enchanting pleasure gardens resplendent with jasmines
sparkling as the playful laughter of lovely women
can entice even a saint's heart serene and passion-free;
Can young hearts turbid with passion remain unmoved?

24
With girdles of golden bells dangling at their waists,
strings of pearls clinging to their breasts,
slender women, soft and yielding from the flames of love,
accompanied by the sweet symphony
of bees and cuckoos in honied spring
ravish the hearts of men.

25
People thrill with joy gazing at hillsides
richly decorated with flowering trees;
rocky hilltops inlaid with lace of alpine flowers,
valleys overflowing with raptures of joyous koels.

26
Seeing the mango trees in full bloom, the traveller,
desolate, parted from his beloved wife,
closes his eyes, grieves, sheds tears,
covers his nose with one hand and cries aloud.

27
The hum of madly excited honey bees,
the cuckoo's sweet melodies, blossoming mango trees;
golden champa gaily festooned with flowers—
with these sharp arrows, the month of flowers, rakes
the proud hearts of noble women
and Love's flames kindle and blaze.

28
His choicest arrow—the lovely spray of mango flowers:
his bow—prettily-curved Kimśuka blooms:
the bowstring—rows of honey bees:
the royal white umbrella, spotless—the moon:
his proud elephant—the balmy southern breeze:
cuckoos his bards:
May bodiless Love, world-conqueror, joined by Spring
grant you all happiness, evermore.

Meghadūtam

(*The Cloud Messenger*)

1

A certain yakṣa unmindful of his appointed duties
and cursed by his lord to endure
a year's grievous separation from his beloved
dwelt exiled, his lustre dimmed, on Rāma's hill
in hermitages thick with shade-trees and waters
hallowed by the touch of Janaka's daughter.

2

The impassioned lover having passed some months
on that hill, parted from her unsupported
—the golden armlet slipping down
to lay bare his wasted fore-arm—
saw on Āṣāḍha's most auspicious day
a cloud embracing the crest of the hill,
strikingly-shaped[1] like a sportive elephant
bent down to butt a river bank.

3

Gazing on that which stirs the ketaka to bloom
the vassal lord of the King of Kings
brooded long,
with effort restraining his tears.
The sight of rain clouds makes even happy hearts
stir with restlessness;
what then of one far from her who longs
to hold him in close embrace.

4

With the month of rains approaching,
desiring to sustain his beloved's life,[2]
hoping to send glad tidings of his wellbeing
through the life-giving cloud, he made with reverence
an offering of fresh blossoms of wild jasmine,
prefacing it with words of affection
and joyously welcomed the cloud.

5

Blended of mists and light, winds and water
can a mere cloud bear messages
that only the living with keen senses
and intelligence can convey?
Unmindful of this the yakṣa entreated it,
overwhelmed by unreasoning eagerness;
indeed, the love-sick, their minds clouded,
confuse the sentient with the insentient.

6

Born in the lofty lineage of swirling diluvial clouds,
I know you are the god of thunder's minister
assuming what shape you will; so, banished
from wife and kinsmen by divine decree, I entreat you;
for it is nobler to address barren pleas
to the virtuous than fruitful to the vile.

7

You are the refuge, O Rain-Giver
for all who burn with anguish;[3] so bear
a message from me parted from my love
by the wrath of the Lord of Treasures;
go then to Alakā, abode of the Yakṣa Lord,
her palaces washed by moonlight
streaming from Śiva's brow
where He is seated in her outer groves.

8

Women whose husbands travel to far lands,
pushing back their straggling hair
will eagerly look up to see you
riding high on the path of the wind,
and draw comfort; for when you arrive
all clad and girt for action,

who can ignore his lonely wife distraught
unless subject like me to an alien will?

9

While a friendly breeze impels you gently
as you loiter along, and here on your left
the cātaka in its pride[4] sings sweetly,
hen-cranes will know the time ripe for mating
and rejoice when they note in the sky
your eye-delighting presence; rest assured
they will attend on you in patterned flight.

10

Arriving there unimpeded you are certain
to see that constant lady,
your brother's wife still living
engrossed only in counting the days;
Hope's slender thread serves to hold
the flower-hearts of women
tender and prone to droop too soon
under the burden of separation.

11

And, hearing your thunder—a sound sweet to their ears—
that can make Earth unfurl her mushroom parasols,
regal swans longing for Mānasa-lake,
gathering tender lotus-shoots for the way
will be your companions in the sky
even up to Mount Kailāsa's peak.

12

Embrace and bid farewell to your loving friend,
this lofty mountain girdled[5] by slopes marked
by the holy feet of the Lord of Raghus
adored by the world.
Time and again, reuniting with you,

it displays its affection, breathing out
burning sighs born of long separation.[6]

13

Listen first, while I describe the way
fitting for your journey which you will follow
resting your foot on mountains when weary,
refreshed when wasted by the clear water of streams:
then you shall hear my message, O Rain-Giver,
drinking it in eagerly with your ears.

14

While simple Siddha maidens with upturned faces,
watching your impetuous power tremble in alarm
and cry: 'Is the wind carrying off the mountain's peak?'
soar high up into the sky facing north,
far above this thicket of sap-filled nicula,
shunning on your path the proud sweep of the heavy trunks
of the elephants that guard the sky's quarters.

15

Here to the east, a fragment of Indra's bow
springs spectacular from the hill top, gleaming
as if blended of the lustres of brilliant gems.
Shot through by its sheen, your dark-blue body
shines resplendent like Viṣṇu's in his cowherd guise,
lit up by irridescent peacock-plumes.

16

While rustic women unversed in eyebrow play
drink you in with eyes moist with happiness
knowing the harvest to depend on you,
ascend the upland plains fragrant from fresh furrowing;
then veering slightly to the west, speed on
keeping ever to the north.

17

As you approach the noble mountain Citrakūta,
he will greet you, O travel-weary Rain-Giver,
and bear you on his head held high: you too
with sharp showers will quench summer's cruel fires.
The tenderness of true feeling in the great
bears fruit in no time, returning kindness for kindness.

18

With his forest fires fully quenched by your sharp showers,
Āmrakūta will bear you gratefully
on his crown, travel-weary as you are;
even the meanest remembering former favours
will not turn his face away from a friend
who seeks shelter; what then of one so lofty!

19

Its slopes all aglow with the ripened fruit
of wild mangoes, and you on its peak set
like a coil of dark glossy hair, the mountain
—seeming Earth's breast—dark-blue centre
encircled by pale-gold expansive curves—
will appear entrancing to celestial lovers.

20

Resting awhile on that mountain
in whose bowers the brides of foresters sport,
and lightened by your waters' outpouring
you'll speedily cross the road beyond
and see Revā's streams spreading dishevelled
at Vindhya's uneven rocky foothills,
inlaying them like ashen streaks
decorating an elephant's body.

21

Your rain disgorged, draw up that river's water
whose flow impeded by rose-apple brakes

is pungent with the scent of wild elephants in rut,
and journey on; gaining inner strength
the wind cannot make light of you, O Rain-Cloud;
for hollowness makes things light; fullness bestows weight.

22

Seeing the green-gold Nīpa flowers
with their stamens half-emerging
and the Kandal is showing their early buds
along the edge of every pool,
savouring the rich fragrance of the earth
in the forests burnt by fire,
antelopes will chart your path as you pass
shedding fresh rain drops.

23

Siddhas watching cātakas
skilled catching falling rain drops,
and pointing out to egrets in flight,
counting them on their fingers,
will pay you their grateful respect,
suddenly obtaining a flurry of unexpected embraces
from their beloved wives clinging to them in alarm
trembling at the sound of your thunder.

24

Even though you would wish to proceed with speed
for the sake of my happiness, my friend,
I foresee delay while you loiter
on peak after peak fragrant with wild jasmine;
though peacocks, their eyes moist with joy may greet you
with welcoming cries, I pray you, try to hasten onward.

25

The Daśārṇas will put on a new beauty
at your approach:
woodlands ringed round by ketakas

with needle-pointed buds newly-opened
will glow a pale gold:
birds starting to nest will throng
the sacred peepuls in the village squares:
rose-apple groves will darken
with the sheen of ripening blue-black fruit
and wild geese settle for a few days.

26

When you reach that royal city, Vidiśā by name
widely renowned, you shall at once obtain
the unalloyed fulfilment of a lover's desire,
tasting Vetravatī's sweet waters as a lover his beloved's lips,
with sonorous thunder passing along her banks
as she flows with knitted brows of tremulous wavelets.

27

There you shall alight seeking rest on Nīcai hill
thrilling with delight at your touch
as Kadambās burst into sudden bloom;
the hill loudly proclaims through grottoes
exhaling fragrances of pleasure,
passions unrestrained of the city's youth
dallying there in love-sports with courtesans.

28

Having rested, go on, sprinkling with fresh rain drops
clusters of jasmine-buds in gardens by woodland streams,
enjoying a fleeting together-ness
as your gift of shade touches
the faces of flower-gathering maidens, who
each time they wipe the sweat off their cheeks, bruise
the wilting lotuses hung at their ears.

29

As your course points due north to Alakā,
the way to Ujjayinī is a detour no doubt,

but do not therefore turn away from a visit to her palace-terraces.
Indeed you would have lived in vain if you do not dally there
with the tremulous eyes of the city's beautiful women
that dart in alarm at the branched lightning's flashes.

30

On your path, when you meet Nirvindhyā
wearing a girdle strung of chiming bells
—a row of water-birds plashing on her undulating waves—
weaving her sinuous course with charming unsteady gait
to reveal eddies forming her navel
—such coy gestures are women's first statements of love—
be sure to be filled with love's fine flavour.

31

Crossing that river, O fortunate lover,
yours will be the happy task to induce Sindhu
visibly grieving at your absence,
her waters shrunk to a thin braid and pale
with the paleness of dry leaves
fallen from trees rooted on her banks,
to cast off the sorrow withering her.

32

Reaching Avantī whose village-elders
are well-versed in the Udayana-tales,
go towards that city already spoken of;
to Ujjayinī glowing in splendour
like a brilliant piece of Paradise
come down to earth with traces of merits
of dwellers in Paradise returning,
the fruit of their good deeds almost spent.

33

At day-break in Ujjayinī, Śiprā's cool breeze
scented with the fragrance of lotuses comes

prolonging the piercing cries of love-maddened sāras-cranes.
Refreshing to the tired limbs of women
after passion's ecstatic play, it removes
their langour like an artful lover
plying his love with amorous entreaties.

34 & 35

Smoke drifting through lattice-screens
from aromatic gums that perfume women's hair
enhances your beautiful form;
Palace-peacocks out of fellow-feeling
present you their gift-offering of dance;
worn out with travel, having passed the night
in her flower-fragrant mansions marked with red lac
from the feet of lovely ladies, approach
the holy shrine of Candeśvara, Preceptor of the Triple-World,
watched with awe by the Lord's attendants,
because your hue is the blue of His throat.
Its gardens are stirred by Gandhavatī's breezes
scented with the pollen of blue-lotuses
and fragrances wafted from unguents
used by young women sporting in her waters.

36

If by chance you reach Mahākāla at a time other than sunset,
stay on till the sun disappears from sight;
by performing the exalted office of the temple-drum
in the evening-rituals offered to the spear-armed Lord
you will enjoy the full fruit, O Rain-Bearer,
of the deep-throated rumblings of your thunder.

37

With jewelled belts tinkling as they move with measured steps,
temple-dancers whose hands tire, gracefully waving
chowries with glittering gem-studded handles,
will taste from the first rain-drops you shed,

pleasure as from a lover's nail-marks and shower on you
sidelong glances streaming like a line of honey-bees.

38

Then bathed in evening's glow red as fresh china rose flowers
when the Lord of Beings commences His Cosmic Dance,
encircling, merging into the forest of His uplifted arms,
dispel His desire to wear the blood-moist elephant-hide,
your devotion observed by Bhavānī
with steady eyes, her terror now calmed.

39

Young women going to their lovers' dwellings at night
set out on the royal highway mantled
in sight-obscuring darkness you could pierce with a pin;
light their path with streaked lightning
glittering like gold-rays on a touchstone,
but do not startle them with thunder and pelting rain
for they are easily alarmed.

40

On the top most terrace of some turreted mansion
where ring-doves sleep,
pass the night with your lightning-wife
much-fatigued by continual play. But pray
resume your journey the moment the sun rises;
surely, those who undertake to help a friend
do not linger over providing that help.

41

Philandering hushands come home at sunrise
called on to comfort their anguished wives
by drying the welling tears of betrayal;
therefore move quickly out of the sun's path;
he too returns at dawn to the lotus-pool
to dry the dew-tears on her lotus-face;
he would be not a little incensed
that you obstruct his bright ray-fingers.

42

Your self intrinsically beautiful
even in its shadow-form will enter Gambhīrā's clear waters
as into a tranquil pool of consciousness;
do not therefore cavalierly dismiss
her welcoming glances—those dazzling upward leaps
of glittering white fishes bright as water-lilies.

43

Her dark-blue waters like a garment
slipping off the sloping bank of her hips,
still cling to the reed-branches
as if lightly held up by one hand;
drawing it away as you bend over her, my friend,
will it not be hard for you to depart?
For who can bear to leave a woman, her loins bared,
once having tasted her body's sweetness?

44

Fragrant with the scent of the earth freshened by your showers,
a cool wind that ripens the fruit on wild fig-trees
is inhaled with delight by elephants
through their water-spout-trunks;
it will waft you gently to the Lord's hill
that you seek to approach.

45

Skanda has made that hill his fixed abode;
transform yourself into a flower-cloud
and shower him with blossoms moist with Gaṅgā's celestial waters;
for he is the blazing energy, sun-surpassing,
that the wearer of the crescent-moon placed
in the Divine Fire's mouth to protect Indra's hosts.

46

Then, let your thunder magnified by the echoing mountain
spur the peacock the fire-born god rides, to dance,

its eyes brightened by the radiance of Śiva's moon;
Bhavānī out of affection for her son
places its fallen plume
gleaming with irridescent circlets on her ear
in place of the lotus-petal she wears.

47

Having thus worshipped
the god born in a thicket of reeds
and travelling some distance
as Siddha-couples bearing lutes
leave your path free, from fear of water-drops,
bend low to honour Rantideva's glory sprung
from the sacrifice of Surabhi's daughters
and flowing on earth changed into a river.

48

Stealing the colour of the god who draws the horn-bow
as you bend down to drink its waters,
sky-rangers looking down will indeed see with wonder
that river from the far distance
as a thin line, broad though she is,
as if Earth wore a single strand of pearls
set with a large sapphire at the centre.

49

Crossing that river go onwards making
yourself the target for the eager eyes
of Daśapura's women accomplished
in the graceful play of curving eye-brows,
their eyes with upturned lashes flashing
with the beauty of gazelles leaping up
and far surpassing the grace of honey-bees
on white jasmines swaying.

50

Ranging with your shadow through the land
of Brahmāvarta stretching below Kuru's field,

do not fail to visit the battleground
that marks the great war of the barons,
where the wielder of the Gāndīva-bow
showered hundreds of sharp arrows on princely faces
as you shoot driving downpours on lotuses.

51

The Plough-Bearer, turning away from that war
out of affection for his kinsmen, renounced
the cherished wine reflecting Revatī's eyes[7]
and worshipped Sarasvatī's waters; you too,
enjoying those waters, O gentle Sir,
will become pure within, dark only in form.

52

From there you should visit Jahnu's daughter
near Kanakhala's hill where she comes down
the slopes of the Lord of Mountains, making
a stairway for Sagara's sons going up to Heaven.
She grasped Śiva's matted hair
clinging with wave-hands to His crest-jewel, the moon,
foam-laughter mocking the frown on Gaurī's face.

53

If you aim to drink her clear crystal waters slantwise,
hanging down by your hind-quarters in the sky
like some elephant out of Paradise,
as your shadow glides along her stream
she would appear beautiful at once as though
she and Yamunā flowed together at that spot.[8]

54

Reaching that river's true birth-place, the mountain
white with snows, its rocks scented by musk deer lying there;
and reclining on its peak to remove
the long journey's weariness, you will wear
a beauty comparable to the stain on the horn
of the triple-eyed lord's white bull rooting in the mud.

55

If a forest-fire born of cedar branches
clashing in the blowing wind
should assail the mountain, and its fiery sparks
scorch the bushy tails of yaks,
pray quench it fully with a thousand sharp showers.
The riches of the great are best employed
to ease the miseries of the distressed.

56

Unable to bear the thunder hurled down,
Śarabhas on the mountain puffed up with pride
will suddenly spring up in fury towards you
who are beyond reach, only to shatter their own limbs;
scatter them with your tumultuous laughter of hail.
Who indeed that undertakes vain-glorious acts
would not become the butt of ridicule!

57

Bending low in adoration, go round
the rock bearing the foot-print of the moon-crested Lord,
perpetually worshipped with offerings by Siddhas;
looking upon it, the body abandoned
and sins shaken off, the faithful gain
the Eternal Station of the Lord's attendants.

58

The wind breathing through hollow bamboos makes sweet music;
woodland nymphs sing with passion-filled voices
of the victory over the triple-city;
if your thunder rumbles in the glens like a drum
would not the ensemble then be complete
for the Dance-Drama of the Lord of Beings?

59

Passing over many marvels on Himālaya's slopes,
you should go north through the narrow Kraunca-pass

—gateway for wild geese and path to glory
for the Bhr̥gu Chief—lengthened out cross-wise,
beautiful like Viṣṇu's dark-blue foot
stretched out to curb Bali's pride.

60

Still climbing higher, be Kailāsa's guest
—mirror for goddesses—the joints of its ridges
cracked by ten-faced Rāvaṇa's straining arms.
Towering up into the sky with lofty peaks
radiant like white water-lilies, it stands
as if it were the wild laughter
of the Parent of the Triple-World[9]
piled up through the ages.

61

When, glistening like smooth-ground collyrium, you lean
dark on its slopes white as ivory freshly cut,
that mountain, I imagine would, like the Plough-Bearer
with a dark-blue mantle slung o'er his shoulder
attain to a grace so arresting
as to hold the gaze entranced.

62

And if Gaurī should stroll on that mountain
created for play, holding Śiva's hand
divested of its snake-bracelet,
hardening your mass of waters within,
form yourself into wave-like steps
and go before her as she climbs the jewelled slopes.

63

When struck by swarms of sparks off Indra's thunderbolt[10]
your water-jets shoot out, celestial maidens there
will surely use you for their bath;
having found you in summer's heat, my friend,

if these girls eager for play will not let you go,
you should scare them with harsh-sounding roars.

64

Sipping Mānasa waters where golden lotuses grow,
joyfully giving Airāvata
the fleeting pleasure of your veiling shade,
fluttering with rain-drenched breezes
the fine silk garments of tender leaves
the Tree of Paradise wears,
amuse yourself on that majestic mountain
whose jewelled slopes glitter in chequered light and shade.

65

Once seen, O wanderer-at-will, you cannot but recognize
Alakā on its upper slope seated as on her lover's lap
—Gangā, her fine garment, falling down—
High over her many-storied mansions
like a woman with her hair piled up
and bound in a net of pearls, she bears
masses of clouds shedding water in the rainy season.

66

Where palaces with their cloud-kissing tops
equal you in loftiness,
and their gem-paved floors rival the glitter
of your glistening rain drops;
where paintings on the walls vie
with your rainbow hues;
and graceful movements of lovely women
rival the lightning's play;
where drums beaten to the sound of music
resemble your thunder, mellow, deep-throated:
And in each particular more than compare with you.

67

Where women toy with a lotus held in the hand,
twine fresh jasmines in their hair;

the beauty of their faces glows pale gold
dusted with the pollen of Lodhra flowers;
fresh amaranth-blooms encircle the hair-knot,
a delicate Śirīṣa nestles at the ear;
and on the hair-parting lie Kadambā blossoms
born at your coming.

68

Where yakṣas accompanied by highborn ladies
resort to their palace-terraces
paved with precious gems star-flower-mirroring,[11]
to partake of passion-kindling flower wines
pressed from the Tree of Paradise,
while drumheads softly struck
throb deep-throated tones like yours.

69

Where at sunrise the path followed at night
by amorous women hastening to midnight trysts
with faltering steps, is marked by telltale signs—
Mandāra flowers fallen from playful curls
and petals of golden lotuses worn at the ears,
dislodged, lie strewn on the ground, with pearls
scattered loose as the threads snapped
of bodices of pearls that closely held their breasts.

70

Where lovers undoing the knot at the waist,
hands trembling with passion,
toss aside silken garments loosening,
yakṣa women with lips like Bimba fruit,
overcome by shy confusion
aim handfuls of aromatic powder
at glittering gems serving as lamps.
Ah! What fruitless throws even though they hit their mark.

71

Where, led to terraces of lofty mansions
by their guide the ever-moving wind,
rain clouds like you stain the paintings
with droplets of water;
then, seeming fearful flee at once
fragmented through lattices,
assuming with practised skill
the shapes of smoke streaming out.

72

Where at midnight moonstones
hanging from networks of threads,
touched by the moon's feet
resplendent as you move away
shed clear drops of coolness
to dispel the languor born
of oft-enjoyed loveplay in women
just released from a loved husband's close embrace.

73

Where, knowing the Supreme One to dwell incarnate,
friend to the Lord of Treasures,
the God of Love out of fear refrains from drawing
his bow strung with honeybees,
his work accomplished by lovely women
displaying their alluring charms, who bend
the bow of their eyebrows to shoot bright glances
unerringly at Love's targets.

74

There, to the north of the palaces
of the Lord of Treasures stands our home
recognizable from afar by its arched gateway
beautiful as the rainbow.
Close by grows a young Mandāra tree

nurtured by my love like a son and now bending
with clusters of blossoms
within reach of her hand.

75

A flight of steps, all emerald slabs—
a pool patterned over
by full-blown lotuses on glossy beryl stems—
Wild geese haunt its waters, freed from restless longing,
no longer resorting to nearby Mānasa-lake
even after they see you coming.

76

By its edge is a miniature hill, wondrous,
with sapphire-inlaid crest, exquisitely blue
and ringed round by golden plantain-trees.
Watching you glitter at the edges with lightning-gleams
my heart trembles struck by the memory of that hill, my friend,
remembering how dear it was to my beloved wife.

77

On it by a fragrant jasmine bower
encircled by a hedge of amaranth
stands a red Aśoka fluttering its tender leaves,
and the dearly-loved Kesara too.
One craves the touch of your friend's lovely foot,
the other longs for the wine of her mouth,
pretending it is blossom-time.

78

And between them a golden rod rising
from a pedestal of jade whose sheen
rivals that of bamboos newly-sprouted
supports a crystal tablet;
your blue-throated friend
settles on it at close of day

after my love clapping her hands has made him dance
to the sweet tinkling of her bracelets.

79

By these tokens of recognition
treasured in your heart, O wise one!
And noting the beautifully-drawn forms
of lotus and conch on the sides of the door,
you will know the mansion, its lustre dimmed
no doubt by my absence: when the sun has set
the lotus does not show forth in all its glory.

80

At once becoming small as an elephant cub
for a speedy descent, seated on the charming crest
of that pleasure-hill I described before,
you may easily dart into the mansion
faint lightning-glances twinkling
like a glittering line of fireflies.

81

There you will see her, in the springtime of youth, slender,
her teeth jasmine-buds, her lips ripe bimba-fruit,
slim-waisted, with deep navel
and the tremulous eyes of a startled doe,
moving languidly from the weight of her hips,
her body bowed down a little by her breasts
—Ah! The Creator's master-work among women.

82

Know her to be my second life,
alone, speaking little,
mourning like a cakravaki
her companion far away.
With the passing of these long days, racked
by intense longing, the young girl
would appear so changed I think,
like a lotus-plant struck by the chilling hoar-frost.

83

Weeping passionately, her eyes would be swollen
and her lips withered by burning sighs;
my beloved's face cupped in the palm of her hand,
only glimpsed through loose tresses flowing down
would surely appear like the miserable moon
stricken pale when shadowed by you.

84

She will come into your view absorbed
in the day's rites of worship or drawing my likeness
imagined wasted by separation
or asking the melodious songster in the cage,
'sweet one, do you remember our lord?
You were a favourite with him.'

85

Or, clad in a drab garment she may place
the lute on her lap, wishing to sing a melody
set to words signifying my name;
succeeding somehow in tuning the strings
wet with her tears, O gentle friend, she forgets
again and again the sequence of notes
even though she composed it herself.

86

Or, beginning with the day of our parting
she may count the months remaining,
laying out in order on the floor,
flowers placed at the threshold;
or, savouring imagined pleasures of love
treasured in her heart:
—such are the only diversions of women
sorrowing in the absence of their husbands.

87

Occupied by day, the pangs of loneliness
would not distress your friend too keenly,

but I fear the nights devoid of diversions
would pass heavy with grief;
therefore, I pray, meet the faithful girl
at midnight with my messages,
standing at the window close to where she lies
wakeful on the ground, and comfort her.

88

Wasted by anguish
she would be lying on her bed of loneliness
drawing herself together on one side,
seeming like the last sliver
of the waning moon on the eastern horizon.
By my side her nights flew by
on winged moments in rapture's fullness;
now they drag on, heavy with her burning tears.

89

With a burning sigh that withers her lips
tender as leaf-buds, you will see her
toss aside those curling tresses
rough with frequent ritual-baths,
that stray down her cheeks uncared for.
Longing for sleep, hoping in dreams at least
she would be one with me in love,
a sudden torrent of tears might wash away those hopes.

90

On that first day of parting, her tresses
with their wreath of flowers stripped off were twisted
and plaited into one single braid
which I shall unwind when the curse is ended
and all my sorrows melted away:
you will see her with untrimmed nails pushing
that tangled braid, rough and painful to the touch,
repeatedly off the curve of her cheek.

91

Remembering past delights her eyes would turn
towards the moonbeams, cool, ambrosial,
streaming in through the lattices,
and turn away at once in sorrow.
Veiling her eyes with lashes heavy-laden with tears
she will seem to be hovering uncertain
between waking and dreaming
—a day-lily on a cloudy day neither open nor shut.

92

Casting aside all adornments,
keeping alive her fragile body in measureless sorrow,
desolate, my love would try in vain
time and again to throw herself on her bed;
the sight I am sure will make you shed some freshwater tears;
for tender hearts ever melt in compassion.

93

I know well you friend's heart is filled with love for me,
hence I believe her brought to this pitiable state
in this our very first parting.
It is not vain self-esteem that makes a braggart of me;
all I have said, my brother,
you will soon see before your very eyes.

94

Lack-lustre without glossy collyrium,
the sidelong glance blocked by straying hair,
the eyebrow's graceful play forgotten
through abstaining from wine,
the doe-eyed lady's left eye
would throb at your coming, I guess,
and match the charm of blue lotuses
quivering as fishes dart among them.

95

And her left thigh—bare of my nail marks,
unadorned by the network of pearls of the long-worn zone
she cast aside struck by the turn of fate,
so used to the gentle stroking of my hands
after love's enjoyment—
pale as a tender plantain's stem will start quivering.

96

If at that time, O Rain-Giver,
she has found happiness, pray wait near her,
just one watch of the night withholding your thunder;
having striven hard to find me, her beloved,
in a dream of love, let not her arms
twined like tender vines round my neck in close embrace,
suddenly fall away from their hold.

97

Awakening her with a breeze
cooled by your fine spray, when revived
along with the fragrant jasmine's
fresh clusters of buds, she gazes intensely
at the casement graced by your presence,
begin to address the noble lady
in vibrant tones courteous,
with your lightning-gleams hidden deep within you.

98

O unwidowed lady! Know me,
your husband's dear friend, a rain cloud
come to tender to you
his messages treasured in my heart.
With deep but gentle tones
I speed weary travellers yearning
to unknot the tangled braids of their grieving wives,
on their way home from distant lands.

99

Thus addressed, like Mithila's princess
lifting her face up to the Son of the Wind,
she will gaze on you, her heart opening
like a flower from eager expectation:
welcoming you at once, with deep respect
she'll listen with rapt attention, gentle friend;
for news of husbands brought by a friend
are to women the closest thing to reunion.

100

O long-lived one! In response to my plea
and to honour yourself, speak to her thus:
your consort lives,
haunting Rāmagiri's hermitages—
parted from you he asks
if all is well with you, tender lady!
Such soothing words should be addressed first
to living beings who fall prey to calamity.

101

Far off, his way barred by adverse decree,
in his imaginings
his body becomes one with your body;
thin with thin,
anguished with intensely anguished,
tear-drowned with tear-drenched
yearning with endlessly yearning,
your hotly-sighing body
with his racked by long drawn-out sighs.

102

Who, before your companions
loved to whisper in your ear
what could well be said aloud indeed,
for he longed to touch your face,
he, gone beyond range of your hearing,

not seen by your eyes, speaks
through my mouth to you, these words
shaped by his intense yearning.

103

In the śyāma-vines I see your body,
your glance in the gazelle's startled eye,
the cool radiance of your face in the moon,
your tresses in the peacock's luxuriant train,
your eyebrow's graceful curve in the stream's small waves;
but alas! O cruel one, I see not
your whole likeness anywhere in any one thing.

104

Scent of warm earth rain-sprinkled, rising fresh,
O my darling, as the fragrance of your mouth, and
the God of Love, five-arrowed, wastes my frame
already wasted, grieving, far from you.
For pity's sake, think how my days pass
now at summer's close, as massed rain clouds
rending the sunshine, scatter the pieces
and cling enamoured to the sky in all directions.

105

With bright ores, I draw you on a rock
feigning anger, but when I wish
to draw myself fallen at your feet,
at once my eyes are dimmed by ever-welling tears.
Ha! How cruel is fate that even here
it will not suffer our reunion.

106

Striving hard I find you in a waking dream,
I stretch my arms out into the empty air
to fold you in a passionate embrace.
Those large pearl-drops clustering on tender leaf-shoots

are surely—are they not—the tears
the tree-goddesses shed watching my grief?

107

Sudden, Himālayan breezes split open
the tightly-shut leaf-buds on deodars,
and redolent of their oozing resin
blow south; I embrace those breezes
fondly imagining they have of late
touched your limbs, O perfect one!

108

If only the long-drawn-out night
could be squeezed into a single moment,
if only the hot summer's day
would glow at all times with a gentle warmth;
my heart, breathing these unattainable prayers
is left a defence-less prey,
O lady with bright-glancing eyes!
To the fierce pangs of separation from you.

109

But no more of me; reflecting deeply
I bear up, drawing on my own inner strength;
you too, lady most blessed,
should resist falling into utter dejection.
Whom does happiness always attend
or misery always befall?
Man's state on earth like the rim of a wheel
goes down and comes up again.

110

With Viṣṇu risen from His serpent couch
my curse shall be ended; closing your eyes
make the four remaining months go by;
then on autumnal nights bright with moonlight

we two shall taste together every desire
eagerly imagined when we were apart.

111

And further he said this: once in bed
asleep, still clinging to my neck
you woke up on a sudden, weeping a little,
and when I asked why again and again,
laughing to yourself you said,
—ah, you cheat, I saw you in my dream
playing with another woman.

112

By this token of recognition
know that I am well; and do not doubt me
O dark-eyed one, believing idle reports
that say for no good reason
that absence destroys the affections;
Ah no, the lack of pleasure makes
the craving intense for what is desired,
piling it up into love's great hoard.

113

I trust, noble friend, you are resolved
to do this kindly service for me?
I cannot think your grave look forbodes refusal;
without a sound you offer cātakas
the water they crave; the answer
noble ones make is to do the thing wished for.

114

Having granted this wish so dear to my heart,
strange as it may seem,
for friendship's sake or out of pity for me, desolated,
wander, O Cloud, in all the lands you choose,
gathering greater glory in the rains;
may you never be parted from the lightning
even for an instant.

Abhijnānaśākuntalam

(*The Recognition of Śakuntalā*)

A Play in Seven Acts

CHARACTERS

PROLOGUE

Chanters of the benediction.

DIRECTOR, *Sūtradhāra* (one who holds the threads); probably plays the hero.

ACTRESS, *Natī*; wife of the Director; probably plays the heroine.

PLAY

KING, Duhṣanta, the hero or *nāyaka*; monarch of the lunar dynasty of Puru.

SUTA, Royal charioteer.

ŚAKUNTALĀ, The heroine or *nāyakī*; Duhṣanta's Queen; adopted daughter of Sage Kaṇva.

ANASŪYĀ, PRIYAMVADĀ, Friends and companions of Śakuntalā.

MADHAVYA, Jester, the King's friend and constant companion.

GUARD, Raivataka, also doorkeeper.

GENERAL, Bhadrasena, *Senāpati* or Commander of the Royal Army.

GAUTAMĪ, Matron of Kaṇva's Hermitage.

HĀRITA, Hermit boy.

KANVA, Head of the Hermitage and foster-father of Śakuntalā.

ŚĀRNGARAVA, ŚĀRADVATA, Disciples of Sage Kaṇva.

CHAMBERLAIN, Pārvatāyana, in charge of the Royal Household.

VETRAVATĪ, Doorkeeper of the Royal Apartments.

SOMARĀṬA, High Priest, the King's preceptor.

CHIEF OF POLICE

SUCAKA, JĀNUKA, Policemen.

FISHERMAN

MIŚRAKEŚĪ, An *apsarā* (celestial nymph), friend to Menakā.

PARABHṚTIKĀ (Little Cuckoo), MADHUKARIKĀ (Little Honey-bee), Maids tending the pleasure garden adjoining the Royal Apartments.

CATURIKĀ, The King's personal attendant.

MĀTALI. Indra's charioteer.

BOY, Sarva-Damana, later the Emperor Bharata, son of Śakuntalā and the King.

SUVRATĀ AND HER COMPANION, Hermit women in Mārīca's Hermitage.

MĀRĪCA, Prajāpati or Primal Parent and Indra's father.

ADITI, Consort of Mārīca and mother of Indra, daughter of Dakṣa.

MINOR CHARACTERS

KARABHAKA, The Queen Mother's emissary.

AN ANCHORITE AND HIS DISCIPLE

PUPIL OF KANVA

TWO HERMITS

ROYAL BARDS

ATTENDANT, Pratīharī

Female bodyguard of the King, who looked after his weapons and attended him on his hunts.

CHARACTERS OFF-STAGE

DURVĀSĀ, A sage reputed for his violent temper and quick to curse.

HAMSAVATĪ, Duhṣanta's junior queen.

Aerial voices: Voices of the tree nymphs in Kaṇva's Hermitage.

Voice of the cuckoo in the Hermitage.

PERSONS MENTIONED

KAUŚIKA, The Royal Sage Viśvāmitra, real father of Śakuntalā.

MENAKĀ, Apsarā (Celestial nymph and dancer at Indra's Court); mother of Śakuntalā.

INDRA, King of the Immortals.

JAYANTA, Indra's son.

NĀRADA, A wandering sage, messenger of the gods.

VASUMATĪ, Royal Consort, Duhṣanta's Chief Queen.

MITRĀ-VASU, The Queen's brother.

PIŚUNA, Chief Minister.

DHANA-VṚDDHI, A wealthy merchant prince, probably head of the guild.

PROLOGUE

BENEDICTION

That First Creation of the Creator: (1)
That Bearer of oblations offered with Holy Rites:
That one who utters the Holy Chants:
Those two that order Time:
That which extends, World-Pervading,
in which sound flows impinging on the ear:
That which is proclaimed the Universal Womb of Seeds:
That which fills all forms that breathe
with the Breath of Life.
May the Supreme Lord of the Universe
who stands revealed in these eight Forms*
perceptible preserve you.

After the benediction enter the Director.

DIRECTOR (*looking towards the green-room*) : Lady! If the preparations in the dressing room are completed, would you be pleased to attend us?

ACTRESS (*entering*) : Here I am, my lord; what are your orders regarding this evening's performance?

DIRECTOR (*looks around*) : Lady, we have here before us, an august audience that is highly educated and most discerning. This evening we wait upon it with a new play composed by Kālidāsa, entitled *The Recognition of Śakuntalā.* Will you see to it that all the actors do their very best?

ACTRESS : With your excellent training and direction, my lord, nothing will be found wanting.

DIRECTOR (*smiling*) : The truth of the matter, my lady, is:

Unless those who know applaud my art, (2)

* The eight forms are in order: Water, Fire, The Priest, Sun and Moon, Space, Earth, Air.

I cannot think I know it well;
even those most expertly schooled
cannot be wholly self-assured.

ACTRESS : Is that so, my lord? Well, now tell me what is to follow, my lord.

DIRECTOR : Let us treat the audience to something that will delight their ears.

ACTRESS : Which of the seasons shall I sing about?

DIRECTOR : About this very season, I should think—Summer, that set in not so long ago and is enjoyable in so many ways. For at the moment:

Days draw to a close in quiet beauty; (3)
plunging in cool waters is delightful;
sleep drops softly in thick-shaded haunts;
woodland breezes blow fresh and fragrant
having consorted with Pātalī flowers.

ACTRESS : Very well. (*sings*)

Exquisite are Śirīṣa blossoms— (4)
see how they sway—
crested with delicate filaments—
kissed, lightly, lightly
by murmurous bees—
lovely women—
exulting in their youth—
place the blossoms
tenderly—
as ornaments over their ears—

DIRECTOR : Beautifully sung, dear lady; aha—just look around you; the audience is still, as if drawn in a picture—spellbound, caught in the web of beauty woven by your singing. Now then, what play shall we put on to honour and entertain them further?

ACTRESS : Why, Sir, what you mentioned right at the beginning—the new play entitled *The Recognition of Śakuntalā.*

DIRECTOR: You do well to remind me, dear lady. Indeed, my memory failed me for an instant; because,

I was carried far, far away, lured (5)
by your impassioned song, compelling,

(*looks towards the wings*)

even as the King, Duhṣanta here,
was, by the fleet fleeing antelope.

(*Exit.*)

End of Prologue

ACT ONE

Scene: The forests in the foothills of the Himālayas; later the Hermitage of Kaṇva, by the river Mālinī.

Enter on a chariot, bow and arrow in hand, in hot pursuit of a deer, the King *with* his charioteer.

SUTA[1] (*looking at the King and the deer*) : O Long-Lived Majesty!

Casting my eye on the fleeting blackbuck (6)
and on you holding the taut-strung bow,
I seem to see before my very eyes
Pinākī,* the Lord, chasing the deer.

KING : We have come a long, long way, Sūta, drawn by this blackbuck; even now he is seen:

Arching his neck with infinite grace, now and then (7)
he glances back at the speeding chariot,
his form curving fearful of the arrow's fall,
the haunches almost touch his chest.
Panting from fatigue, his jaws gaping wide
spill the half-chewed tender grass to mark his path.
With long leaps bounding high upwards, see how
he soars
flying in the sky, scarce skimming the surface of
the earth.

(*puzzled*) How is it that I can hardly see him, even though we are in such hot pursuit?

SUTA : Sire, seeing the ground was uneven, I lightly reined in the horses; the chariot's speed slackened. Therefore, the deer was able to put so much distance between himself and us. Now that we are on level ground, you will soon see that he is not beyond your aim.

KING : Slacken the reins.

---

* Śiva

SŪTA : As His Majesty commands. *(mimes increased speed of the chariot)* See, see, Sire:

The reins hanging slack, (8)
the horses leap forward,
no, they glide over the track—
bodies out-stretched, ears flung back,
the tips of their plumes motionless;
the very dust whirled up
swiftly advancing cannot outstrip them.

KING (*exulting*) : See how they excel even Hari's* bright horses; therefore:

What was minute suddenly looms large; (9)
what's cleft down the middle seems to unite;
the eye sees as straight what's naturally curved:
the chariot rushing along, nothing stays
near or far, even for a moment.

(*A voice off-stage*) : Ho there! Stop, hold, O King! This deer belonging to the Hermitage ought not to be struck down . . . aha! . . . do not kill him, O King.

SŪTA (*listens and looks around*) : Your Majesty, here are ascetics standing shielding the blackbuck who is now right in your arrow's path.

KING (*urgently*) : Quick, rein in the horses.

SŪTA : Yes, Sire. (*stops the chariot*)

Enter an ascetic *accompanied by* his disciple.

ASCETIC (*holding up his hand*) : This deer is of the Hermitage, O King! He should not be killed . . . no . . . no . . . do not strike him down.

How fragile the life of this deer! (10)
How cruel your sharp-pointed arrows, swift-winged!
Never should they fall on his tender frame
like tongues of flame on a heap of flowers.

Quickly withdraw your well-aimed arrow, bound (11)
to protect the distressed, not strike the pure.[2]

---

* Indra

KING (*bowing low in respect*) : It is withdrawn. (*replaces the arrow in the quiver*)

ASCETIC (*pleased*) : This is indeed an act worthy of your Honour, born in Puru's[3] dynasty and the glorious light of kings. May you be blessed with a son who will turn the wheel of empire.[4]

KING (*bowing low*) : I accept a Brāhmaṇa's blessings.

ASCETIC: O King! We are on our way to gather wood for the sacrificial Fire. There, clinging to the slopes of the Himālaya, along the banks of the Mālinī is visible the Hermitage of our Guru, the Patriarch Kaṇva where Śakuntalā dwells like its guardian deity.[5] If other duties do not claim your time, enter and accept the hospitality profferred to a guest. Further:

When you behold the sages rich in holiness (12)
immersed in the tranquil performance of holy rites
free of impediments, you will know how well
your arm scarred by the oft-drawn bowstring protects.

KING : Is the Patriarch at home now?

ASCETIC : Enjoining his daughter Śakuntalā to receive guests with due hospitality, he has gone not long back to Soma-tīrtha, to propitiate the adverse fate threatening her happiness.

KING : I shall pay my respects to her then. She will no doubt inform the great sage of my profound veneration for him.

ASCETIC : We shall then be on our way.

(*Exits with his disciple.*)

KING : Sūta, urge the horses on and let us purify ourselves with a sight of the holy Hermitage.

SŪTA : As Your Gracious Majesty orders. (*mimes increased speed of the chariot*)

KING (*looking around*) : Sūta, even without being told, it is plain that we are now at the outskirts of the penance-groves.

SŪTA : How can you tell, my lord?

KING : Do you not see, Sir? Right here:

Grains of wild rice fallen from tree-hollows (13)
where parrots nest, lie scattered under the trees;
those stones there look moist, glossy, from the oil
of ingudi-nuts split and pounded on them;

all around, deer browse in their tranquil haunts,
unafraid of the chariot's approach; yonder,
drops of water dripping off the edges of bark-garments
in long lines, trace the paths to pools and streams.

And you see further:

Rippling beneath a passing breeze, waters flow (14)
in deep channels to lave the roots of trees;
smoke drifts up from oblations to the Sacred Fire
to dim the soft sheen of tender leafbuds;
free from fear, fawns browse lazily in meadows
beyond, where darbha-shoots are closely cropped.

SŪTA : Yes, Sire, everything is as you say.

They go some distance.

KING : Sūta, let us not disturb the peace of the Hermitage; stop the chariot right here and I shall get down.

SŪTA : I am holding the reins fast; let His Majesty alight.

KING (*alights from the chariot and looks at himself*) : Hermit-groves should be visited modestly attired. So, here are my jewels and bow. (*hands them over to the charioteer*) By the time I return from visiting the residents of the Hermitage, see that the horses are watered.

SŪTA : As His Majesty commands.

(Exits.)

KING (*turns around and looks*) : Ah, here is the entrance to the Hermitage; I shall go in. (*enters and immediately indicates the presence of a good omen*) Ah . . . .

Tranquil is this hermitage, yet my arm throbs;[6] (15)
what fulfilment can await me here?
Yet who knows; coming events find doors
opening everywhere.

(*A voice in the background*) : This way, this way, dear friends.

KING (*listening closely*) : Aha . . . I hear snatches of conversation to the south of this orchard. (*turns and looks around*) I see; here are some hermit-girls coming this way . . . and carrying jars proportionate to their slender frames . . . to water the saplings planted here. O what a charming sight!

If girls bred in a hermitage (16)
can boast of such beauty rare in palaces,
is there any denying woodland vines
far surpass those nurtured in gardens?

I think I shall wait here in the shade and watch them. *(stands observing them)*

Enter Śakuntalā *with* her friends, *occupied as described.*

FIRST : Listen, dear Śakuntalā; it looks to me as if these trees in the Hermitage are dearer to Father Kaṇva than even you are; see, he has appointed you who are as delicate as a newly-opened jasmine-flower, to fill these trenches round the roots with water.

ŚAKUNTALĀ : Dear Anasūyā, it is not merely a matter of Father's injunction; I love them like a sister. *(she mimes watering the trees)*

SECOND : Friend Śakuntalā, the trees of the Hermitage that bloom in summer have all been watered. Shall we now sprinkle those that are past flowering? That would be an act of devotion, not looking for a reward.

ŚAKUNTALĀ : Priyamvadā, my friend, what a lovely thought. *(again mimes watering the trees)*

KING (*to himself*) : What! Is this Kaṇva's daughter, Śakuntalā? (*surprised*) Ah! How utterly lacking in judgement is the venerable Kaṇva to imprison such beauty in a bark-garment.

The sage who would inure to harsh penance (17)
this form ravishing in its artless beauty
is surely attempting to cut acacia wood
with the edge of a blue-lotus petal.

Let it be. Hidden behind these trees, I shall watch her undisturbed. *(stands concealed)*

ŚAKUNTALĀ : Sweet Anasūyā, Priyamvadā has tied my bark-garment so tight that I feel quite uncomfortable; could you loosen it a little? *(Anasūyā loosens it)*

PRIYAMVADĀ (*laughing merrily*) : Blame your own budding youth that's making your bosom swell.

KING: She's right in what she says,

With rounded breasts concealed by cloth of bark (18)
fastened at the shoulder in a fine knot,
her youthful form enfolded like a flower
in its pale leafy sheath unfolds not its glory.

While it is true that bark is not the appropriate dress for her youth, can it be really held that it does not become her like an adornment? Consider,

Though inlaid in duckweed the lotus glows; (19)
a dusky spot enhances the moon's radiance;
this lissom girl is lovelier far dressed in bark!
What indeed is not an adornment for entrancing forms!

ŚAKUNTALĀ (*looking in front of her*) : See, my friends, the mango tree over there fluttering his fingers of tender leaf sprays—as if beckoning to me. I shall go over to him. *(walks over to the tree)*

PRIYAMVADĀ : Dearest Śakuntalā, stand there for a moment.

ŚAKUNTALĀ : What for?

PRIYAMVADĀ : With you beside him, the mango looks as if wedded to a lovely vine.

ŚAKUNTALĀ : You are aptly named—'Sweet-Talker'—aren't you?

KING : Priyamvadā does not speak idly; see how,

Her lower lip has the rich sheen of young shoots, (20)
her arms the very grace of tender twining stems;
her limbs enchanting as a lovely flower
glow with the radiance of magical youth.

ANASŪYĀ : Look, Śakuntalā, the jasmine that you named *Vana-jyotsni** has chosen the mango as her bridegroom.

Śakuntalā *comes close to the vine and looks at it with joy.*

ŚAKUNTALĀ : O Anasūyā, what a charming sight, this marriage of vine and tree. See, the jasmine has this very moment entered into her budding youth. And the mango tree is laden with young fruit indicating he is ready for enjoyment. *(she stands gazing at them)*

---

* Woodland-Moonglow

PRIYAMVADA (*smiling archly*) : Anasūyā, guess why Śakuntalā is gazing upon *Vana-jyotsnī* for so long and with such longing.

ANASUYA : No, I cannot; you tell me.

PRIYAMVADA : Well . . . this is what she is thinking: Just as *Vana-jyotsnī* has married the tree that is a worthy partner for her, so, may I also find a consort worthy of me.

ŚAKUNTALA : That must be your own heart's desire, for sure. *(she pours water from the jar)*

ANASUYA : Hey, Śakuntalā, just look; here is the Mādhavī bush that Father Kaṇva nurtured with his own hands as he nurtured you. You have forgotten her?

ŚAKUNTALA : Then I might as well forget myself. (*comes close to the bush and exclaims in delight)* Look, look, what a surprise! Priyamvadā, listen, I have something to tell that will *please* you.

PRIYAMVADĀ : Please me? What's that, dear?

ŚAKUNTALA : Look, Anasūyā . . . the Mādhavī is covered with buds . . . from the root up; this is not its season for blooming.

BOTH FRIENDS (*come hurrying up*) : Really, is it true, Śakuntalā dear?

ŚAKUNTALĀ : Of course it is true—can't you see?

PRIYAMVADĀ (*viewing the blossoming bush with delight*) : Well, well, now it is *my* turn to tell you something which'll *please* you. You will soon be married.

ŚAKUNTALA (*with a show of annoyance*) : That must be what you wish for yourself.

PRIYAMVADĀ : No, I am not joking; I swear I heard it from Father Kaṇva's own lips that this would signal your wedding.

ANASŪYĀ : Ah! Now we know, don't we, Priyamvadā, why Śakuntalā has been watering Mādhavī so lovingly.

ŚAKUNTALĀ: And why not . . . I love her like a sister. *(waters the Mādhavī)*

KING : I wonder . . . could she be the Patriarch's daughter by a wife not of his own class? Let's be done with doubts:

> It is my firm belief that by the Law[7] (21)
> she can rightly be a warrior's bride,
> for my noble heart yearns deeply for her.
> When in doubt, the truest inner prompting is
> to the virtuous, unassailable authority.

Still, I think I should try and find out the true facts about her.

ŚAKUNTALĀ (*in alarm*) : O help, a bee has flown out of the jasmine bush . . . and it is buzzing round my face. *(mimes attempts to ward off the bee)*

KING (*looking longingly at her*) :

Her lovely eyes rove following (22)
the hovering bee close to her face;
she knits her brows practising already
playful glances though not in love—but fear.

(*with a show of vexation*):

O, you honey-foraging thief! You touch (23)
ever so often her glancing eyes, tremulous,
and softly hum, hovering close to her ear
as if eager to whisper a secret,
sneaking in to taste her ripe lower lip
—the quintessence of love's delight—
even as she piteously flails her hand.
Blessed indeed are you, while I wait
seeking to know the truth—undone.

ŚAKUNTALĀ : Friends, friends, help me, protect me from this villain who keeps harassing me.

FRIENDS (*smiling*) : Who are we to protect you? Call to mind Duhṣanta: the penance-groves are under royal protection.

KING : This is a golden opportunity for me to show myself. O, don't be afraid . . . (*checks himself halfway and speaks to himself*) No, this way, it will be evident that I am the King. Let me think . . . I shall assume the manner of just a plain visitor.[8]

ŚAKUNTALĀ (*rather scared*) : This impudent fellow will not leave me alone. I shall go from this place. (*takes a few steps, stops and throws a quick glance behind*) O help! He follows me.

KING (*hastily steps forward*) : Ha!

While the chastiser of the wicked, (24)
great Puru's scion rules over this rich earth,
who dares behave in this churlish manner
to guileless, young girls of the hermitage.

Seeing the King, *all three are taken aback.*

ANASŪYĀ : O noble Sir, it is nothing very serious; our dear friend here (*pointing to Śakuntalā*) was being bothered by a large bee and became frightened.

KING (*approaching Śakuntalā*) : I trust your devotions go well.

Śakuntalā, confused, is silent.

ANASŪYĀ (*addressing the King*) : All goes well *now*, Sir, since we have the honour of waiting on a distinguished guest.

PRIYAMVADĀ : Welcome to you, noble Sir.

ANASŪYĀ : Dear Śakuntalā, go and bring the proper guest-offering and some fruit. The water we have here will serve to wash the guest's feet.

KING : I have already been welcomed by your gracious words; nothing more is needed.

PRIYAMVADĀ : At least, Sir, do sit down under the spreading shade of this Saptaparṇa tree on this cool seat and rest yourself.

KING : You must all be tired too after performing these pious duties. Do sit down for a while.

PRIYAMVADĀ (*aside*) : Śakuntalā, courtesy demands that we keep our guest company. Come, let us all sit down.

They sit down.

ŚAKUNTALĀ (*to herself*) : How is it that the sight of this person fills me with emotions out of place in a penance-grove.

KING (*looking at them*) : How charming a friendship this of yours, gracious ladies, all of the same age and equally beautiful!

PRIYAMVADĀ (*aside*) : Anasūyā, who could he be—mysterious, majestic in manner, yet he speaks with such easy charm and shows such courtesy?

ANASŪYĀ (*aside*) : I am curious too; let me sound him. (*aloud*) Noble Sir, encouraged by your gracious words, I would like to ask you this: What great lineage does Your Honour adorn—which land now mourns your absence—and what has brought a delicately nurtured noble like yourself on this wearying journey into our Groves of Righteousness?

ŚAKUNTALĀ (*to herself*) : O heart, keep calm; Anasūyā is asking what I wanted to know.

KING (*to himself*) : Now what shall I do? Shall I disclose myself—or—shall I conceal my identity? (*reflecting*) Let me do it this way. (*aloud*) Lady, I am one well-versed in the Vedas whom the Paurava monarch has appointed as Minister in Charge of Religious Affairs. In the course of visiting the holy retreats, I chanced to come to these Groves of Righteousness.

ANASŪYĀ : Why then, the followers of the Right Path have now a guardian.

Śakuntalā shows signs of falling in love.

FRIENDS (*noting the demeanour of Śakuntalā and the King, aside*) : Śakuntalā, if only Father were here!

ŚAKUNTALĀ (*knitting her brows*) : What if he were?

BOTH : He would then make this distinguished guest supremely happy by offering him the sole treasure of his life.

ŚAKUNTALĀ (*pretending to be annoyed*) : O be quiet; you two have some silly notion in your heads and keep prattling; I shan't listen to your nonsense.

KING : We would also like to ask you something about your friend here, if we may.

BOTH : Consider your request a favour done to us.

KING : His Holiness Kaṇva has been known to observe perpetual celibacy; how then can your friend be a daughter begotten by him.

ANASŪYĀ : Hear what I have to say, Sir. There is a Royal Sage of great renown belonging to the Kuśika clan.

KING : Yes, His Holiness Kauśika.

ANASŪYĀ : He is our friend's real father. Father Kaṇva is her father by virtue of having reared her when he found her abandoned.

KING : Abandoned! The word greatly rouses my curiosity. Pray let me hear the story from the beginning.

ANASŪYĀ : Once, a long time back, that Royal Sage was immersed in the most formidable austerities for many years. The gods for some reason became nervous and sent the Apsarā Menakā to disturb his single-minded concentration.

KING : O yes, it is well known that the gods often become afraid of the penances of others. Then what happened?

ANASUYA : Spring had just set in; seeing her maddening beauty. . .(*stops halfway in embarassment*)

KING : What followed is easily understood. So—this lady was born of an Apsarā.

ANASUYA : That's right.

KING : It fits:

How could a form of such matchless beauty (25)
come from the womb of a mortal mother?
The scintillating lightning-flash
does not spring up from the earth.

Śakuntalā, shy, looks down.

KING (*to himself*) : O what good fortune! Now my desires find a firm footing.

PRIYAMVADĀ (*turning to the King with a smile*) : Your Honour was about to say something?

Śakuntalā raises a warning forefinger.

KING : Gracious lady, you have guessed right. Keen to know more about the lives of the saintly, I *am* eager to ask one further question.

PRIYAMVADĀ : Do not hesitate, Sir; ascetics may be questioned freely.

KING : I wish to ask,

Is it only till she is given in marriage (26)
that your friend is strictly bound by hermit-vows
—an unkind bar that shuts out love—
or must she dwell, alas, for ever
with the gazelles so dear to her
whose lovely eyes mirror her own eyes' dear
loveliness?

PRIYAMVADA : Sir, even in the practice of religious duties, she is dependent on another's will. However, it is her father's resolve to give her in marriage to one worthy of her.

KING (*elated, speaks to himself*):

Hold fast, O heart, to your fondest wish: (27)
the troubling doubts are now dispelled.
What you dreaded might be a burning flame,
turns out a glowing gem to touch and hold.

ŚAKUNTALĀ (*pretending anger*) : Anasūyā, I am leaving.

ANASŪYĀ : For what reason?

ŚAKUNTALĀ: To report to the revered Lady Gautamī that Priyamvadā is talking a lot of nonsense. (*rises to leave*)

ANASŪYĀ: Surely, dear, it is not seemly on the part of residents of a hermitage to leave a distinguished guest in this casual manner before he has received all the rites of hospitality.

Śakuntalā without a word prepares to leave.

KING (*to himself*) : How! Is she leaving? (*makes a movement to restrain her, then checks himself*) Strange how a lover's actions mirror his feelings.

Eager to follow the sage's daughter, (28)
vehemently held back by decorum,
no sooner had I left but I returned
it seems, but not stirred from this very spot.

PRIYAMVADĀ (*coming close to Śakuntalā*) : Hey, you headstrong girl; you cannot go.

ŚAKUNTALĀ (*knitting her brows*) : And why not?

PRIYAMVADĀ : Because you owe me two turns at watering the trees; pay me back, then you may leave. (*forces her back*)

KING : I see that the lady is exhausted from watering the trees; as it is,

Her arms droop, languid, her palms glow (29)
reddened lifting up the watering-jar;
her bosom still heaves as she draws deep breaths.
The Śirīṣa blossom adorning her ear,
caught in the sparkling web of beads of sweat,
ceases its delicate play against her cheek.
With one hand she restrains her hair, straying wild,
unruly, released from its knot undone.

Let me release her from her debt to you, if I may. (*offers his ring*)

The friends take it and reading the name on the Signet Ring, look at each other.

KING : O please do not misunderstand; the Ring is a gift from the King.

PRIYAMVADĀ : The more reason then that Your Honour ought not to part with it. Your word is sufficient, Your Honour, to release her from her debt.

ANASŪYĀ: You are free now, friend Śakuntalā—through the magnanimity of this noble gentleman—or—of the great King. Where are you off to, now?

ŚAKUNTALĀ (*to herself*) : Were it in my power to leave, I would.

PRIYAMVADĀ : Why don't you leave now?

ŚAKUNTALĀ : Am I still answerable to you? I shall leave when I please.

KING (*watching Śakuntalā closely, to himself*) : Could it be that she feels towards me as I feel towards her? In that case, my wishes can find fulfilment. For,

Even though she makes no response to my words (30)
she is all ears whenever I speak;
it is true she faces me not, but then
what other object do her eyes ever seek.

(*A voice off-stage*) : Ho there! Ascetics all; get ready to protect the creatures in the vicinity of the penance-groves . . . King Duhṣanta who delights in the chase is in our neighbourhood.

Like swarms of locusts glittering in the sunset glow (31)
the whirling dust threshed by tumultuous hoof-beats
of horses
falls thick upon the trees in the Hermitage
where wet bark-garments hang from the branches.

KING (*to himself*) : Alas! As ill-luck would have it, my armed guards, looking for me are surrounding the penance-groves.

(*Again, the voice off-stage*) : Ho there, listen, ascetics all . . . throwing women, children and the aged into wild confusion, here he comes:

Crazed with fear at the sight of a chariot, (32)
scattering terror-stricken antelope-herds,

holding aloft, skewered on one trunk
a branch sliced off a tree by a violent blow,
and in fury dragging along tangled chains
of trailing wild creepers that form fetters round him,
a tusker rampages in our Grove of Righteousness
—the very embodiment of hindrance to penance.

All listen and rise in alarm.

KING: O what a disaster! How gravely have I wronged the ascetics here; I had better go.

FRIENDS : Noble Lord! We are greatly perturbed hearing these warning cries about the elephant; permit us to return to our cottage.

ANASŪYĀ (*addressing Śakuntalā*) : Listen Śakuntalā, Lady Gautamī will be racked by anxiety on our account; come quickly; let's all be together.

ŚAKUNTALĀ (*indicating some difficulty in walking*) : Ha! A numbness seizes my thighs.

KING: Take care, gentle ladies: go carefully. We too shall take all precautions to prevent damage to the Hermitage.

FRIENDS : Noble Lord! I think we know you well enough to feel that you will forgive us this rude interruption of our welcome; may we request you to visit us once more so that we may make amends for the inadequate hospitality extended to you, Sir.

KING : No, no, that's not true; I am honoured sufficiently by the mere sight of you, gracious ladies.

ŚAKUNTALĀ : See, my foot has been pricked by the needle-like points of fresh blades of Kuśa-grass . . . and my bark-garment is caught in the twigs of this amaranth bush. Wait for me while I free myself.

She follows her friends, gazing at the King all the time.

KING (*sighing deeply*) : They are gone; I too should leave. My keenness to return to the Capital has been blunted by meeting Śakuntalā. I shall set up camp with my companions at some distance from the penance-groves; How hard it is for me to tear my thoughts away from Śakuntalā.

My body moves forward, (33)
my restless heart rushes back
like a silken pennon on a chariot's standard
borne against the wind.

(Exit all.)

End of Act One
entitled
THE CHASE [9]

ACT TWO

Scene: The Forest.

Enter Mādhavya, *the Court-jester and companion of the King.*

MĀDHAVYA : O, this cruel play of Fate: I am reduced to a state of such misery; and why—because I am the friend and constant companion of the King—he is obsessed with the chase. We rattle along forest trails to the cries of 'here's a deer' and 'there's a boar'; even in the intense heat of the noonday sun in Summer, when there is scarcely any shade to be seen. When we are thirsty, what do we drink—phew—the putrid water of mountain streams, tepid, bitter, with rotting leaves floating in them. And for food—we eat at all odd hours—meat most of the time roasted on spits—wolfing it down flaming hot. O, misery upon misery! The bones in my body are all out of joint, galloping without a break on horseback. How can a man sleep well in this state? On top of it all, at the crack of dawn, the beaters with their pack of hounds—those sons of bitches, all of them are up—getting everybody up for the day's hunt. I am rudely awakened by the ear-splitting cacophony of their halloos. But is that the end of the story—no Sir, no indeed. What do you know—the lump has sprouted a boil.[10] Only yesterday, speeding along, His Majesty left us all far behind and went straight into the Hermitage running after a deer. Then, what happened—as my ill-luck would have it, he chanced upon a beautiful hermit-girl—Śakuntalā is the name. From that moment, Sirs, the very idea of returning to the Capital finds no place in his thoughts. Dawn broke this morning on his sleepless lids, thinking of her alone. Can't do a thing about it. At any rate, I shall see him as soon as he completes his morning rituals. Ah! What do I see . . . here comes His Majesty bow in hand, lost in thoughts of his beloved . . . and wearing garlands of wild flowers. I shall approach him now; (*moves a little towards the King*) no, this is what I shall do; I shall stand right here, drooping, bent down, as if my body were all broken with no strength left in it. May be, may. . .be. . .this will bring me some respite.

(*stands supporting himself on his staff*)

Enter the King *as described.*

KING (*lost in deep thought, sighs, speaks to himself*): Aah!

Deeply loved, she is not easy to win; (1)
but watching her ways, my heart is consoled;
though love has not found fulfilment yet,
mutual longing is itself a pleasure.

(*smiling wryly*) Thus indeed does a lover mock himself wishing to believe his beloved's thoughts and feelings reflect his own. However:

That tender glance—the melting glow in her eyes, (2)
though she directed them elsewhere—
her steps languid from the weight of heavy hips,
that seemed love's response patterned in enticing grace—
those words she spoke in scorn when her friend held her back,
saying 'don't go': all this I fancied
had only me for an object—
But alas! Love sees only Himself everywhere.

MĀDHAVYA (*stands without moving a step*) : My friend, my hands are powerless to extend themselves in greeting; I salute Your Honour with words only. May you be ever-victorious!

KING (*looks at him and smiles*) : And what has paralysed your limbs?

MĀDHAVYA : A fine thing to ask; do you hit me in the eye—and then ask why it is watering?

KING : My dear friend, I do not follow; make your meaning clear.

MĀDHAVYA : Now tell me my friend, if the bent reed[11] by the river totters to and fro with the grace of a hunchback's gait, is it from its own force or from the force of the stream's flow?

KING : Why, in the reed's case, the force of the stream's flow is the cause.

MĀDHAVYA : So are you, in mine.

KING : How is that?

MĀDHAVYA (*as if angry*) : Go on; you abandon the affairs of the kingdom; you give up those places where one walks without slipping and you stick around here enamoured of the primitive life of foresters, it seems.

To tell you the truth, my limbs feel as if they are not my own, so bruised and painful are their joints with galloping daily chasing after wild beasts. Do me a favour please; let us rest at least for one day.

KING (*to himself*) : This fellow speaks my own thoughts. My mind is not on the chase either, thinking of Kaṇva's daughter. For:

I cannot bear to draw my well-strung bow (3)
with its perfectly-aimed arrows on these deer
that dwell always beside my own dear love
and bestow on her the loveliness of their eyes.

MĀDHAVYA (*looking at the King*) : You look as if you are communing with your heart; mine was just a cry in the wilderness then?

KING (*trying to smile*) : Thinking that a friend's words ought not to be ignored, I was silent; that was all.

MĀDHAVYA : May you live long. (*prepares to leave*)

KING: No, stay, I haven't finished what I was going to say.

MĀDHAVYA : Command me, my lord.

KING : After you have rested well, Sir, I would like your help in a matter that will not cause you the least bit of exertion.

MĀDHAVYA : Like tasting sweet dumplings perhaps?

KING : I shall let you know.

MĀDHAVYA: I am at your disposal.

KING: Ho there—who is on duty?

Enter the Guard.

GUARD : Your Majesty's command?

KING : Raivataka, let His Lordship, the General, be asked to attend.

RAIVATAKA : As my Royal Master commands.

Goes out and returns with the General.

GENERAL (*looking at the King*) : Much abused though the sport of hunting is, in the case of our Royal Master, it has all been to the good. Just see our great lord:

He carries his magnificent frame (4)
like a tusker that roams the mountains;

a frame spare, instinct with energy,
the sinewy strength hides the loss of rounding flesh;
he endures the sun's hot rays unharmed,
not a trace of sweat showing;
his brawny chest and arms are hard and scored
by the ceaseless recoil of his twanging bowstring.

RAIVATAKA : Sir, His Majesty is looking fixedly in your direction, as if impatient to give you his commands. Let Your Honour approach.

GENERAL (*approaches the King, bowing low*) : Hail, Victory to our Royal Master. The beasts of prey have been tracked down to their lairs deep in the forest. Why then does my lord stay?

KING : Lord Bhadrasena, Mādhavya here has been reviling the chase so bitterly that my ardour for it is cooling off.

GENERAL (*aside*) : Mādhavya, be firm in your opposition; in the meantime, I shall follow the bent of my Royal Master's mind. (*aloud*) My Lord, this blockhead doesn't know what he is talking about. Your Royal Highness is a prime example of the benefits of the chase.

The body light, manly, ready for action, (5)
trim in the waist, fat melted away; knowledge gained
of changing responses of woodland creatures seized
by fear or anger;
the archer's elation as arrows hit perfectly the moving
mark:
falsely indeed is the chase cursed as a vice;[12]
is there another sport so excellent as this?

MĀDHAVYA (*angrily*) : Go away; His Majesty is now recovering his true nature; as for you, you may please yourself roaming from one forest to another until like a witless jackal you walk right into the jaws of some old bear.

KING : Bhadrasena, we are in the vicinity of the Hermitage: therefore I cannot really applaud these words of yours. For the present, my good lord:

Let bisons plunge into forest-pools and revel
splashing, (6)
striking the water repeatedly with their mighty horns;

let the herds of antelopes clustering in groups in the
in the shade,
chew the cud undisturbed;
and let wild boars lining up round puddles
where the marsh-sedge grows fragrant, root peacefully
in the mud:
and let this my bow with its loose-knotted string
be allowed to enjoy its well-earned repose.

GENERAL : So please Your Royal Highness, your wish is my command.

KING : Let the beaters hemming in the game be recalled then; and let the soldiers now encamped in the environs of the holy groves encircling them, be ordered to withdraw. Mark you:

Like sun-crystals[13] cool to the touch (7)
vomit fiery sparks from deep within
if struck by another luminous power,
so, hermits rich in holiness
in whom Tranquillity presides,
have hidden deep a blazing energy
that leaps out to burn when aroused.

MĀDHAVYA : Now, you inciter of strong passions, be off with you and quickly.

GENERAL (*bowing to the King*) : As our Royal Master commands.

(*Exits.*)

KING (*to his attendants*) : Ladies, you may divest yourselves of your hunting costumes; and you too, Raivataka, resume your duties.

RAIVATAKA : As the Great Lord commands.

(*Exit.*)

MĀDHAVYA (*laughing*) : So, now that Your Honour has rid himself of these gadflies, do me a favour; come and sit in comfort in the shade of that tree over there, on that charming stone seat with its canopy of flowering vines, so that I could also sit down and rest.

KING : Lead the way.

MĀDHAVYA : This way, my lord. (*both turn around and sit down*)

KING: Ah! My friend Mādhavya, your eyes have not as yet been richly feasted as they should be; for you have not seen what is truly worth seeing.

MADHAVYA : How do you say that? Is Your Honour not right here before my eyes?

KING: Everyone considers the person dear to him as most worth seeing. But, I am referring to her . . . to Śakuntalā, that exquisite ornament of the Hermitage.

MADHAVYA (*aside*) : I shall not give him room to expatiate on this theme. (*to the King*) Now listen, Your Honour, if she is a hermit-girl beyond your reach, is there any point in seeing her?

KING : O, you blockhead!

Why do people with upturned faces gaze (8)
upon the crescent of the new moon with unblinking
eyes?

Apart from that, you know that Duhṣanta's mind is never drawn to forbidden things.

MADHAVYA : And can you explain that to me?

KING : Like a flower of the fragrant white jasmine (9)
dropped from its parent stalk onto an Arka leaf
she, sprung from a lovely Apsarā, I hear,
is the Sage's daughter only found by him, abandoned.

MADHAVYA (*laughing*) : Oho! So that's how it is, eh! Like one whose palate jaded by enjoying delicate candies made of the sweetest dates hankers after a taste of the sour tamarind, you too, Sir, sated with the pleasure of the Inner Apartments, full of beauties, and each one a gem . . . you are consumed by this passion for a hermit-girl.

KING : It is only because you haven't seen her that you talk like this.

MADHAVYA : Why Sir, then she must be a miracle of beauty indeed . . . to arouse such breathless admiration in *you*.

KING: My friend, she needs not many words:

Contemplating Brahmā's imaging power ineffable, (10)
and her beauty, she flashes on my eye,
a jewel among women
of another order of Creation, extraordinary;
as if the Mighty Creator gathering

rarest elements of beauty,
pictured perfection first,
then quickened it with the Breath of Life.

MĀDHAVYA : Why then, she must put to shame all other beauties for all time.

KING : And I keep thinking . . . she is:

A flower whose fragrance none has dared to smell; (11)
Spring's tenderest shoot no profaning fingers have plucked;
fresh honey whose taste no lip has relished;
a gem glowing inviolate. Who can tell
what sinless mortal Brahmā has named
the blessed enjoyer of such beauty,
the fruit entire of his holy works in many births.

MĀDHAVYA : For that very reason, go quickly, hurry, Sir, and rescue her before she falls into the hands of some forest-dwelling hermit with greasy head and hair plastered down with *ingudi* oil.

KING : Ah! But the lady is not mistress of herself; and her parent is not in the Hermitage at present.

MĀDHAVYA : Now tell me—what are her feelings towards you? Did her eyes express any hint of love?

KING : You know, my friend, hermit-girls are shy and retiring by nature; Yet:

When I turned towards her she turned her gaze away: (12)
her smiles seemed the prologue to some other play;
with her demeanour thus veiled by modesty,
Love neither shone radiant nor was it concealed.

MĀDHAVYA (*laughing*) : What Sir! Did you then expect her to leap into your arms as soon as she set eyes on Your Honour?

KING : But as she was leaving with her friends, her feelings were amply manifest; How?

Having gone some steps, she stopped, unforeseen, (13)
exclaimed—'Ah! My foot is pricked by a darbhā-blade';
sylph-like she stood, still, turning towards me,
busy disentangling the bark-garment
that certainly was not caught on the twigs of any shrub.

MADHAVYA : I see it all now; I see it quite clearly. I trust you have laid in a good stock of provisions. For it looks as if you have turned this penance-grove into a pleasure-garden.

KING : My friend, can you not come up with some pretext or other that will gain us entry into the Hermitage once more?

MĀDHAVYA : Hm . . . now . . . let me think; but do not break my concentration with any of your false lamentations. (*as if deep in thought*) Ah! I have it. Why think of some pretext? Are you not the King?

KING : Yes, so what of it?

MĀDHAVYA : Go right in and demand your one-sixth share of wild rice from the hermits.

KING : They pay a tribute far richer than a heap of priceless gems for the protection we provide them; and we cherish that far more. Think:

> Perishable is the fruit of the yield (14)
> raised from the Realm's Four Estates;
> but imperishable is that sixth part[14]
> the hermits give us of their holiness.

(*Voices off-stage*) : Good, we have succeeded in our search.

KING (*listening*) : From their calm, resonant tones, these must be hermits.

Enter the Guard.

GUARD : Victory to my Royal Lord; here are two young hermits at the entrance.

KING: Usher them in without delay.

GUARD : I shall announce them at once.

Enter two young hermits *with* the Guard.

GUARD : This way, come this way, honourable sirs.

FIRST HERMIT (*seeing the King*) : How admirable! His person radiates such majesty; yet one feels at ease. But that is not surprising in a king who is almost a sage.[15]

> He has embraced the worldly life (15)
> that all must lead to be of use to the world:
> he too practises the Yoga of protection

and garners for himself each day
the purest merit of holy rites:
with all passions under perfect control
and controlling the world's Righteous Way.
To him belongs that hallowed praise-word—Sage
—prefixed merely with the attribute—Royal—
the praise-word so often chanted
by pairs of celestial minstrels
to resound in the Realms of Light.

SECOND HERMIT : **Gautama, *this* is Duhṣanta? Friend to Indra, the** Destroyer of powerful Vala?[16]

FIRST HERMIT : Who else?

SECOND HERMIT :

What wonder then that this heroic King (16)
with arms strong as massive iron beams
that bar the city's great gates should hold
single sway over the All-Supporting Earth
bounded by the dark-blue oceans?
For the celestials, when the battle lines are drawn
against the fierce-encountering Titans
hope for victory only from his taut-drawn bow
and the clashing thunders of Indra,
the oft-invoked[17] Lord of the Realms of Light.

HERMITS (*approaching*) : Blessings be upon you, Sir. (*offer fruits*)

KING (*rises from his seat with respect*) : I welcome you, holy hermits. (*accepts the offering with a deep bow, then sits down*) I am eager to know what has brought you here.

HERMITS : The residents of this Hermitage hearing that you are in the neighbourhood address this request to you.

KING : What are their commands?

HERMITS : In the absence of His Holiness, the Patriarch, demons will begin disturbing the performance of our sacred rites. Therefore they request that you with your charioteer come in and stay for some nights in the Hermitage to guard it.

KING : I am honoured to be asked.

MĀDHAVYA (*aside*) : Good Fortune seizes you by the throat, eh?

KING : Raivataka: go, tell the charioteer to bring round the chariot and my bow and quiver.

GUARD : As Your Highness commands. (*goes off*)

HERMITS (*expressing great satisfaction*) :

The Puru monarchs were first and foremost (17)
consecrated protectors of those in distress;
as befits your noble descent, O King,
you now duly follow in their footsteps.

KING : Go first, Holy Sirs; I shall follow close on your heels.

HERMITS: May victory always attend on you.

(*Exit.*)

KING : Mādhavya, are you not eager to see Śakuntalā?

MĀDHAVYA : At first, yes; I was—with eagerness that was brimming over; but—(*looks fearful*) at the mention of the word 'demons', not a drop of it remains.

KING O, you shouldn't be afraid; you will naturally stay close to me.

MĀDHAVYA : A protector of your chariot wheels then?[18]

Enter the Guard.

GUARD : Your Majesty, the chariot is ready and awaits my lord's triumphal setting out. But—Karabhaka has also arrived—from the Queen's Royal Presence.

KING (*in a reverential tone of voice*) : What! From our Royal Mother?

GUARD : Yes, my lord.

KING : He should have been shown in immediately.

GUARD : I shall do so at once, my lord. (*goes out*)

Enter Karabhaka *with* the doorkeeper.

KARABHAKA (*approaches*) : Hail, hail to His Majesty. The Queen Mother's command runs as follows, Sire: 'On the fourth day after today I shall break the fast that I have undertaken, the fast known as "The Safeguarding of the Son's Succession". My long-lived son[19] should be by my side on that solemn occasion without fail.'

KING : Māḍhavya, look at me; on the one hand I am bound to honour my commitments to the holy sages; on the other the command of a revered parent is laid on me. Neither obligation may be ignored with impunity. How do we cope with such a situation?

MĀDHAVYA (*laughing*) : Hang in between, suspended in mid-air like Triśanku.[20]

KING: I am truly perplexed.

Required to perform duties in places (18)
widely separated, I am in two minds,
like a river that strikes a hill in mid-course,
and forced back parts into two streams.

(*after reflecting*) Mādhavya, my friend, you have always been accepted as a son by our Mother; so—you could leave now, return to the Capital and acquaint Her Majesty with my deep involvement in the affairs of the Hermitage; you could also take my place at the ceremony and carry out for Her Majesty, all the ritual duties that a son has to perform.

MĀDHAVYA : You don't say that because you think that I am afraid of demons, do you?

KING : O no, O Great Brahmin; you—afraid? That is inconceivable.

MĀDHAVYA : Well then, I shall leave; but I must travel in a manner befitting the younger brother of the King.

KING : Indeed you shall, my friend. I shall have my whole retinue accompany you, so that it will no longer be a disquieting presence in the Holy Groves.

MĀDHAVYA (*struts around proudly*) : Ha, I feel already like the Crown Prince.

KING (*to himself*) : This fellow tends to prattle. He may blurt out something about my interest in Śakuntalā to the ladies in the Royal Apartments. That won't do; I should put a different complexion on the whole matter. (*takes the jester by the hand and speaks to him*) My friend, listen carefully to me. I am going into the Hermitage solely out of esteem for the sages, to help them. I have no real interest in the hermit-maiden; just a whim, you know. For you can very well see that:

Between our royal self and that simple girl, (19)
a stranger to love, bred among gentle fawns
as one of them, lies a world of difference.

Do not, my friend,
take in earnest what was spoken merely in jest.

MADHAVYA : Is that all?

(*Exit all.*)

Thus ends Act Two
entitled
CONCEALMENT OF THE TELLING

ACT THREE

PRELUDE[21]

Scene: The Hermitage of Kaṇva.

Enter one of Kaṇva's pupils.

PUPIL (*with admiration*) : O what a mighty monarch Duhṣanta is. No sooner had he entered our Hermitage than all our sacred rites became completely free of all unexpected disturbances.

Why tell a long tale of arrows aimed and shot; (1)
by the mere twang of the bowstring from afar
as if his bow spoke quivering with rage, he made
all hindrances flee terrified from the scene.

Now let me gather Kuśa-grass and take it to the Priest to strew on the altar.

Walks around, notices someone and speaks in the air.

Ho there, Priyamvadā, say, for whom are you carrying these lotus leaves on their tender stalks? And the cooling balsam of the fragrant Uśira-root? (*as if listening to a reply*) What did you say? O, that Śakuntalā has suffered a heat-stroke? That these things are to cool her burning frame? Priyamvadā, listen, let her be looked after with the greatest care, for she is the very life-breath of the Patriarch. I shall also send some hallowed water used for the Sacrifice, with Gautamī; it will soothe Śakuntalā.

(He exits.)

End of the Prelude

Enter the King *deeply in love.*

KING (*pensive, sighing*) :

I know well the Holy Power of penance immense; (2)

that young girl is dependent on another's will,
that I know. But like water flowing down,
my heart is truly powerless to return.

O God who churns men's minds,[22] how is it that your weapons claimed to be flowers, are so sharp? (*as if recollecting*) O yes, I know why:

Śiva's fiery wrath must still burn in you (3)
like Fire smouldering deep in the ocean's depths.
Were it not so, how can you burn lovers like me,
when mere ashes is all that is left of you?[23]

Then again, we of the Brotherhood of Love are cruelly deceived by you and the moon—though we put our fullest trust in both. And why do I say this:

False is the statement to lovers like me (4)
that flowers are your arrows; that moonbeams are cool;
the moon's rays pregnant with ice shoot darts of fire,
and your arrows are tipped with hardest adamant.

On the other hand:

Even if you drive me to distraction, O dolphin-bannered[24] god! (5)
With unsleeping anguish, I would still welcome you,
if only you would assail her too with your darts
—that lovely girl with long, bewitching eyes.

O blessed god, though reproached bitterly, you show no compassion.

Wantonly have I made you greatly grow, O Bodiless One![25] (6)
nourishing you assiduously with a hundred rites and feelings;
now, drawing your bow back to your ear,
it is at *me* you choose to let your arrow fly.

Now that the ascetics, free of impediments, have given me leave to withdraw, where can I find solace for my weary heart? (*sighs deeply*) What other refuge is there but the beloved's presence. (*looking up*) At this hour when the noonday sun blazes down with cruel heat, Lady Śakuntalā with her friends usually retires to the Mālinī's banks where flowering vines form shady bowers. Well, that's where I shall go. (*turns and looks*) I can tell that the beautiful girl has just passed through this avenue of young trées. For:

The cups of flowers she has just plucked (7)
have not as yet sealed themselves,
and these tender shoots, broken off,
are still moist with their milky sap.

(*feeling pleasure at the touch of the breeze*) Aha! How delightful is the breeze blowing here in the woodlands.

This breeze that wafts the fragrance of lotuses (8)
with the cool spray of Mālinī's rippling stream
is able to soothe love-fevered limbs,
enfolding them in a close embrace.

(*noticing something*) Ha! Śakuntalā must be here in this arbour of reeds overhung by flowering vines—it is plain to see,

At the entrance dusted with pale river sand (9)
a line of footprints clearly etched, lightly marked
in front by her toes and indented deeply at the back
by her heels weighed down by wide heavy hips.

Let me look through these twining stems. (*peers in and exclaims with rapture*) My eyes look upon Paradise; there she is, the beloved of my dreams, reclining on a stone slab strewn with flowers and attended by her friends. Let me hear what they are saying in confidence. . . (*stands watching*)

The scene discovers Śakuntalā *with* her friends, *as described.*

FRIENDS (*fanning her*) : Dear Śakuntalā, does the breeze of these lotus leaves soothe you somewhat?

ŚAKUNTALĀ (*in deep distress*) : What! Are my dear friends fanning me? (*her friends look at each other dismayed*)

KING : Lady Śakuntalā does appear greatly indisposed. (*musing awhile*) I wonder if it is the summer's heat that is the real cause of her distress . . . or, is it what I think it is . . . (*reflecting on it*) O well, have done with doubts:

With Uśīra-balm spread thick over her breasts (10)
and a single bracelet of tender lotus stalks

that hangs pale and withered on her wrist,
my beloved's body though racked with pain. . .
how exquisite it looks in its pale loveliness:
Summer's heat can strike as savage as love. . .it's true,
but. . .to burn young girls into such splendour. . .
I cannot think *that* lies in Summer's power.

PRIYAMVADĀ (*aside*) : Anasūyā, ever since she first saw the King, Śakuntalā has been restless and dejected; there can be no other reason for her sickness.

ANASŪYĀ : I suspected as much myself. Very well, I'll ask her. Śakuntalā dearest, I wish to ask you something . . . see how your limbs are simply burning.

KING : Quite so:

Those bracelets of plaited lotus-fibre (11)
bright as moonbeams, now turning brown,
speak of the fever unendurable
coursing like fire through her limbs.

ŚAKUNTALĀ (*raising herself*) : What did you wish to ask me, dear?

ANASŪYĀ : Listen, dear Śakuntalā, we cannot enter your mind and read your thoughts; but we feel that the state you are in is like that of persons experiencing the pangs of love as described in romantic tales. So be frank, tell us the cause of your distress. Without knowing the nature of an illness how can a cure be found for it?

KING : Anasūyā thinks the way I do.

ŚAKUNTALĀ : Indeed, I am deeply troubled; but I cannot blurt it out abruptly.

PRIYAMVADĀ : Dearest, Anasūyā is perfectly right; why are you hiding the cause of your distress? You are wasting away day by day; all that is left is the delicate glow of your loveliness—like the lustre of fine pearls.

KING : Priyamvadā is not exaggerting; just see her:

Wan face with sunken cheeks, breasts no longer firm, (12)
slender waist grown more slender, shoulders drooping
despondent,
complexion dulled by pallor—O how woebegone she
looks,
limp, struck by maddening love, yet how lovely

—a Mādhavī, its leaves touched by a scorching wind.

ŚAKUNTALĀ (*sighing*) : Whom else can I speak to of my heartache? But it will be a source of anxiety for you both.

BOTH : That's why we insist on knowing; grief shared is easier to bear.

KING : Asked by friends who share her joys and sorrows, (13)
the young girl cannot but speak of the ache
hid within her heart.
Although I saw her turn round many a time
gazing at me with hungering eyes,
my heart beats now like a coward's
fearing to hear the answer she makes.

ŚAKUNTALĀ (*shyly*) : From the moment that Royal Sage who is the protector of penance-groves came within my sight. . . (*breaks off overcome by shyness*)

BOTH : Go on, tell us, dear.

ŚAKUNTALĀ : From that instant I am pining for love of him.

BOTH : Fortunately, you have set your heart on one truly worthy of you. But then where else would a great river flow except to the ocean!

KING (*ecstatic*) : I have heard what I longed to hear.

Love, the creator of my anguish (14)
now brings a touch of cooling balm,
as days dark with clouds at summer's end
bring relief to the world of living things.

ŚAKUNTALĀ : My friends, if you approve, counsel me as to how I can find favour in the eyes of the Royal Sage; otherwise I shall be just a memory.

KING : Her words remove all doubts.

PRIYAMVADĀ (*aside*) : Anasūyā, she is too far gone in love and cannot brook any delay.

ANASŪYĀ : Priyamvadā, what plan can we devise to fulfil our friend's desire secretly and without any delay.

PRIYAMVADĀ : Hm . . . without delay, why that's easy . . . but secretly . . . ah! That bears some thinking.

ANASŪYĀ : And how's that?

PRIYAMVADĀ : Why, the Royal Sage looks at her with so much tenderness in his eyes; and these days he appears rather wasted . . . as if he spends wakeful nights.

KING : How right she is; such is my state:

Hot tears welling up of anguish within, as I lie (15)
night after night, my cheek pillowed on my arm,
dull the brilliance of gems set in this gold armlet
that unimpeded by the welt raised by the bowstring,
slips down as often as I push it up from my wrist.

PRIYAMVADĀ (*after reflecting*) : Listen, let Śakuntalā write a love letter; hiding it under some flowers that I shall pretend were part of those offered to the deity, I shall manage to give it to the King.

ANASŪYĀ : My friend, it is a pretty plan, I like it. What does our Śakuntalā have to say about it?

ŚAKUNTALĀ : Can the arrangement be questioned?

PRIYAMVADĀ : Right then, now you think of an elegant song that'll convey your feelings to the King.

ŚAKUNTALĀ : I can think of something, but my heart trembles at the thought of being rebuffed.

KING : He from whom you fear a rebuff, O timid girl! (16)
He stands here, yearning to enfold you in his arms.
The man who woos Fortune may win her—or he may not,
but does Fortune ever fail to win the man *she* woos?

again:

Longing for your love, the man you assume (17)
wrongly as one who would spurn that love,
he, is here, close to you, beautiful girl!
A gem is sought for, it does not seek.

FRIENDS : O you who belittles her own worth! Who on earth will think of unfurling an umbrella to keep off the cooling autumnal moonlight!

ŚAKUNTALĀ (*smiling*) : I am admonished.

KING : My eyes forget to wink while I stand gazing on my beloved; and no wonder;

With one eyebrow raised, curving deep as a tendril (18)
as she shapes her feelings into words,
her face, a blush mantling her cheek, proclaims
the passionate love she feels for me.

ŚAKUNTALĀ : Dear friends, I have a little song running through my head; but there are no writing materials at hand to set it down.

PRIYAMVADĀ : Why don't you incise the words with your nail on this lotus leaf soft as a parrot's downy breast?

ŚAKUNTALĀ : Now listen to the song and tell me if the words are well-chosen to convey my feelings.

FRIENDS : Go ahead, we are listening.

ŚAKUNTALĀ (*reading*)[26] :

I do not know your heart, (19)
but my nights and days, O pitiless one!
Are haunted by Love,
as every part of me
yearns to be one with you.

KING (*coming out at once*) :

Love burns you, true, my slender girl! (20)
But me, He consumes utterly—relentless;
Day wipes out the moon[27] from view
but not the water-lily.

FRIENDS (*rising with the greatest joy*) : Welcome, welcome to the immediate answer to our inmost wish. (*Śakuntalā tries to get up too*)

KING : Fair lady, no, no, do not exert yourself.

Your limbs aflame with pain that bite (21)
into the bed of flowers, fast fading
your bracelets of lotus-fibre, need not
bend in the customary courtesies.

ŚAKUNTALĀ (*thrown into confusion, to herself*) : O my heart, are you so overcome that you find nothing to say?

ANASŪYĀ : Let His Majesty grace one end of this stone slab.

Śakuntalā *moves away a little.*

KING (*sitting down*) : Priyamvadā, I trust your friend's fever is somewhat abated?

PRIYAMVADĀ (*with a smile*) : With the right medicine at hand it ought to improve, Sir. Your Majesty, the love you bear to each other is plain to see. But the love I bear my friend prompts me to say something.

KING : Say what is on your mind, gracious lady. What is intended to be said, if left unsaid, becomes a matter of regret later.

PRIYAMVADĀ : Well, I shall say it then, Your Honour. It is the duty of the King to relieve the sufferings of the residents of a hermitage . . .

KING : What higher duty can there be?

PRIYAMVADĀ : The god of love, mighty as he is, has reduced our dear friend here to this state for love of you. You are bound therefore to sustain her life by taking her.

KING : Dear lady, this is a mutual wish and entreaty. I am most highly favoured.

ŚAKUNTALĀ (*with a smile but feigning annoyance*) : That's enough, Priyamvadā, do not hold back the good King who must be impatient to return to the Inner Apartments of the Royal Palace.[28]

KING :
O Lady enshrined in my heart! if you consider my heart (22)
devoted to none but you, as otherwise, then think of me
slain once by the arrow of the god who makes men mad,
as slain once more,
O lady whose glances pour into me like delicious wine!

ANASŪYĀ : Sire, one hears that kings have many loves. Pray act in such a manner as not to bring sorrow and bitter tears to her kinsfolk.

KING : Gracious Lady! I shall just say this:
Though many a wife may grace our palace-courts (23)
none but two shall ever be the glory
and mainstay of our race—the Earth[29]
sea-girdled, and, this lady, your friend.

Śakuntalā is overjoyed.

FRIENDS : We are reassured.

PRIYAMVADĀ (*aside*) : Anasūyā, just observe our dear friend; see how she revives each minute like a pea-hen that feels the touch of the breeze from fresh rain clouds.

ŚAKUNTALĀ : Listen, friends, beg the Protector of the Earth's pardon for what might have been spoken among ourselves, that went beyond the bounds of propriety.

FRIENDS (*smiling*) : Whoever said something of the sort should beg his pardon; is anyone else to blame?

ŚAKUNTALĀ : Pray forgive whatever was said in your presence; people say many things behind a person's back.

KING (*smiling*) :

I may overlook the offence, (24)
O girl with tapering thighs! If
out of kindness, you offer me a place
on this bed of flowers
sweet from the touch of your limbs,
to allay my weariness.

PRIYAMVADĀ : Would that be sufficient to make her happy?

ŚAKUNTALĀ (*with a show of being peeved*) : Stop it, you naughty girl; how dare you tease me . . . and in the state I am in.

ANASŪYĀ (*glancing outside*) : Priyamvadā, look, this little fawn is anxiously searching here and there . . . must be looking for his mother. . . he seems to have lost her; let me take him to her.

PRIYAMVADĀ : O, this little one . . . he is like quicksilver, nimble and wayward, my friend; you are no match for him single-handed. Let me help you.

They prepare to leave.

ŚAKUNTALĀ : Friends, dear friends, do not leave me alone; let one of you go. I am helpless with no one to turn to.

FRIENDS (*smiling*) : He whom the whole world turns to for help is by your side.

(*They leave.*)

ŚAKUNTALĀ : What, have they gone already. . . and left me alone?

KING (*looks around*) : My love, do not be uneasy. Am I not near you, your suitor who adores you utterly? Now, tell me:

Shall I raise cool breezes, waving over you (25)
these broad lotus-leaf fans, moist and refreshing
to relieve your languid weariness?

Shall I place your lotus-pink feet on my lap,
O Lady with beautiful tapering thighs!
And press them tenderly to ease your pain?

ŚAKUNTALĀ : I shall not bring dishonour on those whom I should honour.[30]

Gets up to leave; the King barring her way addresses her.

KING : Beautiful girl! The day is not cool as yet; look at your condition:

Leaving your couch of flowers, throwing off (26)
the cool wrap of lotus leaves placed on your breasts,
your delicate body all worn out with pain,
how will you brave this fierce noonday heat?

(saying this the King forces her to turn around)

ŚAKUNTALĀ : Let go of me, release me, I am not free to do as I please. But what can I do when I have only my friends to help me?

KING : O misery! You make me feel ashamed of myself.

ŚAKUNTALĀ : I don't mean to, Your Majesty; I am just blaming my Fate.

KING : Why do you rail at a fate that is favourable to you?

ŚAKUNTALĀ : And why won't I rail against my Fate that tempts me when I am not my own mistress, with qualities not my own.

KING (*to himself*) :

It is not Love who torments virgins[31] to gain
his ends, (27)
it is they who torment Love, letting the moment
slip by;
great though their own eagerness, shrinking
from the advances of the beloved,
and fearful of yielding their bodies
though longing for the pleasure of union.

(Śakuntalā does leave.)

KING : What! Shall I not please myself? (*advances and seizes her by her garment*)

ŚAKUNTALĀ (*with a show of anger*) : Paurava![*] Act with decorum; ascetics

[*] Ruler of the Puru dynasty.

constantly move about here.

KING : Fair Lady! Such fear of your elders? His Holiness Kaṇva is well-versed in the Law; you will not cause him any distress. Listen,

Many are the daughters of sages, (28)
married by the Gāndharva rite,[32] we hear;
and once married, felicitated
with joyful acceptance by their fathers.

(*looking around*) What! I have walked into the open, have I? (*lets go of Śakuntalā and retraces his steps*)

ŚAKUNTALĀ (*takes a step forward, turns around; bending*) : Paurava! Even though your wishes remain unfulfilled and you know me only through conversation, do not forget me.

KING : My beautiful girl!

However far you may go from me, (29)
you shall never go from my heart,
as the shadow of the tree at evening
never leaves its base on the eastern side.

ŚAKUNTALĀ (*going a little way, to herself*) : Alas! What shall I do? Hearing these words my feet refuse to move forward. Let me hide behind this amaranth hedge and observe how his feelings incline. (*stands still*)

KING : How could you go off like this, my love, without a thought, forsaking me whose unchangeable love is for you and for you only.

How delicate is your body to be loved most gently! (30)
And how hard your heart like the stalk of the Śiriṣa-
flower!

ŚAKUNTALĀ : Ah! Hearing this I am powerless to leave.

KING : What'll I do now in this bower, empty of my beloved's presence. (*looking in front*) O, what's this . . . my way is barred.

This bright bracelet of lotus-stalks fragrant (31)
with Uśīra-balm from her body
lies here before me, fallen from her wrist
to become a chain around my heart.

(he picks it up adoringly)

ŚAKUNTALĀ (*looking at her arm*) : O dear, the bracelet was so loose, it must have slipped off and fallen without my noticing it.

KING (*placing the bracelet on his breast*) : O for its touch!

This charming ornament of yours, my love, (32)
having left your lovely arm to rest here,
consoles this unhappy man more than you have,
though it is only an insentient thing.

ŚAKUNTALA : Ha! I cannot hold back any longer. Using this bracelet as a pretext, I shall discover myself. (*approaches the King*)

KING (*seeing her is overjoyed*) : Ah! Here is the lady who is my very life; no sooner had I begun to lament my fate than Fate came to my aid to do me a favour.

Parched with thirst, the bird has only to crave for
water (33)
and a shower from a fresh rain-cloud falls into its
mouth.

ŚAKUNTALĀ (*standing before the King*) : Sire, when I was half-way I remembered the bracelet that had slipped off my arm; I have come back for it knowing in my heart that you would have taken it. Let me have it back lest it betray us both to the sages.

KING : Well . . . I'll give it back on one condition.

ŚAKUNTALĀ : And what's that?

KING : That I myself restore it to the place it once occupied.

ŚAKUNTALĀ (*to herself*) : There's no way out. (*comes closer to him*)

KING : Let's sit here on this same stone slab.

They both turn around and sit.

KING (*taking hold of Śakuntalā's hand*) : O, to feel such a touch!

Has Fate rained down a shower ambrosial[33] (34)
to make the tree of love
once burnt to ashes by Siva's wrath
put forth a fresh shoot once more?

ŚAKUNTALĀ (*feeling the touch of his hand*) : Quickly, hurry up, my lord.

KING (*filled with happiness, to himself*) : How this inspires confidence in me; for she has addressed me by the word used for a husband in speaking. (*aloud*) Oh beautiful girl! The ends of this bracelet of lotus-stalks are not joined very firmly; if you permit me, I'll re-do it.

ŚAKUNTALĀ (*with a smile*) : If you wish.

KING (*artfully delays and finally fixes the bracelet*) : See, lovely girl!

Leaving the sky in search of richer beauty, (35)
the new moon in the form of lotus-stems,
joining the points of its crescent, has placed itself
on your arm lovely as a śyāmā-vine.

ŚAKUNTALĀ : I cannot see very well; the pollen-dust from the lily at my ear shaken by the breeze, has fallen into my eye blurring my sight.

KING (*with a smile*) : If you permit me, I can blow it away.

ŚAKUNTALĀ : That would be kind . . . but . . . what if I don't trust you?

KING : Why not? A new servant does not overstep his master's instructions.

ŚAKUNTALĀ : It is just this excess of gallantry that I can't quite trust.

KING (*to himself*) : I am certainly not going to pass up an opportunity so pleasant, to minister to her comfort. (*about to raise her face up to his, Śakuntalā resists at first, then gives up*)

KING : O, you with your intoxicating eyes, why don't you stop suspecting me of dishonourable behaviour. (*Śakuntalā glances up at him, then hangs her head*)

KING (*raising her face lightly with two fingers, to himself*) :

My love's lower lip, soft and unbruised, (36)
trembles with such alluring charm
as if granting me who thirst for it
the permission I wait for eagerly.

ŚAKUNTALĀ : My lord is taking his time to do what he promised, it seems.

KING : The lily adorning your ear, sweet lady, was confusing me by its likeness to your eye to which it lies so close. (*blows the pollen dust away*)

ŚAKUNTALĀ : I can now see clearly. But I am sorry, my lord, I have no way of returning the kind favour you have done me.

KING : No matter, there is no need to, beautiful lady!

To inhale the fragrance of your face (37)
is itself a favour granted to me;
is the honey-bee not well-content
with the mere fragrance of the lotus?

ŚAKUNTALĀ (*with a smile*) : But if it were not, what would he* do?

* The bee stands for the King; the Skt. word is in the masculine.

KING (*decisively brings his face close to hers*) : This . . . this . . .

(*A voice off-stage*) : Little bride of the sheldrake, come bid your mate farewell; Night is here.[34]

ŚAKUNTALĀ (*flustered*) : My lord! Lady Gautamī is on her way here, to ask after my health, I'm sure. Hide behind this tangle of vines.

KING : Yes. (*goes into a secret place*)

Gautamī *enters with a goblet in her hand.*

GAUTAMĪ : My child! Here is the sanctified water for you. (*looks at her and helps her up*) A fine state of affairs. . . unwell, and only the gods to keep you company.

ŚAKUNTALĀ : Priyamvadā and Anasūyā went down just this minute to the Mālinī.

GAUTAMĪ (*sprinkling Śakuntalā with the holy water*) : Dear child, may you live long and in good health. Is your fever somewhat abated now? (*touches her*)

ŚAKUNTALĀ : There is a change for the better, Mother.

GAUTAMĪ : The day is drawing to its close; come, child, let us return to our cottage.

ŚAKUNTALĀ (*rising with difficulty, to herself*) : O heart! At first you drew back like a coward, fearing to taste the happiness that came knocking at your door. Now to your great regret, the time of parting has come; how bitter is your anguish. O fragrant bower of creepers! Soother of my anguish! I bid you farewell and take leave of you only to meet again and enjoy your company. (*leaves*)

KING (*returning to his former seat and sighing deeply*) : O misery! Many a hindrance lies between desire and its fulfilment:

She turned aside that lovely face (38)
with beautifully-lashed eyes:
again and again she guarded with her fingers
her lower lip, all the more tempting
for the faltering words of denial
murmured indistinct:
after much gentle persuasion
I raised her face to mine—
but could not kiss it, alas!

Where, where shall I go now? No, I shall stay right here; here in the bower of creepers where my beloved rested. *(looks round)*

Here on the stone-slab is the bed of flowers (39)
crushed by her body; here lies languishing
her message of love confided to the lotus-leaf;
an ornament of fine lotus-stalks, banished
from her hand lies there pathetic, abandoned;
my eyes cling to each object that I see;
how can I leave this arbour of reeds
all of a sudden, deserted though it be.

(*reflecting*) Alas! It was surely a mistake on my part to have delayed and wasted time once I had won my beloved. So now:

When next I find myself alone with her (40)
—that girl with a face of chiselled loveliness—
I'll lose no time: for happiness, as a rule,
is hard to come by: thus my foolish heart,
frustrated by stumbling-blocks, spells it out.
But, in the beloved's presence,
it stands somewhat abashed.

(*A voice in the air*) : O, King!

The evening rituals are in solemn progress; (41)
flesh-eating demons prowl and press round the altars
where the Holy Fire blazes.
Like massed thunder-clouds that reflect the sunset glow,
their shadowy forms, lurid,
move around in many ways
fear-instilling.

KING (*listens, then resolutely speaks*) : Ho there, ascetics . . . do not fear . . . here I am . . . I am coming.

(*Leaves.*)

End of Act Three
entitled
LOVE'S FRUITION

ACT FOUR

PRELUDE

Scene: The Hermitage.

Enter Śakuntalā's friends *gathering flowers.*

ANASŪYĀ: Priyamvadā, although I rejoice greatly knowing that Śakuntalā is happily married to a husband of her own choice who is worthy of her in every respect, I feel rather uneasy about something.

PRIYAMVADĀ: And what may that be?

ANASŪYĀ: The Royal Sage has been given leave to depart by the sages grateful for the successful completion of the Sacrifice; and he has returned to his Capital. Now, in the company of his Queens, will he remember all that happened here in the Hermitage . . . or will he not?

PRIYAMVADĀ: O, surely you should not feel uneasy on that score; such a noble form cannot house a nature so totally at variance with it. But I am anxious about something else; how will Father take it when he hears of all this on his return?

ANASŪYĀ: If you ask me, this marriage will be sealed with Father's approval and blessing.

PRIYAṂVADĀ: Why do you think that?

ANASŪYĀ: It is the paramount consideration in the mind of a parent to give a young daughter in marriage to a groom endowed with all noble qualities. If the gods themselves send one without any effort on the part of the parent, would he not congratulate himself on being most fortunate?

PRIYAMVADĀ (*looks into the basket*): Anasūyā, don't you think we have picked enough flowers for the worship of the divinities of the home?

ANASŪYĀ: But we also need some flowers for the adoration of Śakuntalā's Goddess of Fortune who watches over her marriage.

PRIYAMVADĀ: Yes, you are right.

They gather more flowers.

(*A voice off-stage rings out*): Ho there, I am here, at your door!

ANASŪYĀ (*listening carefully*): That sounds like a guest announcing himself.

PRIYAMVADĀ: Surely Śakuntalā is not far from the cottage; Ah . . . hm . . . but I'm afraid her heart is far away.

ANASŪYĀ: Then we must go; these flowers will do.

They are about to leave.

(*The same voice off-stage rings out again*): Woe to you, woe, you insolent girl who disregards the honoured guest standing at your door.

You who do not notice me, (1)
a hoard of holy merit
standing at your door,
because you are lost in thoughts of one
to the exclusion of all else,
you shall be lost in his thoughts:
though you goad his memory hard,
he shall fail to remember you,
even as a man drunk remembers not
thereafter, the tale he told before.

Hearing this, the girls are dismayed.

PRIYAMVADĀ: Alas, alas, the worst has happened. Our darling Śakuntalā, absent-minded, has offended some guest worthy of great reverence.

ANASŪYĀ (*looking ahead*): And it is not just any guest, O cruel Fate! It is the great sage Durvāsā quick to anger. Look where he is going after cursing her so cruelly . . . striding off briskly shaking with passion; it will not be easy to intercept him.

PRIYAMVADĀ: What has the power to burn other than Fire? You must go quickly, Anasūyā; fall at his feet and try to calm him down while I hurry and get water and a guest-offering to welcome him.

ANASŪYĀ: Yes, I am going. (*goes out in haste*)

PRIYAMVADĀ (*takes a few hurried steps, then stumbles*): O, an ill omen! This is what comes of hurrying. The basket has slipped from my hand

and the flowers lie all scattered on the ground. I had better pick them up. (*starts picking up the flowers*)

ANASŪYĀ (*entering*): O my friend, anger incarnate that he is, do you think he is one to accept anyone's entreaties? But I managed to squeeze a little compassion out of the old crust.

PRIYAMVADĀ (*smiling*): Even that 'little' is a lot for him; what happened, tell me.

ANASŪYĀ: When he peremptorily refused to turn back, I pleaded with him in these words: 'Most Venerable Holiness, your daughter is unaware of the great power you possess through your austerities; this is also her very first offence; considering these, please, revered Sir, forgive her.'

PRIYAMVADĀ: Then what did he say, go on.

ANASŪYĀ: He said: 'My curse cannot prove false; but its power will cease the moment she presents some ornament as a token of recognition.' With these words he vanished into thin air.

PRIYAMVADĀ: At least we can console ourselves a little with that. There *is* a token. When the Royal Sage was taking leave of Śakuntalā, he slipped the signet-ring with his name inscribed on it on her finger, as a remembrance. She does have in her possession the means of ensuring recognition.

They turn round and see Śakuntalā *at the cottage door.*

PRIYAMVADĀ: Look, Anasūyā, do you see our dearest friend there? Still, as if drawn in a picture, her cheek resting on her left hand . . . her mind so totally absorbed in thoughts of her absent lord that she does not seem to be aware of her own self . . . how could she have noticed the presence of a visitor.

ANASŪYĀ: I tell you what; let us keep this matter of the curse between our two selves. Delicate by nature, our dear friend should be spared a shock.

PRIYAMVADĀ: Naturally, who would sprinkle a tender jasmine with boiling water.

(*Both leave.*)

End of the Prelude

Enter a pupil of Kaṇva, *just got up from sleep.*

PUPIL: I have been asked by His Holiness, just returned from his pilgrimage, to look out and see what time it is. Let me go out into the open and ascertain how much of the night remains. (*turns and looks around*) O, it is daybreak already, I see.

Here, the moon, lord of healing herbs (2)
sinks behind the western mountain,
there, on the other, Dawn heralds
the advance of the rising Sun.
The rise and setting of the two Lights simultaneous
regulate the vicissitudes of life on earth.

And further,

Now that the Moon has set, the pool of moon-lotuses (3)
delights not my eye—her beauty is but a memory.
the grief of women left alone when loved ones
travel far are beyond measure hard to bear.

See how:

Daybreak's rose-red glow flushes the dew on the
jujube trees (4)
the peacock wakened leaves the cottage roof of
darbha-grass;
the blackbuck springs up from the altar's edge, hoof-
marked,
stretches his limbs and draws himself up to his noble
height.

And now:

The same moon who, stepping on the crown of
Sumeru, (5)
Parent of Mountains, dispelled the darkness, and
traversed
the middle regions of Viṣṇu's abode,
now falls down the sky in a pitiful glimmer of light:
the ascent too high of even the great ends in a fall.

Entering with a toss of the curtain.

ANASŪYĀ (*to herself*): Even one unacquainted with the ways of the world cannot help thinking that the King has behaved badly towards our Śakuntalā.

PUPIL: Well, I had better go now and inform our Preceptor that it is time for the oblations to the Sacred Fire. (*he departs*)

ANASŪYĀ: Dawn is breaking. I have woken up early. But now that I am awake, what is there for me to do? My hands refuse to go about their normal morning duties. Let the god of love be now happy since he has brought my pure-hearted friend into contact with a perfidious man. On the other hand, the Royal Sage may not be to blame. Perhaps, Durvāsā's curse is working itself out. Otherwise, how is it possible that after all the protestations he made, the king has not sent word to her in all this time? (*reflects a moment*) Then, shall we send him the Ring he left for remembrance? But with whom? Which of these austere hermits, serene and devoid of passions can we ask? And we can't get our friend into trouble by informing Father Kaṇva that Śakuntalā is married to Duhṣanta and now bears his child. In such a situation what can we do?

PRIYAMVADĀ: Anasūyā, Anasūyā, come quickly, hurry; the festive ceremonies for Śakuntalā's departure are on.

ANASŪYĀ: What? What is all this? (*astonished*)

PRIYAMVADĀ: Listen, just now I went to Śakuntalā's bedside to ask if she had slept well.

ANASŪYĀ: Then, then?

PRIYAMVADĀ: What do I see: Father Kaṇva, embracing Śakuntalā whose head was bowed low as if in shame, was felicitating her saying: 'Fortunately, my child, even though the smoke was blinding the sacrificer's eyes, the oblation he made fell right into the Fire.[35] You are like knowledge imparted to a good pupil—not to be regretted. I shall arrange to send you to your husband this very day with an escort of ascetics.'

ANASŪYĀ (*astonished*): But who informed Father Kaṇva of all that had happened during his absence?

PRIYAMVADĀ: As he was entering the Sanctuary of the Mystic Fire, a bodiless voice chanted a verse.

ANASŪYĀ: Repeat it to me.

PRIYAMVADĀ (*speaks in Sanskrit in the metre of the sacred texts*):

As the Holy Tree (6)
is with the Mystic Fire pregnant,
so is your daughter;
know, O Great Brāhmaṇa,
she holds Duhṣanta's glowing energy
pledged for the well-being of the world.

ANASŪYĀ (*embracing Priyamvadā, ecstatically*): O, what great news; I am happy, happy beyond all measure; yet, my mind is poised between joy and regret; regret that dear Śakuntalā will be leaving this very day.

PRIYAMVADĀ: We shall get over our regrets soon enough; let the poor girl taste some happiness.

ANASŪYĀ : Of course. It is for such an occasion that I put away a garland of Kesara flowers whose fragrance is lasting; there it is, in that casket of palm leaves hanging over there from a branch of the mango tree. Will you take it down and wrap it in lotus leaves while I go and prepare all the auspicious materials for Śakuntalā's adornment: yellow orpiment, holy earth, and Dūrvā sprouts? (*goes out*)

Priyamvadā takes down the casket of Kesara flowers.

(*A voice back-stage*) : Gautamī, bid Śārṇgarava and the other hermits get ready to escort Śakuntalā.

PRIYAMVADĀ : Anasūyā, hurry, hurry. They are calling the hermits who are to escort Śakuntalā to the Capital.

Anasūyā *enters with a tray of toiletries in her hand.*

PRIYAMVADĀ (*looks ahead*) : Anasūyā, there, do you see Śakuntalā, her hair freshly washed at sunrise with hallowed water. She is surrounded by the wives of sages who are congratulating her and invoking blessings holding grains of wild rice sanctified by prayers in their hands. Let us go and join them.

Śakuntalā *is seen seated with* Lady Gautamī *and* wives of sages.

ŚAKUNTALĀ : I bow to you all, revered ladies.

GAUTAMĪ : Daughter, may your lord confer on you the title of Chief Queen[36] as a mark of his high esteem.

SAGES' WIVES : Child, may you give birth safely to a son who will be a hero.

Having blessed her they leave, all except Gautamī.

FRIENDS (*approaching her*) : May the Holy Bath shower all happiness on you, dear Śakuntalā.

ŚAKUNTALĀ : Welcome, welcome to my dearest friends; sit near me, both of you, won't you.

FRIENDS : Now sit still while we apply the auspicious adornments on your person.

The two friends *sit down and pick up the tray containing the auspicious cosmetics.*

ŚAKUNTALĀ : I value this affectionate service you do me today more than I did at any other time. When will I be adorned again by my dear friends? (*weeps*)

FRIENDS : Dearest friend, you should not weep on such a happy occasion as this. (*wipe away her tears and begin to apply the decorations on her face*)

PRIYAMVADĀ : These simple adornments are all we have in the Hermitage; they do no justice to your beauty that richly deserves fine jewels and adornments to set it off.

Enter a hermit boy *bearing gifts for Śakuntalā.*

BOY : Here are rich ornaments to adorn Lady Śakuntalā.

Everybody looks at him in amazement.

GAUTAMĪ : Hārīta, my child, where did you get these?

HĀRĪTA : I found them, Lady, through Father Kaṇva's favour.

GAUTAMĪ : Created by his mind-power?

HĀRĪTA : No, not quite; he directed me saying: 'Go, bring lovely blossoms from the great forest trees for Śakuntalā's adornment.' So I went:

A certain tree produced as if by magic (7)
a garment of silk, pale-bright as moonbeams,
fitting for this most auspicious occasion;
another noble tree poured out rich rose-red juice
to tint beautifully her tender feet;
in the branches of other stately trees
woodland nymphs unseen, held out their hands
rivalling in beauty delicate leaf buds
unfurling, to offer rich gifts of rare jewels.

PRIYAMVADĀ (*looking at Śakuntalā*) : The Queen-bee though born in a tree-hollow deserves nothing less than the honey of the lotus.

GAUTAMĪ : Dear child, the bestowal of such rare gifts augurs well for the great honours that await you in the palace of your lord.

Śakuntalā, bashful, looks down.

HĀRĪTA : I shall go now and inform Father Kaṇva who went down to the Mālinī for his ablutions, about this homage rendered him by the Lords of the Forest.

ÁNASŪYĀ : Śakuntalā, my friend, how can we adorn you? We are not used to handling such fine ornaments. (*reflects for a moment*) Drawing from our knowledge of paintings, we shall place these jewels on you as they should be.

ŚAKUNTALĀ (*with a smile*) : O, I know how clever you both are.

The two friends begin adorning Śakuntalā with the ornaments. Enter Sage Kaṇva *having finished his ablutions.*

KAṆVA : Śakuntalā leaves us today—sobs my heart (8)
grief-stricken; unshed tears choke my voiceless throat;
a pale cast of troubled thoughts dims my very sight.
If affection can make me, a hermit grown old
in the forest's hard school, so distraught,
O, how much more bitter must the anguish
of the first parting from a daughter be
to fathers who dwell in the heart of home and family.

FRIENDS : Śakuntalā, dear, you are now properly adorned; put on this pair of silk garments[37] that have been blessed by prayer.

Śakuntalā gets up and puts them on.

GAUTAMI : Look, dear child, your father is standing there, watching you as if he were embracing you with eyes brimming with happy tears. Greet him with due reverence.

Śakuntalā shyly makes reverential obeisance.

KAṆVA : My beloved child:

Be held in high esteem by your lord (9)
as Śarmiṣtta was by Yayāti;
as she bore Puru, may you too bear
a son to whom the whole world will bow.

GAUTAMI : Worshipful Sir, this is a boon, not a blessing.

KAṆVA : Daughter, come, go round these sacred fires into which oblations have just been offered.

Śakuntalā walks sun-wise round the fires.

KAṆVA (*chants, using a Vedic metre*):

May these Sacrificial Fires (10)
ranged round the Holy Altar
that blaze fed with sacred wood
within the circle of strewn darbhā grass,
whose oblation-fragrant smoke
billows out chasing away
all evil, keep you good and pure.

My darling, now start on your journey. (*Glancing around*) Where are Śārṇgarava and his companions?

They enter with— 'Holy Sir, here we are.'

KAṆVA : Śārṇgarava, show your sister the way.

ŚĀRṆGARAVA: This way, come this way, gracious lady.

All walk around.

KAṆVA : Hear, O hear, all you noble trees of the Holy Grove with indwelling divinities:

She who never had a drink of water (11)
before you had all drunk your fill,
she who never plucked your tender buds
for love of you, though fond of adorning herself,
she to whom it was a joyous festival
when you first burst into bloom; she, Śakuntalā,
leaves us today for her husband's home:
All grant her leave to go.

A koel sings.

ŚĀRṆGARAVA :

Kin to her during her woodland sojourn (12)
the trees now give her leave to go,
answering your request, Sir, in the Koel's notes.
Śakuntalā can now bid the grove farewell.

(*Voices in the sky; invisible spirits sing*) :

May her path be safe and gracious,[38] (13)
as gentle breezes blow,
pleasant be her way dotted by lakes
where green lotus-creepers grow;
may the burning rays of the sun
filter mellowed through thick shade-trees;
let the pollen of water-lilies drift
to lie as softest dust beneath her feet.

All listen in great amazement.

GAUTAMĪ : Dear child, do you hear the divinities of the Holy Grove bidding you farewell in as loving a manner as your own kinsfolk? Bow to them with due reverence.

ŚAKUNTALĀ (*walks around bowing, then speaks aside*) : Oh! Priyamvadā, even though my heart yearns to see my lord once more, now that I am deserting the Hermitage, my feet move forward with painful reluctance.

PRIYAMVADĀ : The bitterness of parting is not yours alone; look around and see how the Holy Grove grieves, knowing the hour of parting from you is near:

> The doe tosses out mouthfuls of grass, (14)
> the peacocks dance no more:
> pale leaves flutter down
> as if the vines are shedding their limbs.

ŚAKUNTALĀ (*recollecting*) : O Father, I have to say goodbye to Mādhavī, my woodland sister.

KAṆVA : Yes, my child, I know how much you love her; here she is, to your right.

ŚAKUNTALĀ (*coming close to the jasmine, throws her arms round it*) : O, Mādhavī, beloved sister, twine your branching arms round me; from today, I shall be far, far away from you. Dear Father, do care for her as if she were me.

KAṆVA : My love,

> What I had contemplated from the first for you, (15)
> a worthy husband, by your own merits you have
> obtained.
> Freed from needful care for you, I shall now make
> the Mango by her side, the loving bridegroom of this
> vine.

So come this way and start on your journey.

ŚAKUNTALĀ (*approaches her friends*) : I leave her in your hands, dearest friends.

FRIENDS : And in whose care are you leaving us, dearest? (*they burst into tears*)

KAṆVA : O for shame, Anasūyā, Priyamvadā, dry your tears. It is at a time like this that Śakuntalā needs your support to be firm.

All walk around.

ŚAKUNTALĀ : Father, you see that young doe keeping close to the cottage and moving very slowly because she is near her time—when she fawns safely, will you send someone to give me the happy news? You won't forget, dear Father?

KAṆVA : I shall not forget that, my love.

ŚAKUNTALĀ (*feeling something holding her back*) : Hello! Who's this at my heels, tugging again and again at the hem of my garment? (*turns to look*)

KAṆVA : My darling:

> It is the little fawn, your adopted son, (16)
> whom you fondly reared with handfuls of millet,
> whose mouth you dabbed with healing ingudi oil
> when lacerated by sharp blades of kuśa-grass:
> It is he who will not move out of your path.

ŚAKUNTALĀ (*addressing the fawn*) : My fondling, why do you keep following me who abandons her companions? No sooner were you born than your mother died and I brought you up. Now, abandoned by me, it is Father who is left to take care of you. So go back, my little one, go back. (*weeping, she moves on*)

KAṆVA : O my child, do not weep like this; keep your chin up and see where you are going:

> Brace your will and check this flow of welling tears (17)
> that veil the light of those eyes with up-curving lashes;
> your steps are faltering on the uneven ground
> where your path winds, its ups and downs unnoticed.

ŚĀRṆGARAVA : Your Holiness, as you know, a loved one is to be accompanied only up to the water's edge. And this, is the edge of the lake; so give us your instructions and turn back at this point.

KAṆVA : Well then, let us withdraw into the shade of this milk-bearing tree. (*they retire into the shade of the fig-tree*) Now . . . what would be a suitable message to send to His Honour Duhṣanta? (*reflects deeply for a while*)

ANASŪYĀ : Śakuntalā dearest, have you noticed that there is not one sentient being in the Hermitage that is not sorrowful now at the thought of losing you. See:

> The cakravāka answers not the call of his love (18)

hidden behind lotus-leaves:
with lotus-fibre dangling from his beak,
he gazes only at you.

ŚAKUNTALA: Ah! Anasūyā, the cakravākī, not seeing her beloved companion just a lotus-leaf away from her, really shrills in distress . . . (*fearful*) . . . indeed . . . what a hard lot to bear . . .[39]

PRIYAMVADA:

She too spends the night away from her beloved, (19)
the night stretching out long from sorrow:
the heart's heavy with the pain of parting,
but hope's slender thread still supports it.

KAṆVA: Śārṅgarava, my son, present Śakuntalā to the good King with these words of mine . . .

ŚĀRṄGARAVA: Command me, Your Holiness.

KAṆVA: Consider us, who are rich in self-restraint, (20)
and consider your own exalted lineage,
consider well her love, spontaneous,
that flowed towards you unprompted by her kin.
Regard her then as worth equal esteem
as your other consorts; more than that rests
on what Fortune has in store for her:
The bride's kin ought not to speak of it.

ŚĀRṄGARAVA: I have grasped the message, Your Holiness.

KAṆVA (*addressing Śakuntalā*): My beloved child, I should now give you some advice. Though I am a forest-dweller, I am conversant with worldly matters.

ŚĀRṄGARAVA: No matter is outside the purview of the wise, Your Holiness.

KAṆVA: My child, you are now leaving for your husband's home; when you enter it:

Serve your elders with diligence; be a friend to your
co-wives; (21)
even if wronged by your husband do not cross him
through anger;
treat those who serve you with the utmost courtesy;
be not puffed up with pride by wealth and pleasures:

Thus do girls attain the status of mistress of the home;
those who act contrary are the bane of their families.

What does our Gautamī think of this?

GAUTAMĪ: The best advice for a young bride. (*to Śakuntalā*) Dear daughter, keep these precepts always in mind.

KAṆVA: My beloved child, come, embrace me and your two friends.

ŚAKUNTALĀ: O Father, will my dear friends have to turn back right here?

KAṆVA: My darling, they also have to be given in marriage. It would not be proper for them to go with you. Gautamī will accompany you.

ŚAKUNTALĀ (*clasping her father in her arms*): Rent from my dear father's lap like a sapling of the sandalwood tree uprooted from the side of the Malaya mountain, how can I ever survive in an alien soil? (*weeps bitterly*)

KAṆVA: O my darling, why ever are you so distressed?

Occupying the honoured place of consort (22)
to your nobly-descended lord, you will
each moment be engrossed in great affairs
consequent to his imperial estate:
And like the East the bright and holy sun
soon you will give birth to a royal son:
The grief of parting from me will then
count but little with you, my darling.

ŚAKUNTALĀ (*falling at her father's feet*): Father, I bow to you in reverence.

KAṆVA: My child, may all that I wish for you come true.

ŚAKUNTALĀ (*coming close to her friends*): My dear, dear friends, hold me close, both of you together.

FRIENDS (*embracing her*): Śakuntalā dear, listen, if the good King be at all slow to recognize you, be sure to show him the Ring inscribed with his name.

ŚAKUNTALĀ: You are voicing misgivings that make my heart tremble.

FRIENDS: No, no, don't be afraid; affection always makes one over-anxious.

ŚĀRṆGARAVA (*looking up*): The sun has mounted over the tree-tops, Your Holiness, the lady had better hurry.

ŚAKUNTALĀ (*again throwing her arms round her father*): Dear Father, when shall I see this holy Hermitage again?

KAṆVA : When you have long been co-wife with this great Earth (23)
extending to the far horizons; and borne
Duhṣanta a son, a warrior unrivalled,
who shall bear the yoke of sovereignty,
then you shall set foot in this Hermitage
once more with your lord, seeking tranquillity.[40]

GAUTAMĪ : Daughter, the favourable time for starting your journey is fast going by. Let your father go back. No, she will not let him go for a long while. Your Honour had better turn back.

KAṆVA : My love, the performance of my holy rites is being interrupted.

ŚAKUNTALĀ : Dear Father, the affairs of the Hermitage will keep you from missing me. But as for me, I am already beginning to miss you, Father.

KAṆVA : O, child, child, how could you think I would be so uncaring. (*sighing deeply*)

How can my grief ever leave me, (24)
O my beloved child, when I see
grains of wild rice already scattered by you
sprouting green shoots at the cottage door.

Go, my love, and may your path be blessed.

(Gautamī, Śārṇgarava *and* Śāradvata *leave with* Śakuntalā.)

FRIENDS (*following Śakuntalā with their eyes for a long time speak sorrowfully*) : Alas, alas, Śakuntalā is now hidden from view by a line of trees.

KAṆVA : Anasūyā, Priyamvadā, your friend and companion is gone. Check your grief and follow me.

(*All leave.*)

FRIENDS : O Father, we shall be entering the Holy Groves that will be desolate, bereft of Śakuntalā's presence.

KAṆVA : Your great affection for her makes you feel this way. (*walking about deliberating*) O well, now that I have sent Śakuntalā away to her home, my mind is at peace. Consider it:

A daughter is wealth belonging to another; (25)

I have sent her this day to him who took her by the hand;
At once, my inner being is calm and clear, as if
I have restored what was left with me in trust.

End of Act Four
entitled
ŚAKUNTALĀ'S DEPARTURE

ACT FIVE

PRELUDE

Enter the Royal Chamberlain.[41]

CHAMBERLAIN (*sighing*) : Alas, how the years have taken their toll of me.

This ceremonial staff of cane I took (1)
when chosen to head the Royal Household
has with the passage of time become
the support of my faltering steps.

I shall see His Majesty in the Inner Apartments to inform him of some business that he has to attend to himself immediately. (*going a little way*) Yes, but what was it? (*pondering*) Ah! I have it. Some ascetics, pupils of Kaṇva wish to see him. O, how strange!

Wakeful one moment, (2)
shrouded in darkness the next,
my ageing mind
is like the flame of a dying lamp.

(*turns round and sees the King*): Here is His Majesty,

Wearied caring for his subjects (3)
as if they were his own children,
he now seeks the peace of seclusion
as a lord of elephants who led his herd
to graze all day, burned by the noonday sun
finds at last a quiet, cool spot to rest.

To tell the truth I hesitate to tell His Majesty who has just risen from the seat of judgement that Kaṇva's pupils are here. But then, where do the protectors of the earth find time to rest. That's how it is,

The Sun yoked his coursers just that once; (4)
the fragrant wind blows night and day;
the Cosmic Serpent[42] ever bears Earth's burden;
And this is the Law that binds him who claims a sixth.

Turns around; then enter the King *with* the jester *and* retinue *in order of rank.*

KING (*wearied by the burden of administrative duties*) : Every man who gains the object of his desire is happy. Only to kings does the gain itself bring misery. For,

Attainment of sovereignty merely lays to rest (5)
the eager craving of expectancy; guarding
what is gained lays on one a weight of care.
Kingship, like an umbrella[43] held in one's own hand
tires more than it removes tiredness.

(*Voices of two bards, off-stage*) : Victory to our lord.

FIRST BARD :

Unmindful of your own ease, you toil (6)
each day for the world's sake—such is your way of life;
the tree bares its crown to the blazing heat
while it refreshes those who shelter in its shade.

SECOND BARD :

Grasping the rod of justice, you bring to heel (7)
those who are set on evil paths; you bring calm
where contentions rage; and afford protection.
Where wealth abounds kinsmen come flocking.
But in you, O King, all find kinship's perfect pattern.

KING (*listening*) : This is great; hearing these words have revived my spirits worn out by the task of governing the kingdom.

MĀDHAVYA : Tell the bull he is king of the herd and his tiredness disappears.

KING (*with a smile*) : Well, let's sit down.

They both sit down while the retinue stands in order of rank; the sound of a lute is heard in the background.

MĀDHAVYA (*listening intently*) : Listen carefully to the sounds coming from the Hall of Music, my friend. Do you hear the pure, clear tones of a lovely melody played on the *vina*, keeping perfect rhythm? I think it is Lady Hamsavatī practising her singing.

KING (*listening*) : Now be quiet, Mādhavya, and let me listen.

CHAMBERLAIN (*watching the King*) : Oho! His Majesty seems lost in deep thought. I had better wait for the right moment to approach him. (*he stands on one side*)

(*A voice off-stage, singing*) :

O you honey-pilfering bee! (8)
Greedy as ever for fresh honey,
once you lovingly kissed
the mango's fresh spray of flowers—[44]
is she then forgotten so soon?
You are content now merely to stay
within the full-blown lotus.[45]

KING : O, how brimful of passion comes this song borne on the air.

MĀDHAVYA : So . . . you have understood every word of the song?

KING (*smiling*) : Yes; once I loved her deeply. She is taunting me now for my neglect of her. Mādhavya, my friend, do go to Queen Hamsavatī and tell her that I have taken to heart the reproof that she has conveyed so subtly.

MĀDHAVYA : As Your Honour commands. (*gets up*) Look here, my friend, you are getting someone else to catch a bear by its tail for you. Like a shaven monk still in the grip of passion, I have no hope of release.

KING : Come, come, my friend, speak to her like the cultivated man-about-town that you are.

MĀDHAVYA : I see; there seems to be no way out for me.

(*He exits.*)

KING (*to himself*) : That song I just heard . . . a restless, yearning sadness steals into my heart . . . though I am not separated from someone I love deeply. Or . . . can it be that:

When a sadness ineffable falls (9)
suddenly like a shadow over the heart
—even while one is wrapped in happiness—
the mind trills spontaneous, unknown to itself,
to an intimation from the past
quickened by some fleeting loveliness

or, haunting sounds of exquisite music heard:
lasting impressions of love's remembrance
live on in us from former lives, perhaps,
clinging like fragrance to our migrant soul.

He remains bewildered as if trying to recollect something.

CHAMBERLAIN (*approaching the King*) : Victory, victory to His Majesty. Sire, some hermits who dwell in the forests at the foothills of the Himālayas are here with a message from Kaṇva; they are accompanied by women. Your orders, Sire.

KING (*surprised*) : What—hermits with a message from Kaṇva and accompanied by women, did you say?

CHAMBERLAIN : Yes, Sire.

KING : Send word to our Preceptor, Somarāṭa, requesting him to welcome the ascetics from the Hermitage with all due Vedic rites and then accompany them to our presence. I shall await their coming in a place suitable for receiving holy guests.

CHAMBERLAIN : Your commands, Sire. (*he leaves*)

KING (*rising*) : Vetravati, lead the way to the sanctuary of the Mystic Fire.

VETRAVATĪ : This way, Your Majesty. (*turns around*) Gracious Sire, here is the terrace of the Fire Sanctuary, newly washed and the cow that gives milk for the holy rites stands close by. Let His Majesty ascend the steps.

KING (*mimes ascent and stands leaning on an attendant*) : Vetravati, I wonder why sage Kaṇva has sent these sages to our presence.

Has the penance of sages of strict vows, (10)
possessed of spiritual energy immense
been defiled perchance by impediments?
Or has someone practised evil on creatures
roaming free in the Groves of Righteousness?
Or—has some misdeed[46] of my own, alas!
Stopped the flowering of plants? My mind's bewildered
in the face of so many possible guesses.

VETRAVATĪ : How could this be, in a hermitage free from trouble, defended by your arm? It is my guess that the sages highly pleased with Your Majesty's noble conduct have come to honour you.

Then enter Kaṇva's pupils *accompanied by* Gautamī, *bringing* Śakuntalā; the Chamberlain *and* the Preceptor *are in front leading the way.*

CHAMBERLAIN : This way, this way, honoured ones.

ŚĀRṄGARAVA : Śāradvata, my friend:

Granted, this King of unblemished nobleness (11)
does not swerve from the path of rectitude;
true, none of his subjects, even those
in the lowliest walks of life, resort to evil ways;
even so, my mind enjoying continual solitude,
prompts me to view this place thronged with people
as a house encircled by blazing fires.

ŚĀRADVATA : You have become deeply disturbed from the moment we entered the city. It is understandable, for I feel the same:[47]

As a man freshly bathed views one smeared with oil, (12)
as one pure the impure, as one wakeful the sleeper,
as one who can move freely sees one in bondage,
thus I, freed of the world's will, regard these, bound
to the world.

HIGH PRIEST : Therefore persons like you are great.

ŚAKUNTALĀ (*feeling a bad omen*) : O you gods! What means this throbbing of my right eye?

GAUTAMĪ : May all evil be averted; and may happiness always attend you.

They walk around.

HIGH PRIEST (*pointing in the King's direction*) : O holy sages! *There* is His Honour, the protector of the four estates; risen already from his seat he waits for you. Behold him.

ŚĀRṄGARAVA : Most commendable, I grant you, O great Brāhmaṇa; even so, we view it all with an equal eye:

Trees bend down when laden with fruit; (13)
rain clouds filled with water
hang low almost to the ground;

wealth does not make the good haughty:
this is the true nature
of those who do good to others.

VETRAVAI : From the serene expression on their faces, it is evident that the sages have come on a mission of goodwill.

KING (*looking at Śakuntalā*) : That lady?

Who may she be, standing veiled, I wonder, (14)
the loveliness of her form, like a bud
not burst into bloom, is barely-revealed;
she appears in the midst of ascetics,
a tender sprout among yellowing leaves.

VETRAVATI : Surely she does appear to be very beautiful, worth looking at, Sire.

KING : Enough, it is highly improper to stare at another's wife.

ŚAKUNTALĀ (*laying a hand on her bosom, speaks to herself*) : Why are you trembling, O heart? Remembering the love my lord has for me, calm yourself.

HIGH PRIEST (*coming forward*) : Good Fortune attend you, Sire; the sages have been honoured with all due rites. They have a message for you from their Preceptor. Will Your Majesty be pleased to hear it?

KING : I am all attention.

SAGES (*approaching the King, they raise their hands in blessing*) : May the King be ever victorious!

KING (*with folded hands*) : I greet you all.

SAGES : Good Fortune attend you.[48]

KING : Do the penances prosper?

SAGES : While you protect the virtuous (15)
who dares disrupt their pious rites?
When the bright sun blazes bright
can darkness show its face?

KING (*to himself*) : By this praise, my title of ruler gains its true meaning. (*aloud*) Is Sage Kaṇva in good health?

ŚĀRṆGARAVA : The well-being of those who have attained superhuman powers lies in their own control. He makes kind enquiries of Your Honour's good health and then addresses you thus. . .

KING : What are the commands of His Holiness?

ŚĀRNGARAVA : You took her, my daughter, in secret, as your wife; pleased, I have assented to the marriage.

We regard you as foremost among those of high worth (16)
and Śakuntalā is Virtue's embodiment;
having brought together a bride and groom of equal merit,
the Creator after a long time incurs no reproach.[49]

She bears your child; so take her as your lawful wife and partner in all religious duties.

GAUTAMI : Gracious Sir, I wish to say a few words at this point, though it is not my place to speak.

KING : Speak freely, Lady.

You did not approach the elders in the matter, (17)
She did not seek advice from her kinsfolk;
when it was all agreed upon between you two,
what in the world can one say to either?

ŚAKUNTALĀ (*to herself*) : What will my lord say now?

KING (*listens to all this with his mind troubled by doubts*) : What kind of proposition is this that is being placed before me?

ŚAKUNTALĀ (*to herself*) : Ha! His words are fire in my ears.

ŚĀRNGARAVA : What means this? This talk of a proposition being placed before you? Your Honour is doubtless quite conversant with the ways of the world.

The world suspects even the most virtuous woman (18)
as otherwise, when with her husband living,
the parental home becomes her sole resort:
hence, her kinsfolk wish that she *be* beside him
who took her by the hand as his wife,
be she dear to him, or be she not.

KING : Are you saying that this lady is already married to me?

ŚAKUNTALĀ (*despondent, to herself*) : O, my heart, your fears are proving true.

ŚĀRNGARAVA :

Is this revulsion from a deed done? (19a)
Or disregard for one's own actions?

Or turning away from one's duty?

KING : This is a case of proceeding on a wrong assumption.

ŚĀRṆGARAVA :

Such fickleness generally swells (19b)
and comes to a head in those drunk with power.

KING : I am being taken to task too harshly.

GAUTAMĪ : Daughter, lay aside your bashfulness for a while; let me remove your veil. Your lord will not fail to recognize you then.

KING (*gazing ardently at Śakuntalā, speaks to himself with astonished admiration*) :

This glowing loveliness that is proffered unsought, (20)
was this held by me once as my own, or not?
My mind hovers uncertain, like a bee
circling at daybreak over the jasmine's dew-filled cup.
I cannot permit myself to possess it;
nor can I bring myself to relinquish it.

VETRAVATĪ (*to herself*) : O, admirable is His Majesty's regard for right action. Who else would stop to consider right from wrong, when such beauty comes sweetly on its own and offers itself?

ŚĀRṆGARAVA : O King, what means this silence?

KING : O, hermits, rich in holiness, try as I might, I cannot recall to my mind accepting the hand of this lady in marriage at any time. Seeing that she is plainly pregnant, how can I receive her when I have doubts about being the husband?

ŚAKUNTALĀ (*aside*) : Alas, my cruel fate! Even the marriage is now in doubt; where are all those high-mounting hopes of mine?

ŚĀRṆGARAVA : Then don't:

Assenting gladly to your seizure of his daughter (21)
the good sage makes you worthy of such a gift,
as a robber is offered the goods he seized:
for this he deserves your refusal—does he not?

ŚĀRADVATA : That is enough Śārṅgarava; cease expostulating. Śakuntalā, we have said what we had to say; the King has spoken as he has. Now, it is for you to give a fitting reply.

ŚAKUNTALĀ (*to herself*) : What can I say? When such a love has suffered such a change, what use is it reminding him of it now? On the other hand, I should defend myself and clear my name. (*aloud*) Dear Lord, (*stops in the middle*) no . . . my right to address you as such has been questioned. Prince of the Purus! In the Hermitage you deceived me, a simple girl, trusting and open by nature; *then* you made a solemn compact . . . now . . . to disown me with such words . . . is this becoming of you?

KING (*stopping his ears*) : Perish the sinful thought.

Why are you out to sully your family's honour, (22)
and to make me fall; you are like a river
that crumbles its banks to muddy its crystal stream,
and uproots the tree growing by its edge.

ŚAKUNTALĀ : If you are proceeding in this manner under the impression that I am another man's wife, I can remove your suspicions by showing this highly-prized token.

KING : A proper procedure.

ŚAKUNTALA (*feeling for the ring*) : Ha! I am lost. The Ring is missing from my finger.

Looks at Gautamī, shattered.

GAUTAMI : The Ring must have slipped off and fallen into the water when you immersed yourself in holy Śacī's Pool[50] next to Indra's Landing.

KING (*smiles ironically*) : A good example of the ready wit that is womankind's gift.

ŚAKUNTALA : Alas, Fate shows its inexorable power. But I shall relate something, an incident.

KING : Ah, now we have something that is to be heard.

ŚAKUNTALA : You do remember that day in the bower of canes covered by vines—you held a cup of lotus leaves filled with water?

KING : I am listening.

ŚAKUNTALA : Just at that moment, the little fawn, my adopted son, whom I had named 'Liquid Long-eyes' came trotting up. Feeling affectionate towards him, you held the cup out saying, 'let him drink first' and coaxed him to drink. But he would not come near, because you were a stranger to him. When I took the cup from you and held it in my hand, he was happy to drink. And you laughed saying 'One trusts one's own kind, you are both creatures of the woods'.

KING (*laughs sarcastically*) : By such honeyed words are pleasure-loving men lured by young women out to gain their own ends.

GAUTAMĪ : Gracious Prince, you should not speak to her like that. Brought up in a sacred grove, this girl is a stranger to guile.

KING : Ascetic matron, listen:

Intuitive cunning is seen even in females (23)
of lower creatures: what then of those
endowed with reason and understanding:
the cuckoo, as we know, has her young reared
by other birds before they take to the air.

ŚAKUNTALĀ (*in anger*) : Ignoble man! You who are like a well covered with grass . . . you judge every one by the measure of your own heart . . . who would stoop to imitate your conduct . . . practising falseness while putting on the mantle of virtue?

KING : The lady's anger is real—the spontaneous outburst of one who lives in the green world.

Her eyes red with anger look straight at me, (24)
her words flung out harsh, not smoothed into a drawl;
her lower lip like a ripe bimba-fruit
is all quivering as if struck by an icy blast;
her eyebrows, graceful curves,
knot together in a twisting frown.

Further, her anger fell concentrated on me whose mind is clouded over with uncertainties. Therefore,

When I cruelly denied our secret love (25)
then did she dart flaming glances on me,
fiercely bending the graceful curve of her brow,
it seemed she snapped the bow of Love itself.

(*aloud*) Gracious lady, Duhṣanta's life lies an open book before his subjects; it's there for you to read too.

ŚAKUNTALĀ : O, so,

You are the sole measure, and you, only you know (26)
the firm Rule of Righteousness for the world;

women, who have set aside their modesty,
they understand nothing—they know nothing, is it?

Very well; so be it; putting my trust in the fame of Puru's lineage, I have fallen into the clutches of a man whose mouth is honey, but whose heart is stone . . . and now, I am made out to be a self-willed wanton. (*she covers her face with the end of her veil and weeps*)

ŚĀRṆAGARAVA : Thus does unbridled impulse destroy a person.

Therefore, a marriage, specially one made in secret (27)
should be contracted after careful scrutiny;
affection quickly turns to hate in hearts
that have known each other but slenderly.

KING : O, Sir, you are hurling words of concentrated anger upon me, relying only on the testimony of this lady here.

ŚĀRṄGARAVA (*disdainfully*) : O no, that would be quite preposterous, would it not?

The words of one who from birth (28)
has grown up uninstructed in deceit,
should carry no weight; but those who study
the deception of others as an esteemed art,[51]
are infallible speakers of truth.

KING : O, speaker of truth, supposing we are as you say we are, what is gained, do you think, by deceiving her?

ŚĀRṄGARAVA : Downfall.

KING : This is incredible; would the Pauravas court their own downfall?

ŚĀRADVATA : O King, why this bandying of words? We have carried out our Preceptor's orders; we shall leave presently.

This then, is your wife, accept her, or abandon her; (29)
a husband's dominion over his wife is absolute.

Gautamī, lead the way.

The sages *prepare to leave.*

ŚAKUNTALĀ (*calling out piteously*) : What's this; here I am, betrayed by this cheat; are you also abandoning me?

Tries to follow Gautamī.

GAUTAMĪ (*stopping*) : Son, Sārṇgarava, here is Śakuntalā following us, wailing pitifully. Cruelly repudiated by her husband, what can the poor child do?

ŚĀRṆGARAVA (*turning back*) : You forward girl, are you asserting your independence?

Śakuntalā stops, frightened, trembling.

ŚĀRṆGARAVA :

If you are what the King says you are, (30)
what will your father have to do with you—
a stain on his family? But, as you know
your own conduct to be pure, even servitude
in your husband's house will be welcome to you.

Stay here; we are leaving.

KING : O ascetic! Why do you give this lady false hopes?

The moon wakes only night-blooming lilies, (31)
the sun day-lotuses only:
the man with mastery over his passions
turns away from the touch of another's wife.

ŚĀRṆGARAVA : Assuming that Your Honour has forgotten past events through impressions created by fresh interests, why this fear on your part of losing your virtue?

KING : Very well, I shall ask you this; you tell me, which is the greater and which the lesser evil of the two?

Am I deluded, or, is she false? (32)
this is the question: should I incur
the blame of forsaking my own wife,
or the stain of adultery, alas,
with the wife of another?

HIGH PRIEST (*after some thought*) : Supposing we do it this way.

KING : Instruct me, Your Reverence.

HIGH PRIEST : Let the gracious lady who is with child, stay in my house till she gives birth. I shall tell you why I suggest this: the seers have already foretold that your first-born is destined to be Sovereign of the World. If the sage's daughter should give birth to a son bearing all the marks of sovereignty on his person, then, offering her your felicitations, receive her into your Royal Apartments; if it turns out otherwise then the only thing to do is to take her back to her father.

KING : As my revered Preceptor deems right.

HIGH PRIEST : Child, follow me.

ŚAKUNTALĀ (*weeping*) : O gracious Goddess, Mother Earth, open wide and take me in.

(*Exit the sages and Śakuntalā with the High Priest.*)

The King remains musing over Śakuntalā but his memory is still clouded.

(*A voice off-stage*) : O, a marvel, a marvel has occurred.

KING : What could this be?

The High Priest *enters in great astonishment.*

HIGH PRIEST : My lord, something quite marvellous has just occurred.

KING : What is it?

HIGH PRIEST : No sooner had Kaṇva's disciples left on their journey back than:

The young girl cursing her stars, (33a)
wept aloud, flinging her hands up.

KING : And then?

HIGH PRIEST :

A flash of light in a woman's shape (33b)
from Apsarā Pool, snatched her up
and vanished straightaway.

Everyone is amazed.

KING : Reverence, we have already settled this matter and dismissed it; what is the point of pursuing it further? Your Honour may go and rest.

HIGH PRIEST : Be victorious.

(*Exits.*)

KING : Vetravati, I am deeply disturbed; lead the way to my sleeping-chamber.

VETRAVATĪ : This way, this way, my lord.

KING (*to himself*) :

I have spurned the sage's daughter, it is true, (34)
having no recollection of marrying her;
yet, the poignant ache in my heart validates
it seems, the truth of her assertion that I had.

(All exit.)

End of Act Five
entitled
THE REPUDIATION OF ŚAKUNTALĀ

ACT SIX

PRELUDE

Scene: Duhṣanta's Capital.

Enter the Chief of the City Police *with* two policemen *behind him, leading* a man *with his hands tied at the back.*

POLICEMEN (*beating the prisoner*) : Hey, you thief! Tell us how you came by this Royal Signet-Ring set with a priceless gem and the King's name engraved round it in the setting. Come on, tell us.

MAN (*in great fear*) : O, please worthy Sirs, please; I am no thief, indeed I am not.

FIRST POLICEMAN : O, is that so? Did the King then give this Ring to you as a gift? Because he regarded you highly as some distinguished Brahmin?

MAN : Please Sir, listen to me; I am but a poor fisherman living at Śakrāvatāra.

SECOND POLICEMAN : You foul thief! Did we ask where you lived or what you lived by?

CHIEF : Sūcaka, let him tell his story in his own way, from the beginning, in order; and don't interrupt him, either of you.

POLICEMEN : As Your Honour commands, Sir. Speak, vermin, speak.

MAN : Well, worthy Sirs, I support my family by catching fish with hooks and nets and other such devices, Sirs.

CHIEF (*laughing*) : A most clean and virtuous livelihood, I'm sure.

MAN : O Master, do not laugh at my trade.

For it's said, a fellow shouldn't give up (1)
the trade he's born to, however low it may be,
the most soft-hearted of butchers engages
in the cruel job of slaughtering animals.

CHIEF : Yes, yes, go on.

MAN : One day as I am cutting up this big carp into pieces, what do I see lying in its belly—O Sirs, I see this Ring, its huge gem flashing. Then, Sirs, as I am hawking it around here, hoping, of course, for a good sale—I am then seized by these worthy masters. That's all I've to tell you as to how I got this Ring. Now, either you kill me, or, you set me free.

CHIEF (*sniffing the Ring*) : O yes, it's been in a fish's belly alright; such a stink of raw fish pours out of it. But—how it got into that damn fish in the first place—that has to be carefully investigated. So come; to the palace we must go now.

POLICEMEN : Yes, Your Honour. Move, cut-purse, move it, quick.

They walk around.

CHIEF : Sūcaka, you two look sharp and wait here for me at the tower-gate, while I go in to the Palace and inform the King about finding this Ring and return with his Majesty's orders.

POLICEMEN : Yes, Your Honour. Go in, Your Honour, where royal favour awaits you.

(*The Chief goes out.*)

SŪCAKA (*after a while*) : His Honour has been away quite a while, it seems, Jānuka.

JĀNUKA : O you know how one has to wait and approach a king at just the right moment.

SŪCAKA : I tell you, my friend, my hands, they just itch to finish off this cut-purse.

FISHERMAN : O Sir, you wouldn't want to kill someone without good reason, would you now?

JĀNUKA (*looking*) : There is our Chief coming towards us with a letter in his hand; that must be the Royal Decree. (*to the fisherman*) Hey you, fellow, you will either make your acquaintance soon with the fangs of bloodhounds or become an offering to vultures.[52]

CHIEF (*entering*) : Quickly, make haste, this . . .

FISHERMAN (*cuts in, terrified, before the sentence is completed*) : O misery, misery, I am done for . . .

CHIEF : Hey you, release him, fellows; release the fisherman, I say. It is now quite clear how the Ring came into his hands.

SŪCAKA : As you command, Your Honour. (*unties the bonds*)

JĀNUKA : You might say that this man entered Death's kingdom and returned, mightn't you?

FISHERMAN : O, Master, I owe my life to you. (*falls at his feet*)

CHIEF : Get up, you, and here, take this; the King has graciously ordered that this reward, equal in value to the Ring, be given to you. (*gives him money*)

FISHERMAN (*accepting it with a deep bow*) : Your Honour, I am most highly favoured.

SUCAKA : Indeed, you might well describe it as a favour. For here is a man who has been taken off the point of an impaling stake and set on the back of an elephant.[53]

JĀNUKA : Your Honour, the princely reward indicates that His Majesty must set great store by this Ring with its priceless gem.

CHIEF : Hm . . . no, I don't think it was the rare gem that mattered so much to his Majesty.

BOTH POLICEMEN : Then what?

CHIEF : Somehow, I got the impression that the Ring made His Majesty remember someone he had loved very much . . . because, as soon as he saw it—for a moment he was much moved—and by nature, His Majesty is very poised and dignified.

SUCAKA : A great service has then been done to His Majesty by Your Honour.

JĀNUKA : To this enemy of little fishes here, I'd say. (*glares resentfully at the fisherman*)

FISHERMAN (*taking the hint*) : Worshipful Master, let half of this be yours—drink-money, Sirs.

JĀNUKA : Fisherman, as of this very instant, you have become my very best friend. The beginning of such a friendship should be pledged with some good flower-wine. Come, let us go to the tavern.

(*All exit.*)

End of Prelude

Scene: The Pleasure Gardens attached to the Royal Apartments.

Enter the Apsarā Miśrakeśi *flying through the air.*

MIŚRAKEŚI : Having completed my spell of duty guarding Apsarā Pool during the season of pilgrimage to its sacred waters by pious devotees, I have a little time now to see with my own eyes how it goes with the Royal Sage. Śakuntalā is like my own flesh and blood because of my great friendship with Menakā; and Menakā had requested me earlier to do this for the sake of her daughter. (*looking around*) How is it that no preparations are seen in the palace-grounds for the commencement of the season's festivities?[54] And today is the day of the Festival? Sure, I have the ability of knowing all that goes on through exercising my powers of mental contemplation; but, out of respect for my friend's high regard for me, I should see it all myself. Therefore, making myself invisible, I shall stay close behind these two girls who seem to be employed to tend the gardens, and learn what has been happening here. *(alights on the ground and waits)*

Enter a female gardener *looking at the sprays of mango blossom;* another *comes behind her.*

FIRST GIRL :

O Mango-Blossom, turning from rich copper (2)
to pale-green! O loveliness
breathed by Spring's first fragrant month!
Hail to you! My eyes have been blessed with a
sight of you,
auspicious harbinger of the Festival!

SECOND GIRL (*approaching*) : Hallo there, Parabhṛtikā!* What are you muttering to yourself?

PARABHṚTIKĀ : Ah, my friend, seeing the spray of mango blossom, the little cuckoo is intoxicated—mad.

SECOND GIRL (*with joy*) : You mean Spring is already here?

* Little Cuckoo

FIRST GIRL : Yes, Madhukarikā,* it is now your time to dance with glancing movements and sing your rapturous melodies.

MADHUKARIKĀ : Let me have your support, dear friend, so that I can stand on tiptoe and pluck one little mango blossom and offer it in worship to the God of Love.

PARABHṚTIKĀ : Certainly, if half the fruit of the worship is mine.

MADHUKARIKĀ : O my dear friend, do you have to ask in so many words . . . when our hearts are one, though our bodies may divide us? (*leaning on her friend, she plucks a* mango flower) Ah! How exquisite! Even though this bud hasn't opened its eye as yet, the snapping of its stalk releases a divine perfume. (*folds her hands together in prayer*) O Lord Love! O dolphin-bannered God! I bow before you.

O Mango-blossom, here, I offer you to Love (3)
who already holds his bow firmly in his hand;
may this flower be the most potent
of his five flower-arrows, to aim
at the young wives of men who travel far.

(*tosses the flower up in the air*)

Enter the Chamberlain, *with a toss of the curtain, and very angry.*

CHAMBERLAIN : You there, stop, you impudent girl; what do you think you are doing, plucking mango buds when His Majesty has expressly forbidden the celebration of the Spring Festival.

BOTH (*alarmed*) : Please, Your Honour, we had not heard about it.

CHAMBERLAIN : Hm . . . so, you have not heard about it, is it? . . . When even the trees that bloom in the Spring, and the birds nesting in them, seem to have . . . and show their respect for His Majesty's decree? Just look around:

The Mango has long since put out its wealth of buds, (4)
but the pollen does not gather golden within:
the amaranth is all set for blossom-time,
but the buds still linger, tight-folded in their sheaths:
though winter is past, the melodious koel,

* Little Honey-Bee

strangles in his throat his rich burst of song;
even Love hovers uncertain, withdraws timidly,
his arrow half-drawn out of the quiver.

MIŚRAKEŚĪ : Now there is no room for doubt; the Royal Sage possesses great powers.

PARABHṚTIKĀ : Honourable Sir, it is only a few days back that Mitrā-vasu, the Inspector-General of Police, sent us both to wait on his sister, the Queen; and we have been detailed to perform various duties here in the pleasure-gardens. That's why we had not heard about all this.

CHAMBERLAIN : Very well; let this not happen again.

BOTH : Your Honour, we feel very curious. If it is proper for people like us to know, can you tell us why His Majesty has forbidden the holding of the Spring Festival, please?

MIŚRAKEŚĪ : Kings are usually fond of festivities; so the reason must be a good one.

CHAMBERLAIN : Seeing as the matter is common knowledge, there is no reason for not telling you. Has the gossip relating to the repudiation of Śakuntalā not reached your ears as yet?

BOTH : It has, Your Honour; we also heard from the King's brother-in-law about the finding of the Ring.

CHAMBERLAIN : Then there is little left to tell. From the moment His Majesty set eyes on the Ring, he remembered that he had married Lady Śakuntalā in secret and then repudiated her through some strange lapse of memory. Since then His Majesty has been struck with bitter remorse.

He loathes all beautiful things; to his ministers (5)
he is not free of access as before;
he passes nights sleepless, tossing in bed;
to the queens in the Royal Apartments,
he extends all formal courtesies, but,
addresses them wrongly, mistaking their names;
then, he remains long plunged in painful
embarrassment.

MIŚRAKEŚĪ : This pleases me.

CHAMBERLAIN : On account of the King's distraught state of mind, the Festival has been cancelled.

BOTH : A very proper decision, we'd say.

(*A voice off-stage*): The King, the King; come this way, Your Majesty.

CHAMBERLAIN (*listening*) : Our Lord is headed this way; now go, attend to your work.

THE GIRLS : Yes, Your Honour.

Both *exit; then enter* the King *costumed to indicate grief, attended by* Vetravatī *and accompanied by* the jester, Mādhavya.

CHAMBERLAIN (*watching the King*) : O how handsome our lord looks, notwithstanding his grief. Those blessed with fine looks always present a pleasing appearance, whatever the circumstances.

Spurning the splendour of dress and adornment (6)
he wears a single bracelet of gold,
now slipping down his forearm:
the lower lip blanched, scorched by his hot breath,
those eyes shorn of their brilliance
by unquiet wakefulness; his form,
glowing with intrinsic lustre, though wasted,
scarcely seems so, but dazzles the eye
like some magnificent gem cunningly fined down
and polished with exquisite art.

MIŚRAKEŚĪ (*scrutinizing the King*) : No wonder our dear Śakuntalā though humiliated by his harsh repudiation of her, still pines for him.

VETRAVATĪ : Let His Majesty walk on.

KING (*pacing slowly in deep thought*) :

Rudely awakened by penitent grief (7)
this cursed heart, then insensible
when my doe-eyed beloved tried hard
to rouse it from sleep, is now painfully awake.

MIŚRAKEŚĪ : Ah, such is that poor girl's unhappy lot.

MĀDHAVYA (*aside*) : There he goes again; the Śakuntalā-fit is upon him. How on earth do we get this sickness of his treated?

CHAMBERLAIN (*approaching*) : Hail, Your Majesty. I have inspected the various spots in the pleasure-gardens; Your Majesty can safely resort to any of them as you please.

KING (*to the attendant*) : Vetravatī, go, take this message from me to the

Chief Minister, the Honourable Piśuna, and say: 'Having spent a long sleepless night, I feel unfit to preside today at the Court in the Hall of Justice. Let those cases of our citizens that Your Honour has personally attended to, be written out and dispatched to me.'

VETRAVATĪ : As His Majesty commands. (*leaves*)

KING : Pārvatāyana, you also attend to your business.

CHAMBERLAIN : As Your Highness commands.

(*He exits.*)

MĀDHAVYA : That has done it; there are no more flies buzzing around. Now you can relax in peace and enjoy the gardens, so pleasant now with the cold weather gone.

KING (*sighing*) : Ah, Mādhavya, my friend, is it not a true and tried saying that misfortunes strike a person all at once through chinks in his armour? Look at this:

> No sooner is my mind freed from the darkness (8)
> that eclipsed the memory of my love
> for the daughter of the sage,
> than the mind-born God* chooses this moment
> to fit the arrow of the mango's flower to his bow,
> O my friend—and strikes me down.

And further

> With memory restored by the Signet Ring, (9)
> of the beloved spurned without real cause,
> I weep for her with remorse and longing,
> now that the fragrant month** is here with its joys.

MĀDHAVYA : How dare he, just wait; I shall destroy Love's arrow with this stick. (*lifts his stick to knock down the spray of mango blossom*)

KING (*smiling*) : Well done; I have witnessed your Brahminic power. Now find me a pleasant spot, my friend, where I can divert my mind watching flowering vines that resemble my beloved a little.

MĀDHAVYA : Did I not hear you instructing your attendant, Caturikā, saying to her, 'I shall pass the hour in the jasmine bower; bring me the

---

* Kāma or Eros

** Spring

drawing-board on which I had painted Lady Sakuntala's portrait'?

KING : It is the only way I have to console myself. Well, lead the way then to the jasmine-bower.

MĀDHAVYA : This way, this way, Your Honour. (*they turn around, Miśrakeśī follows*)

MĀDHAVYA : See, here is the bower of the spring-creeper with its marble seat, so secluded, it seems to be waiting expectantly for you, extending a silent welcome. Let us enter and sit down. (*they do so*)

MIŚRAKEŚĪ : I shall stand here hidden behind the vines and take a look at my friend's portrait; then I can let her know of the great love her lord bears her. (*stands still*)

KING (*sighing deeply*) : Ah! My dear friend, at this moment, all the events relating to my very first meeting with Śakuntalā pass through my mind. You remember I spoke to you about it; however when I disavowed her, you were not there by my side. But even before that you never once mentioned her name. Did you also forget her as I did?

MIŚRAKEŚĪ : It is for this reason that the lords of the earth should not allow a companion close to their heart, leave their side even for a moment.

MĀDHAVYA : O no, I did not forget. But after telling me all about her, you said at the end that it was all in jest—that there was no truth to it. And I, having a lump of clay for my brains accepted this. Well, when all is said and done, we have to accept that Fate is all-powerful.

MIŚRAKEŚĪ : How true.

KING (*after brooding for a while*) : Help me, my dear friend, help me.

MĀDHAVYA : Hey, hey, what's all this? What has come over you, my dear friend? How can noble men allow themselves to be overcome like this by grief? Mountains stand firm in the fiercest storm.

KING : O my dear friend, when I remember how distraught my love was when she found herself harshly repulsed, I feel totally shorn of all defences. There she was:

Cruelly spurned by me and starting to follow her kin, (10)
but sternly halted by the command—*'stay'*—
of her father's pupil, like a father to her,
she turned once again her eyes welling with tears
on me, O so pitiless:
How that look burns me like a poisoned dart.

MIŚRAKEŚĪ : O you gods! Such concern for right conduct!

MĀDHAVYA : An idea just struck me. Do you think some celestial being has carried off the lady?

KING : Who else would dare touch a chaste wife? I learnt from her friends that it was the celestial dancer Menakā who gave birth to her. My heart tells me that one of her mother's companions took her away.

MIŚRAKEŚĪ : What is surprising is not that he has come out of a state of blank confusion but that he ever got into such a state in the first place.

MĀDHAVYA : Listen, if that's the case, take heart, Sir. You are sure to be reunited with the lady.

KING : What makes you say that?

MĀDHAVYA : Because no mother, or father, can bear to see a daughter separated from her husband for long.

KING : Ah! My friend,

Was it a dream? A magical vision (11)
of loveliness? A hallucination?
Or, the fruit of my good deeds past,
reward in strict measure, and no more?
It is gone, I am quite certain,
never to return: Wishes?—they have fallen,
all, off the edge of a precipice.

MĀDHAVYA : No, no, don't talk like this. The Ring itself proves that reunions that are destined to happen can come about in the most unexpected manner.

KING (*looking at the Ring*) : This thing—that fell from a place so hard to gain—it deserves to be pitied.

The merit of your good deeds, O Ring, (12)
was as slender as mine, as we see
from the reward you gained.
You won a high place on her fingers,
whose nails are pale-rose like dawn, enchanting—
then alas, you took such a fall.

MIŚRAKEŚĪ : If it had been on any other hand, it would have really deserved to be pitied. O, Śakuntalā, dear friend, you are so far and I alone have the happiness of hearing words so sweet to the ear.

MĀDHAVYA : Tell me, my friend, what was the occasion on which you gave this Signet-Ring to the lady?

MIŚRAKEŚĪ : He is voicing the same curiosity that possesses me.

KING : I'll tell you, my friend, listen; when I was leaving the Holy Grove to return to the Capital, my beloved asked me weeping—'And when will my lord send for me?'

MĀDHAVYA : And then?

KING : Then, putting the Ring on her finger, I said to her:

MĀDHAVYA : What did you say?

KING :
Count off each day one letter of my name (13)
on this Ring; and when you come to the last,
an escort will present himself, my love,
to lead you to my Royal Apartments.

But in blank confusion I acted cruelly.

MIŚRAKEŚĪ : A charming arrangement, no doubt; only Fate stepped in and broke it.

MĀDHAVYA : How on earth did the Ring enter the carp's mouth as if it were a hook?

KING : It slipped off your friend's finger* when she was worshipping the waters at Sācī's Pool.

MĀDHAVYA : Ah! That explains it.

MIŚRAKEŚĪ : Is that why the Royal Sage, afraid of committing a sin, began to have doubts about his marriage to our unfortunate Śakuntalā? On the other hand, does a love such as this really need a token of recognition? How can that be?

KING : Well; let me scold this Ring.

MĀDHAVYA (*grinning*) : I shall also scold this stick; O stick! Why are you so crooked when I myself am so straight?

KING (*as if not hearing him*) :
How could you abandon that hand (14)
with its delicate curving fingers,
to drown in the water, O Ring?

But consider :
A mindless thing cannot see perfection—
How could I have brushed aside my sweet love?

* Śakuntalā, a formal way of referring to one's wife.

MIŚRAKEŚĪ : Just what I was about to say; he has said it himself.

MĀDHAVYA : Look, why am I always left to die of hunger?

KING (*paying no attention to him*) : My darling! Pity this man whose heart burns with bitter remorse from having abandoned you without any cause; let him see you again.

Enter Caturikā *with a painting.*

CATURIKĀ : Your Majesty, here is the portrait of the Queen. *(shows the board)*

KING (*gazing at it*) : Aho! What a beautiful subject for a painting. Just look:

A pair of long expansive eyes, graceful curves of
tendril-like eyebrows (15)
the lower lip bathed in the radiance of smiles bright
as moonbeams
the luscious upper glowing rose-hued with the sheen
of jujube-berries:
This, is her face that seems to speak even in a picture,
a dazzling beauty bursts forth in streaming rays.

MĀDHAVYA (*looks at it*) : O, what a lovely painting, so full of feeling; my eyes almost trip over those ups and downs in the landscape. Expecting it to come alive I am eager to start a conversation with it—why say more.

MIŚRAKEŚĪ : What an accomplished artist the Royal Sage is; I could have sworn that my dear friend stood before me.

KING : My friend,

Whatever did not come out right was done again; (16)
yet this painting but hints at her glowing beauty.

MIŚRAKEŚĪ : Spoken like one whose love has been strengthened by remorse.

KING (*sighing*) :

Once she stood before my eyes and I spurned her, (17)
now, I adore her painted in a picture.
Having passed by a full-flowing stream,
I pant after a mirage, my friend.

MĀDHAVYA : I see three figures here, all beautiful. Which one is Lady

Śakuntalā?

MIŚRAKEŚĪ : O this poor man has not the slightest inkling of my friend's beauty. Of what use is the gift of sight to him, if he has never seen her?

KING : Come on, guess, which one is it?

MĀDHAVYA (*scrutinizing the painting*) : This, I think, as she is painted here—standing by the side of the Aśoka tree whose soft young leaves glisten sprayed with water—the hair-knot having become loose, the flowers in her lovely mass of hair falling off—drops of sweat forming on her face—her vine-like arms drooping limp—the knot of her lower garment coming undone—looking rather tired—*this*, is the Lady Śakuntalā. The other two are her companions, I guess.

KING : You are clever, Sir; do you see here the marks of my emotion?

Her portrait is soiled round the edges (18)
from marks left by my sweating fingers;
and on her cheek where I let fall a tear,
the paint has swelled and blistered.

Caturikā, the landscape is only partly painted in; go, get my paints.

CATURIKĀ : Sir Mādhavya, will you hold this painting while I go and fetch the paints?

KING : I'll hold it myself. (*takes it from her; she leaves*)

MĀDHAVYA : Now tell me, friend, what else remains to be painted in?

MIŚRAKEŚĪ : I guess he wishes to paint each favourite spot that my dear friend loved to haunt.

KING : See, my friend:

Mālinī's stream has yet to be drawn where wild-goose
pairs rest on sandy banks, (19)
and circling her, the holy foothills of Gaurī's Parent[55]
where deer recline;
Then, under a tree where bark-garments are hung out
to dry,
I wish to draw a doe rubbing her left eye against
a blackbuck's horn.

MADHAVYA (*aside*) : The way he goes on, I can just see him filling up the board with scores of bent longbeards.

KING : And there is something else I have forgotten that I had planned to put in—Śakuntalā's ornaments.

MĀDHAVYA : Such as?

MIŚRAKEŚĪ : Something appropriate to a sylvan way of life and to her maiden state, no doubt.

KING : The Śirīṣa blossom nestling at her ear, (20)
its filaments hanging down her cheek; lying snug
between her breasts, a necklace of lotus-fibre
soft as autumnal noonbeams: these are not drawn,
my friend.

MĀDHAVYA : Why does the lady appear unduly alarmed and covering her face with a hand radiant as a red lotus, if I may ask? (*looks*) O, yes, I see now; there's that bastard, that honey-looter, that rogue of a bee, coveting the lotus of her face.

KING : Then why don't you drive the impertinent fellow off?

MĀDHAVYA : Only you can chastise shameless knaves.

KING : Quite right. Hey you, you welcome guest of flowering-vines! Why do you bother to keep whirling around here?

There on that flower sits Lady Honeybee (21)
waiting, enamoured of you, Your Honour;
though thirsty she will not drink
the sweet honey until you join her.

MIŚRAKEŚĪ : The bee has been most courteously dismissed.

MĀDHAVYA : This sort of creature can turn perverse if driven away.

KING (*getting angry*) : Hey! You won't obey my command, is that so? Then hear me now:

If you dare bite my love's lower lip, like a bimba fruit, (22)
and alluring as fresh sprouts of a young tree—that lip
I drank so tenderly celebrating love's raptures,
I'll have you shut up, O Bee, in the heart of a lotus.

MĀDHAVYA : Such a terrible punishment . . . yet the fellow isn't a bit afraid . . . (*laughing, speaks to himself*) He is quite mad . . . and I, constantly in his company . . . I am also going crazy.

KING : What! He has been driven off . . . yet, he hangs around.

MIŚRAKEŚĪ : Ah! How love can affect the steadiest mind!

MĀDHAVYA (*aloud*) : Look, my friend, this is just a picture.

KING : *Just* a picture?

MIŚRAKEŚĪ : He says what I was thinking to myself; but, the King was living in a world of his own.

KING : O, what gratuitous cruelty! How could you do this to me?

With my heart wholly lost in her as if she stood (23)
right here before my eyes, what supreme joy was mine;
waking up my memory you have trans-formed
my beloved into a lifeless image once again.

(*he sheds tears*)

MIŚRAKEŚI : His behaviour before and now . . . what a strange pattern they weave of inconsistency.

KING : O, my friend, what unrelenting anguish am I being subjected to:

Denied sleep I cannot dream (24)
she is in my arms; and my tears,
they will not let me gaze on her
even re-presented in a picture.

MIŚRAKEŚI : You have completely wiped off Śakuntalā's grief at having been spurned, my friend; I have seen it for myself.

CATURIKĀ (*entering*) : Your Majesty! I was on my way here with the box of paints . . .

KING : Yes? What happened?

CATURIKĀ : Her Highness, Queen Vasumatī . . . accompanied by Pingalikā . . . met me and snatched the box out of my hands, saying, 'I shall take this to my noble lord myself'.

MĀDHAVYA : And how did you escape then?

CATURIKĀ : While her maid was freeing the Queen's veil that had got caught on a branch, I slipped away.

(*A voice in the wings*): This way, this way, Your Highness.

MĀDHAVYA (*listening*) : Ah! Here comes the tigress of the Royal Apartments ready to pounce on Caturikā and gobble her up as if she were a doe.

KING : Mādhavya, my friend, the Queen is approaching and she is very concious of the high honour I hold her in. You had better look after this portrait and keep it safe.

MĀDHAVYA : Keep *you* safe you mean—why don't you add that? (*picks up the painting and gets up*) If you manage to get away from the entrapments of the Royal Apartments, shout for me in the Palace of Clouds.

And I'll hide this where none but the pigeons can get a look in. (*walks away with quick steps*)

MIŚRAKEŚĪ : Even though his heart belongs to someone else now, the King continues to be considerate to his first love, it seems. He is a man of steady affections.

ATTENDANT (*entering with a letter in her hand*) : Victory, victory to our lord.

KING : Vetravati, did you not meet Queen Vasumatī on your way here?

ATTENDANT : Yes, my lord; but seeing me carrying a document, Her Majesty turned back.

KING : Her Highness is well aware of the proprieties; she would take care not to interrupt me in my work.

ATTENDANT : The Chief Minister begs to make this known to His Majesty: 'The work relating to revenues being very heavy, only one civil case could be reviewed. The papers are sent herewith for His Majesty's consideration.'

KING : Here, show me the document. (*the attendant hands it over*)

KING (*reading*) : 'Be it known to His Majesty as follows: A wealthy merchant by name Dhana-Vṛedhi, who carried on a flourishing trade overseas, is known to have been lost in a shipwreck. He is childless and his wealth runs into millions. As of now it becomes state property. His Majesty's decision is awaited.'

KING (*greatly dejected*) : Childlessness is a misery, Vetravati . . . . Since he was so wealthy, he must have had many wives. Let enquiries be therefore made if any one of them is pregnant.

ATTENDANT : We are informed, Sire, that very recently, the daughter of a merchant prince of Śaketa had her Pumsavana rites[56] duly performed.

KING : Then in that case, the child in the womb has the right to the father's property. Go, tell the Chief Minister so.

ATTENDANT : Your commands, Your Majesty. (*prepares to leave*)

KING : No—come here.

ATTENDANT (*returning*) : Here, Your Majesty.

KING : On the other hand, what does it matter whether there is an heir or not:

Proclaim thus to my subjects: Whosoever (25)
suffers the loss of one dearly loved
shall find in Duhṣanta one to take his place

in all relations deemed lawful and holy.

ATTENDANT : This proclamation shall be made. (*she leaves, then re-enters*) My lord, your proclamation was received with joy by the leading citizens, like rain at the proper time.

KING (*heaving a deep sigh*) : This is how the wealth of families rendered supportless by the break in succession, passes to strangers when the life of the head of the family comes to an end. And this again will be the fate of the fortunes of Puru's lineage when my own end comes.

ATTENDANT : Perish such inauspicious thoughts.

KING : A curse on me for turning my back on Fortune when she came to me.

MIŚRAKEŚĪ : It is my dear friend alone whom he has in mind when he reproaches himself—I have no doubt.

KING : My wife by right, the firm base of my lineage, (26)
abandoned, though I had implanted myself in her—
like the rich Earth sown with seed in due season—
deserted
before the promise of the rich harvest came true.

MIŚRAKEŚĪ : She will not be deserted by you any longer.

CATURIKĀ (*aside*) : Lady, our lord is now doubly desolated as a result of the Chief Minister sending him that document. Perhaps you ought to go to the Palace of Clouds and fetch His Honour Mādhavya to console His Majesty.

ATTENDANT : An excellent idea.

(*She leaves.*)

KING : O misery! The shades of Duhṣanta's ancestors are beset by mounting doubts, wondering:
'After him, who in our line will prepare with
ordained rites (27)
and offer us the oblations of remembrance—'
My washed tears that I, unblessed with offspring
pour out,
the ancestors, I am certain, drink as their libations.

MIŚRAKEŚĪ : Though there is light, because it is covered, the good king remains shrouded in darkness.

CATURIKĀ : Sire, do not torture yourself any further. You are in the prime of life and there will be fine sons born to your other queens, who will discharge your debts to the ancestors. (*to herself*) His Majesty pays no heed to my words. But then it is the right medicine that can cure the disease.

KING (*overcome by sorrow*) : From earliest times:

This, the dynasty of Puru, pure from its roots, (28)
descending in one uninterrupted succession,
will now have its setting in my life, unfruitful,
like Sarasvati's stream lost in barbarous sandy
wastes.

He loses consciousness.[57]

CATURIKĀ (*alarmed*): Courage, my lord, take heart.

MIŚRAKEŚĪ : Should I not free him now from his grief? No, I had better not. For I have heard the Mother of Gods speak of this when consoling Śakuntalā—heard from her own lips that the gods themselves in their concern for the continuity of the sacrifices and to secure their own share in them, would see to it that before long, her lord welcomes Śakuntalā as his lawful wedded wife. Well, I should not really linger here any more; let me go and acquaint my dear friend with the happy turn of events. That should cheer her up. (*she ascends into the sky and flies away*)

(A voice off-stage): Help! A sacrilege, a sacrilege.

KING (*regaining consciousness*) : Hey! What's that; it sounds like Mādhavya's piteous call for help.

CATURIKĀ : Sire, I do hope poor Mādhavya hasn't been caught red-handed by the worthy Madam Pingalikā with the painting in his possession.

KING : Go, Caturikā, go and convey my displeasure to the Queen for not disciplining her servants.

CATURIKĀ : As Your Majesty commands.

(*She leaves.*)

(The same voice off-stage): Help! A sacrilege, a sacrilege.

KING : The Brahmin's voice sounds truly altered by terror . . . Ho there, who's there?

CHAMBERLAIN (*entering*) : Your commands, Majesty.

KING : Go, and find out why our little Mādhavya is crying out so piteously.

CHAMBERLAIN : I shall find out. (*he goes out, then returns in great agitation*)

KING : Pārvatāyana, nothing terrible has happened, I trust?

CHAMBERLAIN : Yes, it has, Sire.

KING : Why are you trembling like this? I see you—

Already trembling from age, your limbs now tremble
even more, (29)
like a pipal tree, shaken by the wind blowing through it.

CHAMBERLAIN : Let His Majesty come at once and save his friend.

KING : Save him from what?

CHAMBERLAIN : Great danger.

KING : Make your meaning clear, man.

CHAMBERLAIN : The palace known as the Palace of Clouds . . . from where one can see far into the distance, in all directions . . .

KING : Yes, what of it?

CHAMBERLAIN :

From its topmost turret which even the palace-
peacocks (30)
cannot fly up to without frequent pauses,
some being, invisible,
has seized your friend and carried him off.

KING (*getting up at once*) : Ah! My own home . . . haunted by evil spirits? But it is known that kingship bears responsibility for many offences.

Each day of our own life we slip and fall into error (31)
through negligence that we are unaware of;
how then can we fully know what paths
the life of each one of our subjects takes?

(A voice in the background) : Ho! Protect me, here, protect me, here.

KING (*listening, begins to walk fast*) : My friend, don't be afraid, don't be afraid.

(The voice in the background) : How can I not be afraid . . . when someone is forcing my head back . . . and trying to break my neck into bits as if it were a piece of sugarcane.

KING (*casting a glance around*) : My bow, bring my bow.

Enter a female bodyguard *carrying the bow.*

BODYGUARD : Sire, here is the bow and arrows and your hand-guard.

The king takes them from her.

(A voice off-stage):

Thirsting for the fresh blood that'll gush from your throat, (32)
I'll kill you here, as a tiger kills the animal
struggling in its grasp: Let Duhṣanta who wields his bow
to free the distressed of their fear now be your refuge.

KING (*angrily*) : How dare he address me thus. Ha! Hold, hold, you foul eater of corpses. From this instant you will cease to live. (*stringing his bow*) Pārvatāyana, lead the way to the staircase.

CHAMBERLAIN : This way, this way, Your Majesty.

All proceed in great haste.

KING (*looking all around*) : But this place is completely empty.

(A voice off-stage) : Protect me, protect me. I can see you, but alas! You cannot see me . . . like a mouse in a cat's paw, I despair for my life.

KING : Hey! You! You who wax arrogant possessed of the powers of invisibility! Do you imagine that my missile cannot see you either? Just wait. And don't be too confident that you can safely hide behind my friend. I am activating *that* missile[58]—

Which shall strike you who deserves to die and save him, (33)
the twice-born who deserves to be protected,
just as the swan only takes in the milk
and leaves the water mixed with it behind.

Saying this he aims his weapon; then enter Mātali *and* Mādhavya *with him.*

MĀTALI : May you be blessed with long life.

The Titans are your arrows' target (34)
by Indra ordained; on them should you bend your bow.
The noble direct towards their friends
serene eyes and gentle—not cruel arrows.

KING (*de-activating his missile with alacrity*) : Ah! It's you, Mātali, welcome, welcome to the charioteer of the Lord of the Immortals.

MĀDHAVYA : Hm . . . so . . . he was about to slay me as if I were a sacrificial beast . . . and here . . . you welcome him with open arms.

MĀTALI (*smiling*) : Gracious lord, now let me tell you why Indra has sent me.

KING : I am all attention.

MĀTALI : There is a race of Titans, the invincible brood of the demon Kālanemi.

KING : I once heard of them from Nārada.

MĀTALI : Destined for destruction at your hands alone (35)
in the battle's forefront, they are inviolable
before your comrade, the Lord of a Hundred Powers.*
Where the Sun with His spreading beams
cannot spring forth to break Night's massed darkness,
the Moon appears and chases it away.

So let Your Honour mount the celestial chariot as you are with your bow ready and strung and ride forth to victory.

KING : I am indeed highly honoured by this singular mark of Indra's favour. But tell me, Mātali, why did you act the way you did towards poor Mādhavya?

MĀTALI : O, I shall explain that too. I found you deeply dejected on account of some sorrow or other. Accordingly, I acted to rouse your anger. For:

A fire stirred blazes brightly, (36)
a cobra provoked spreads its hood;
every form of life possessed of energy

* Indra

glows into brilliance invariably, when roused.

KING : My friend, the command of the Lord of Heaven cannot be transgressed. So, go to the Chief Minister, Piśuna, acquaint him with all that has transpired and give him this message from me:

Let your wisdom alone protect the subjects while I am away; (37)
this drawn bow of mine other duties has to accomplish.

MĀDHAVYA : As Your Honour commands.

(*He leaves.*)

MĀTALI : Let my gracious lord mount the chariot. (*the King does so*)

(All exit.)

End of Act Six

entitled

SEPARATION FROM ŚAKUNTALĀ

ACT SEVEN

Scene: First the celestial regions; then the Hermitage of Mārīca.

Enter King Duhṣanta *and* Mātali *by the Aerial Path, mounted on Indra's chariot.*

KING : Mātali, although I have carried out the mission entrusted to me by Indra, the Munificent, I feel that I have rendered him too slight a service to merit that special welcome he accorded me.

MĀTALI (*smiling*) : It seems neither of you feels truly gratified.

To you those services you rendered Indra, (1)
Lord of Mighty Storms, look trifling
beside the high honours you received;
while He, marvelling at your glorious deeds
reckons not high the honours He bestowed.

KING : O no, Mātali, that's not so; the honour He did me at the time of my leave-taking went far beyond my wildest expectations. Mark you, in the presence of all the assembled Immortals, He made me share His royal seat. And:

Glancing up with a smile at Jayanta, his son, (2)
who stood beside him longing inwardly for the same,
Hari[*] placed round my neck the Mandāra-garland,
tinged with golden sandal rubbed off his chest.

MĀTALI : What indeed does Your Honour not deserve that the Lord of the Immortals can bestow? Just think:

Once before Paradise was rid of thorns, the Titans, (3)
by the fierce claws of godhead descended lion-like:
now, once again it is freed by your smooth streamlined arrows,
for Hari to savour His pleasures in peace.

[*] Indra

KING : But Mātali, in this case, the glory of the Lord of Hundred Powers alone, is to be celebrated.

Those delegated to perform momentous deeds, (4)
know them, O Mātali, to succeed
only by virtue of the high esteem
they are held in by their masters:
could Aruṇa dispel darkness if the thousand-rayed
Sun
did not place him in the forefront as His charioteer?

MĀTALI : Such words accord with the nobility of your mind, Sire. (*drives the chariot a little further*) Gracious Prince, can you see from here how the splendour of your fame spreads across the high vault of the sky?

With pigments left from cosmetics blended (5)
for the lovely women of Paradise,
celestials inscribe on scrolls
that hang from the Wish-Granting Vine,
your deeds of glory that form the themes
for the well-wrought poems they sing.

KING : Mātali, the other day during our ascent into the ethereal regions, I was burning with such ardour to meet and do battle with the Titans that I did not pay much attention to the Celestial Path we were traversing. So, tell me, which of the Paths of the Seven Winds are we on now?

MĀTALI : The Path of the Wind Pravaha, hallowed (6)
by Viṣṇu's wide-stepping second stride,
and free of all worldly taints:
its current bears along the Triple-Streamed Gangā
—her home and resting place the firmament—
and propels on their circling course
the luminous orbs of the sky, spraying
their beams of light evenly around.

KING : No wonder then that my inmost being and my outward-looking senses as well experience such tranquillity. (*looking down at the wheels*) We have descended into the Path of the Clouds, I believe, Mātali.

MĀTALI (*smiling*) : How do you know that?

KING : The rims of the wheels glisten misted with spray; (7)

cātaka birds dart in and out through their spokes;
the horses gleam bathed by flickers of lightning;
it is clear that your chariot now rides
over clouds whose bellies are swollen with rain.

MĀTALI : In an instant Your Honour will be landing on the Earth that you rule over.

KING (*looking down again*) : Mātali, see with what rapidity we are descending; the world of mortals presents a most marvellous sight. Look:

As the mountains rear upwards, the land climbs (8)
precipitately down their great peaks, it seems;
trees whose forms were merged within the dense leafage
emerge distinct as their branching shoulders
thrust into view: those fine lines display themselves
as great rivers brimming with water:
see how the Earth looms at my side
as if some mighty hand had flung her up to me.

MĀTALI : An acute observation, Sire. (*looking down with profound admiration*) O, what enchanting beauty is this, of the Earth!

KING : Mātali, what range of mountains is that, glowing with liquid gold, stretching like a bar of clouds drenched in sunset colours and plunging deep into the eastern and western oceans?

MĀTALI : That range of mountains, Your Honour, is known as Hēma-Kūta, the home of Kimpuruṣas; it is there that the highest forms of penance are wrought. And listen further, Gracious Prince:

The Lord of Beings, born of The Light (9)
sprung from the Self-Existent Itself,
He, the revered Parent of Gods and Titans,
leads with his consort, here, a life of penance.

KING (*speaking in reverential tones*) : In that case I should pay my respects to His Supreme Holiness before proceeding any further; such a rare opportunity for receiving blessings must not be passed by.

MĀTALI : An excellent thought, Sire. (*mimes descent of the chariot*) There, we have landed.

KING (*in a tone of utmost wonder*) : How's this, Mātali!

The wheels glide noiseless; no jolting is felt; (10)
no dust is seen whirling around;
they do not touch the surface of the Earth;
nothing marks the chariot's descent.

MĀTALI : This, needless to say, is the difference, gracious lord, between the chariot of Indra, Lord of Heroic Fury and that of Your Honour.

KING : Mātali, whereabouts is the Hermitage of Sage Mārīca situated?

MĀTALI (*pointing with his hand*) : There:

Where stands that sage, still as a tree stump (11)
and faces the disk of the noonday sun,
his form half-buried in an ant hill,
with the slough of a snake a second sacred thread,
his throat squeezed tightly round
by twining tendrils of a dried-up vine;
and wears coiled on his head a tangled mass of matted hair
where birds build nests and dishevel strands
that fall loose about his shoulders.

KING : I humbly bow to you, O Practiser of Cruel Penance!

MĀTALI (*pulling in the reins*) : Now, gracious lord, we are entering the Hermitage of the Lord of Beings, where the holy Aditi, his consort, tends the young Mandāra trees herself.

KING : O wondrous! This is a spot far more blissful than Paradise itself. I feel as if I am immersed in the Pool of Nectar.

MĀTALI (*bringing the chariot to a stop*) : Dismount, gracious lord.

KING (*dismounting*) : And you, Sir?

MĀTALI : Seeing that the chariot is on level ground and well secured, I can also get down. (*does so*) Gracious lord, come this way and look around you; these are the penance-groves of the Perfected Seers.

KING : I look around at the penance-groves and at the Seers; and I am filled with wonder.

In groves where trees abound that grant all desires, (12)
air is the sole means of life-support for these Seers;
ablutions for holy rites are performed
in waters that glow with the sheen
of a host of golden lotuses;

meditations are practised in jewelled caves
and restraint in the presence of celestial nymphs.
The Seers here lead lives of penance in this place
that other ascetics seek to win through penances.

MĀTALI : The aims of the truly great soar high. (*he walks around and speaks in the air*) Venerable Śākalya, how is the Holy Mārīca occupied now? (*as if listening to a reply*) Ah, I see; that questioned by Aditi, daughter of Dakṣa, about the conduct of a virtuous wife, he is expounding these truths to her and the wives of other sages? I think we should wait till the discourse is finished. (*addressing the King*) Sire, Why don't you stay in the shade of this Aśoka tree, while I go and wait for the opportune moment to announce your arrival to Indra's Parent.

KING : Yes, whatever you think best.

(Mātali exits.)

KING (*indicates feeling a good omen*) :

I see no hope for my fondest wish— (13)
yet you throb, O, my arm, all in vain;
Good Fortune once brushed aside
turns to misfortune without fail.

(*Voice offstage*) : No, don't do that; don't be so wayward; his true nature repeatedly breaks out.

KING (*listening*) : This is hardly a place for undisciplined behaviour; who is being rebuked, I wonder. (*following in the direction of the voice, exclaims in astonishment*) And whom have we here? Just a child. . . he is being held back by hermit women. . . his strength is certainly not that of a child.

To amuse himself in play, he pulls (14)
roughly from its mother's half-sucked teat,
a lion's cub; tousling its soft mane
he drags it along by sheer force.

Enter as described a little boy *followed by* two hermit women.

BOY : Come little lion, come, open wide your jaws; I wish to count your teeth.

FIRST HERMIT LADY : O you naughty boy, why do you hurt our animals that we love tenderly like our own children? Really. . . each day your ways become wilder and more wayward. The sages have well named you Sarva-Damana.*

KING : Who can this child be for whom I feel an affection as if he were my own? (*reflecting*) O well, I guess that being childless, my heart fills with tenderness for him.

SECOND LADY : The lioness over there will spring on you if you don't let go of her little one, you know?

BOY (*grinning*) : O what a shame! I am really scared now. (*pouts his lower lip*)

KING : This boy strikes me as the tiny germ (15)
of mighty valour that waits
like a fiery spark for kindling,
before it bursts into a blazing fire.

FIRST LADY : Darling, let go of this little lion cub; I shall give you something else to play with.

BOY : What is that? Give it to me. (*holds out his right hand*)

KING (*looks in astonishment at the boy's outstretched hand*) : Why, this is incredible, he bears on his palm the mark of a Sovereign of the World.

With fingers close knit, palm slightly hollowed, (16)
the hand he stretches out in eager expectation
to hold the wished-for plaything, resembles
a single lotus bud, its petals tightly shut,
just prized open by Dawn's first flush of rose.

SECOND LADY : Suvratā, we cannot fob this child off with mere promises; so go to my cottage, you will find there a clay peacock painted in many colours that once belonged to Mankaṇaka, the child of one of the hermits. Bring it and give it to him.

FIRST HERMIT LADY : Very well.

(She exits.)

BOY : In the meantime I shall play with this little lion, shan't I? (*looks at the hermit woman and laughs*)

* All-Tamer

KING : O how my heart goes out to this wayward little fellow. (*sighs*)

Blessed are they whose garments get soiled (17)
from the dust of the limbs of their little sons
who clamour in words sweetly indistinct,
to be lifted on to their laps, and for no reason
laugh to reveal glimpses of their budding teeth.

HERMIT LADY (*shaking her forefinger at the child*) : Very well, so you won't listen to me. (*turns around to look for help*) Is any one of the younger hermits around? (*notices the King*) Gracious Sir, please come and free this little lion cub from the iron grip of this small boy who takes a childish pleasure in tormenting it.

KING (*approaches, smilling*) : Listen, son of a great sage:

Why do you act in this wanton manner (18)
alien to the life of a hermitage
where the spirit finds its tranquil home?
Why do you flout that rule of gentleness
towards all living things,
like the young of a black serpent that spoils
for other creatures, the pleasant sanctuary
that is the fragrant sandalwood tree?

HERMIT LADY : Gracious Sir, he is not the son of a sage.

KING : His actions that suit his appearance proclaim loudly that he is not. But meeting him in a place such as this, I thought he might be. (*doing what was requested of him, the King feels the touch of the child, and speaks to himself*):

If such pleasure can thrill through my whole body (19)
from a touch of this child—a stranger's offspring—
what bliss must he not then bring to the heart
of the lucky man from whose loins he has sprung?

HERMIT LADY : How extraordinary! O, it is a marvel. . .

KING : What is?

HERMIT LADY : The likeness, Gracious Sir; the likeness of this boy's appearance to yours, even though you are not related. It astonishes me. Further, wild as he is, he does not shy away from you who are a stranger to him; I am amazed by that.

KING (*fondling the child*) : If he is not the son of a hermit, to which family does he belong?

HERMIT LADY : Puru's family.

KING (*to himself*) : The same as mine? That *is* strange. Therefore the noble lady fancies a resemblance between us. It's true though that the descendants of Puru observe one last family vow.

> As rulers of the earth they wish to pass (20)
> in mansions abounding in sensuous delights
> their early years: thereafter they make
> the roots of trees their home and live
> bound by the hermit's single vow.

(*aloud*) But mortals cannot reach these regions on their own, noble lady.

HERMIT LADY : Yes, Gracious Sir; what you say is true. But this boy's mother related as she was to an *apsarā*, gave birth to him here in this Hermitage presided over by the Father of the Immortals.

KING (*aside*) : My hopes are stirred a second time running. (*aloud*) And the name of the Royal Sage whose wife his noble mother is, if I may ask?

HERMIT LADY : Who would ever think of even uttering the name of one who abandoned his lawful wife.

KING (*to himself*) : The remark points straight at me, I'm afraid. If I could only ask the name of the boy's mother. (*reflecting*) No, I shouldn't. It is highly improper to exhibit curiosity about another man's wife.

Enter the other hermit woman *with the clay peacock in her hand.*

HERMIT LADY : Look, Sarva-Damana, see how pretty the *śakunta** is.

BOY (*looking around*) : Mamma, Mamma, where is she?

Both women laugh.

FIRST LADY : So fond is he of his mother that the similarity in sound of the two words has misled him.

SECOND LADY : Darling, she means this clay peacock; she was pointing out to you how pretty the toy is.

KING (*to himself*) : So, his mother's name is Śakuntalā; but it is not an

---

* A bird

uncommon name. Will these events turn out after all to be a mirage that will lead me into further misery?

BOY : Yes, dear Aunt, it is; I like this pretty peacock. (*takes the toy from her*)

HERMIT LADY (*in great alarm*) : Look, look, what has happened, great gods; the protective amulet—it is not on his wrist . . .

KING : O, please don't be alarmed, worshipful ladies; here it is. It must have slipped off during his playful scuffle with the lion cub.

Stoops to pick it up.

BOTH LADIES : No, no, don't, don't touch it. . . that is very strange. . . he *has* picked it up. (*they clasp their hands on their bosoms and stare at each other in amazement*)

KING : Why did you ask me not to touch it?

FIRST LADY : Illustrious monarch, listen: this is an amulet of divine power, made out of a herb of immense virtue, named 'Invincible'; and it was tied on the child's wrist at the time of his natal rites, by His Holiness Mārīca. If it falls on the ground, no one except himself or his parents can safely pick it up.

KING : And if someone else does?

FIRST LADY : It is transformed at once into a serpent that bites him.

KING : And have you worthy ladies seen this happen, with your own eyes?

BOTH : Many times.

KING (*overcome with joy*) : How can I not rejoice with my whole heart that this moment, my heart's desire has at last found its fulfilment.

He embraces the child.

SECOND LADY : Suvratā, come, let us go straight to Śakuntalā who is engaged in the unfailing performance of her ritual vows and inform her of all that has happened.

(Both exit.)

BOY : Let me go, let me go; I wish to go to my Mamma.

KING : My little son, we shall both go together to your mother and make her happy, shall we?

BOY : You are not my father; Duhṣanta is my father.

KING (*with a smile*) : His hot rebuttal is the last bit of proof I need.

Enter Śakuntalā *with her hair done in a single braid.*

ŚAKUNTALĀ : Even after I was told that Sarva-Damana's amulet did not turn immediately into a serpent, I was afraid to believe that good fortune would greet me again. . . . but I do remember Miśrakeśī mentioning something that hinted at just such a possibility.

KING (*sees Śakuntalā*) : Ha! Here is Lady Śakuntalā . . . it is *she* . . .

Dressed in dusky garments (21)
her face fined thin from observing strictest vows,
her hair bound in a single braid; pure, upright,
she keeps the long vow of cruel separation
from me who acted so heartless to her.

ŚAKUNTALĀ (*seeing the King pale with remorse*) : This does not seem to be my noble lord. Who then is this man? Defiling by his embrace my child who was protected by the sanctified amulet?

BOY (*running to his mother*) : Dearest Mamma, here is some stranger who calls me his little son.

KING : My beloved, the cruelty I showed you has come full circle now; it is I who have to plead now to be recognized by you.

ŚAKUNTALĀ (*to herself*) : Take courage, O my heart; envious Fate seems to have relented at last; this is indeed my noble lord.

KING : Dear love:

The light of memory has pierced through (22)
the sightless night of my dark delusion;
by Fortune's grace, you now stand before me,
O Lady of the most gracious face!
Like Rohini in conjunction with the Moon
appearing at the end of an eclipse.

ŚAKUNTALĀ : Hail! Vic. . . . . (*breaks off in the middle, her voice choked by tears*)

KING : Though the greeting of 'victory' (23)
was strangled by your tears, I have more than won—
for my eyes have looked upon your face

with their pale, unadorned, parted lips.

BOY : Who is this, Mamma, who is this?

ŚAKUNTALĀ : Ask your fortunes, my little one. (*weeps bitterly*)

KING : Cast off from your heart, O lovely lady, (24)
the bitter pain of cruel rejection; believe
that some strange overpowering blank confusion
took hold of my heart on that fateful day.
Place a wreath on a blind man's brows
and he tears it off, fearing it to be a snake:
It so happens that minds wrought upon by utter darkness
meet the good and beautiful with a perverse response.

With these words, the King falls at her feet.

ŚAKUNTALĀ : O my lord, rise. It must be that I had to reap the consequences of some wrongdoing on my part in a former birth; otherwise how could my noble lord, so compassionate by nature, have acted in such an unfeeling manner towards me.

The King rises.

ŚAKUNTALĀ : How did the memory of this most unhappy person return to you, my lord?

KING : Once I have plucked this wounding dart of grief from my heart, I shall tell you all.

O fair lady! The tear drop that once stood (25)
trembling on your lower lip
—and I watched uncaring, lost in delusion—
while it still clings to your gently-curving lashes,
I shall now wipe away, my beloved,
to free myself of remorse.

ŚAKUNTALĀ (*as he wipes away her tears, notices the Ring*) : O my lord, this is the Ring.

KING : Yes, and it was its amazing recovery that restored my memory.

ŚAKUNTALĀ : Where I failed in convincing my lord, this thing has succeeded and done just that.

KING : Then let the vine receive once more the blossom that is the symbol of its union with the springtime.

ŚAKUNTALĀ : No, no, my lord, I don't trust it. Let my lord wear it himself.

Enter Mātali.

MĀTALI : Indeed, Fortune has blessed you, gracious lord, by granting you the happiness of meeting again your lawful wife and of seeing the face of your son.

KING : My cherished desires have more than amply borne fruit because their fulfilment has been brought about through the aid of my friend. Mātali, tell me, do you think that the Destroyer of Darkness* knew this would happen?

MĀTALI (*with a smile*) : What is beyond the knowing of the Lords of the Universe? Come, Sir, His Holiness Mārīca is waiting to receive you.

KING : Dearest, hold our child, I wish to present myself before His Holiness with you leading the way.

ŚAKUNTALĀ : I feel that it is indecorous to appear before elders in the company of my husband.

KING : It is the proper way of doing things on auspicious occasions; come, my love.

All turn around. Then Mārīca *is seen enthroned with* Aditi *by his side.*

MĀRĪCA (*seeing the King*) : O Daughter of Dakṣa!

Here is the one who is in the forefront of your
son's battles (26)
He, called Duhṣanta, is Lord of the Earth; because
of his bow,
the myriad-pointed thunderbolt of the Lord of Riches*
giving up its office has become a mere ornament.

ADITI : His mien does proclaim his greatness.

MĀTALI : Lord of the Earth! The Parents of the Universe regard you with eyes that reveal the affection for a son. Approach them, Your Honour.

---

* Indra

KING : Mātali:

Is this The Twain sprung from Dakṣa and Marīci,
but one remove from the Creator. (27)
Whom the seers extol as The Cause of The Effulgence
that manifests Itself in Twelve Forms,
Who begat The Protector of the Triple-World and
Ruler of the gods offered oblations,
in Whom the World's Self, higher even than the Self-
Born placed Itself to be born into the world.

MĀTALI : Who else?

KING (*prostrates himself before them*) : I, Duhṣanta, ever the servant of Indra, humbly bow before you both.

MĀRĪCA : My son, long may you protect the Earth.

ADITI : Be invincible in battle, my child.

Śakuntalā with her son falls at their feet.

MĀRĪCA : Daughter,

With a husband the equal of The Breaker of Dark
Clouds* (28)
With a son like his son, Jayanta, no other blessing
fits you but this: Be the equal of Paulomī.

ADITI : My child, may you always be highly esteemed by your lord; and your little son live long and be the ornament to both your families. Sit down here.

All sit down.

MĀRĪCA (*Pointing to each in turn*) :

Here, Śakuntalā, the virtuous wife, (29)
here, your fine son and here Your Honour:
Faith, Promise, Performance—
The three have happily come together.

KING : Supreme Holiness! This is indeed an unprecedented favour that you have granted us now—first comes the fulfilment of our wishes, then,

* Indra

the gracious sight of Your Holiness. As a rule, Holiness:

> The flower appears first, then the fruit, (30)
> dense clouds gather followed by rain,
> this is the law of cause and effect:
> but good fortune has preceded your grace.

MĀTALI : Long-Lived Majesty! This is the way the Parents of the Universe bestow their blessings.

KING : Supreme Holiness! Having married your handmaid here by the rites of mutual love, I cruelly repudiated her because of an unfortunate lapse of memory, when her kinsfolk brought her to me after a period of time; and in so doing, I have gravely wronged your kinsman, His Holiness, Kaṇva. Subsequently, on seeing this Ring, I realized that I had in fact married her. All this strikes me as most strange:

> Just as a man sees an elephant pass by (31)
> before his very eyes but doubts its existence,
> then, noticing its footprints, ceases to doubt,
> such changes has my mind passed through.

MĀRĪCA : You have reproached yourself sufficiently, my son. The delusion you were labouring under was quite natural. Listen to what I have to say.

KING : I am all attention.

MĀRĪCA : The moment Menakā flew in from Apsarā Pool and came to Aditi, bearing Śakuntalā grief-stricken on account of her repudiation, I knew from meditating upon it that this unhappy girl, your partner in religious rites, had been repulsed by you under the influence of Durvāsā's curse. And, that the effect of the curse would cease as soon as you saw this Ring.

KING (*sighing with relief*) : Then I am free from blame.

ŚAKUNTALĀ (*to herself*) : Thank my good stars! My lord did not really wish to spurn me. He did so only because he had forgotten all about me . . . But . . . I have no recollection of ever having been cursed. Or. . . is it possible that being absent-minded on account of the separation from my husband, I was oblivious of a curse? I wonder if that was why my friends asked me to be sure and present the Ring to my lord.

MĀRĪCA (*addressing Śakuntalā*) : Dear child, you know all the facts now. Therefore do not harbour any feelings of resentment towards your partner in all religious rites. Remember that:

You were harshly repulsed by your Lord (32)
when the curse clouded darkly his memory;
now that the darkness has lifted,
sovereignty over him is yours.
Tarnished by grime, the mirror's surface
returns no image; polished, its brightness reflects one.

KING : It is as Your Holiness observes.

MĀRĪCA : My son, I trust you have greeted with joy your son born of Śakuntalā; I have myself performed the birth rite and all other sacraments for him.

KING : Supreme Holiness, the enduring glory of my line rests with him.

MĀRĪCA : YES, THAT SHALL BE. O King who will live for many years, know this—he will be a Sovereign of the World. Know this too:

Crossing the oceans in a chariot gliding smooth, (33)
he shall conquer and rule unopposed
the rich Earth with her seven continents:
named All-Tamer here, because he subdues all
creatures
by his strength, the future will see his name
proclaimed *Bharata*: He who bears the world.

KING : When your Divine Self has performed all the sacraments for him, all this and more may be expected of him.

ADITI : Divine Lord, should the venerable Sage Kaṇva not be informed in detail of all the events that has led to the fulfilment of his daughter's hopes and wishes? Menakā, out of love for her daughter, has been living here, attending on us, and knows it all.

ŚAKUNTALĀ : Her Holiness has put in words the longings of my heart.

MĀRĪCA : By the Divine Vision acquired through penance, everything that has happened is present to the eyes of His Reverence Kaṇva. (*on reflection*) Even so, it is our obligation to formally acquaint the Sage with the happy turn of events. Ho there, is anyone there?

Enter a disciple.

DISCIPLE : Supreme Holiness! Here I am.

MĀRĪCA : Gālava, my son, go by the Aerial Path at once to His Reverence,

Kaṇva and convey my joyful message to him: that, on the termination of the curse, Śakuntalā with her son has been duly received by Duhṣanta, whose memory has been restored.

DISCIPLE : Your command shall be carried out at once, Your Holiness.

(He exits.)

MĀRĪCA (*to the King*) : My son, you too should mount the chariot of Indra, your friend, with your son and wife and return to your Capital.

KING : Your Holiness' command shall be obeyed.

MĀRĪCA : Honour the gods in full measure (34)
with holy rites and all due offerings;
May the God of gods* in return
bless your people with abundant rains;
Let Time run its round in this pattern
woven of acts of mutual service:
May both the Worlds enjoy Glory and Plenitude
built on such an enduring friendship

KING : For my part, Divine Holiness, I shall strive to the best of my power to establish this blessed state.

MĀRĪCA : Is there some other blessing that I may bestow on you, my son?

KING (*worshipping him with great joy*) : If His Divine Holiness wishes to grant me any further favours, let them be these:

May kings ever work for the good of their subjects: (35)
May the utterance of those blessed by the Word
be ever honoured:
May the Self-Existent Lord who unites in Himself
the Dark and the Light,[59]
Whose Infinite Power pervades this Universe
annihilate forever the round of my births.

(Exit all.)

End of Act Seven
entitled
ŚAKUNTALĀ'S PROSPERITY

Thus ends the play entitled *The Recognition of Śakuntalā*

---

* Indra

Glossary

Aditi	'Boundless', the infinitude of space. In myth Aditi is called the 'mother of the gods'; she is the daughter of the Primal Ancestor, Dakṣa.
Airāvata	The celestial elephant who rose from the ocean when it was churned for *Amṛta* (ambrosia) at the Beginning; the mount of Indra.
Alakā	Kubera's capital on Mt. Kailāsa.
Apsarā	'Born of the waters'; celestial dancers; guardians of pools.
Āmra-kūta	'Mango Peak'; source of the Narmadā or Revā, in the eastern Vindhyas. Identified with the modern Amara-kantak.
Arjuna or Kakubha (i)	A tree that blooms at the beginning of the year, bearing creamy spikes of flowers; Terminalia Arjuna. Kakubha is another name for this tree.
Arjuna (ii)	'Bright'; the name of the middle Pāndava brother; one of the foremost warriors in the epic *Mahābhārata*; he was the son of Kunti by Indra, Lord of the Immortals. The Pāndavas were sons of Pāndu, born by levirate.
Aromatic gums	A fragrant and resinous rock that is powdered and burnt in a brazier like incense, the smoke dries and perfumes women's hair after it is washed.
Aruṇa	The very first light of dawn; the word signifies a coppery-red; Aruṇa is the charioteer of the sun.
Ārya-putra	'My lord'; the respectful form of address used

by a wife to her husband.

Āṣāḍha — The last month of summer, mid-June to mid-July. The rains begin at the end of Āṣāḍha.

Ash — The residue of the universe when it is burnt and destroyed at the end of a great epoch (*mahā-kalpa*) by fire, wind and water. A new universe is created out of the ashes after a long period of rest. Ash is therefore a symbol of dissolution and recreation. Sacred ash is given to devotees as symbolic of this cosmic process. Temple elephants are decorated with lines of ash and other colours, red, yellow, black. Seen from a height the grey rocks of granite in central India, streaked with silvery streams and branches of rivers that divide to go round rocks, look like supine elephants basking in the sun.

Aśoka — An evergreen blooming in Spring; the compact clusters of blossoms varying in colour from pale orange to scarlet, depending on their age, cover the tree completely; the flowers have a delicate fragrance. The Aśōka (*a-śōka*) meaning 'sorrow-less' is a tree celebrated in myth and legend. The flower is one of the five flower-arrows of Kāma, god of love; Sītā, the heroine of the epic *Rāmāyana* who was abducted by Rāvaṇa, the demon-king of Lankā, spent a year in his Aśoka-grove, waiting in sorrow for Rāma to come and rescue her. The tree was believed to bloom at the touch of the richly-jewelled left foot of a lovely young woman.

Atimukta — A variety of fragrant jasmine; the petals are sparkling white; the tubes and underside of two of the petals are a pale purple, clearly noticeable in the buds; probably what is commonly known as *chameli.*

Avanti — The ancient name for Malwa, now the western part of the state of Madhya Pradesh. Avanti is a very ancient kingdom, mentioned in the *Mahābhārata* as one of the 16 great kingdoms—*mahā-janapada.* In the time of Gautama Buddha (sixth century BC), it was very powerful under its ruler Pradyōta; Ujjayinī was its capital. Avanti was a rich kingdom because of its overseas trade which passed through Ujjayinī.

Bakula or Kesara — A beautiful timber tree bearing clusters of small, pale-cream flowers that retain their fragrance when dry. Mimusops Elengi is the botanical name of this tree.

Bali — Literally 'offering'; the name of an ancient king famed for his magnanimity; see under 'Bali and Viṣṇu's Three Strides' in Appendix II: Myths.

Bandhūka — Jungle geranium; *Ixora Goccinea.* A small shrub that blooms all the year round but specially luxuriant during the rains; the tubular flowers form thick heads, a brilliant orange in colour.

Betel — A vine whose leaves are chewed after meals; the juice is a digestive.

Bhavānī — 'Becoming' as opposed to 'Being'; the feminine formed from 'Bhava' one of Śiva's epithets. It is one of the many names for Śaktī, Śiva's inherent power, that brings the world into existence.

Bhṛgu-chief — Paraśu-rāma (Rāma, wielding the axe) decimated the Baronage. The legend implies some enmity of Brahmins and Kṣatriyas (warriors). Paraśu-rāma is believed to have thrown his battle-axe and made the cleft in the mountain, known as the Kraunca Pass or modern Niti Pass in Ladakh.

Blossoming time — Certain trees were believed to bloom from contact with a lovely young woman; either from the touch of her hands or her jewelled foot, or by being sprinkled with wine from her mouth. This is a poetic convention known as *'dohada'*—the longings of a pregnant women.

Blue of his throat — Śiva swallowed the deadly poison spewed out by the Ocean when it was churned at the Beginning, according to a myth of Origins, and retained it in his throat to save the newly-created universe from destruction by being burnt by the poison; an ambivalent myth, because the churning produces treasures as well as poison. In this context, it underlines the highest *service* that can be done, to serve the good of others at great cost to one's own well-being.

Blue- throated friend — Peacock.

Bodiless One — Kāma, the god of Love; puffed up with pride, Kāma had the temerity to assail the Great Yogi, Śiva, seated on Mt. Kailāsa in meditation, to break the Lord's single-minded contemplation. A spark from Śiva's third eye—the inner eye of wisdom—burnt Kāma to ashes. This myth is beautifully developed in the third canto of *Kumārasambhavam* by Kālidāsa.

Brahmā — 'One with Brahma or holy creative power'; the Creator.

Brahmāvarta — 'The Holy Land': 'the land where the gods came down'; original home of the Vedic people; it lay between 'the divine rivers Sarasvatī and Dṛṣadvatī': the land west of the Jamunā and modern Delhi; in Vedic times the great sacri-

	fices were performed here and the gods invoked to come down and partake of the oblations offered into the fire.
Brother's wife	A term of respect in addressing and referring to a lady; no relationship is involved; the term *'bhabhi'* (brother's wife) is still used in the Indian languages.
Caṇḍeśvara	'The Wrathful Lord'; one of the names given to Śiva. It denotes the destructive aspect of Time, for all things are born in Time and are destroyed by Time.
Cakravāka (m) Cakravāki (f)	The sheldrake or ruddy goose; also known as Brahminy Duck; these birds formed loving pairs and became a symbol in literature for connubial love and constancy; they were believed to have been cursed by a sage or by Rāma, to spend nights apart; in fact they forage at opposite sides of a stream or pool and call constantly to each other.
Carmaṇvatī	The river Chambal, a mighty river that rises in the Vindhyas and flows north, gathering the waters of many rivers in Malwa—Śiprā, Sindhu, Nirvindhyā and smaller streams mentioned in *Meghadūtam*—to join the river Yamunā. Further, myth speaks of the innumerable sacrifices of the pious monarch Rantideva who ruled over the kingdom of Daśapura (modern Mandasor District) through which the Chambal flows, and the stream of blood of the sacrificial cows that flowed as the river.
Cātaka	The crested cuckoo, sometimes identified as the hawk-cuckoo. Because of its persistent and peculiar call, it is also known as the brain-fever bird. The cātaka is believed to subsist only on rain drops; as it disdains to drink any other water, it has become a symbol in literature of

pride and self-respect; it is associated with clouds and rain. To see a cātaka on the left is a good omen; in st.9 of *Megh.* three good omens are listed: the cātaka on the left, a gentle breeze and hen-cranes eager for mating.

Chowries — Fly-whisks and fans made of the soft hair of yaks' tails and bound and set in ornamental handles were used ceremonially for deity and royalty.

Citra-Kūta — The peak mentioned in the *Rāmāyana* as one of the places that Rāma spent his years of exile with Lakṣmaṇa and Sītā.

Crest-jewel (i) — Popular belief that the cobra had a priceless gem encrusted in its hood. Cf. Shakespeare: '. . . the toad, ugly and venomous, / wears yet a precious jewel in his head' (*As You Like It*, 2:13, 14)

Crest-jewel (ii) — The moon is depicted in iconography as Śiva's crest jewel; it might symbolize the life-sap contained in the bowl of the moon (see under, Tree of Paradise) or be a residual feature derived from the iconographical representation of an ancient horned god depicted on Indus seals (second and third millennium BC) and identified with an early form of Śiva; the bull as Śiva's mount might also be linked to this old conception and representation of deity. The moon is represented as a crescent on Śiva's topknot in iconography.

Cosmic dance — The dance of creation and destruction; the two acts are inseparable; nothing can be formed without something else being destroyed; all creative acts are acts of *trans-forming*. Everything is born and destroyed in and by Time (*Mahākāla*). The metaphor of the dance is used in Śaiva myth and metaphysics to figure the

	process of creation; dance is movement, 'a becoming' in space and time.
Dance drama	Same as the cosmic dance. *The Burning of the Triple-City* was the first drama said to have been composed by Brahmā, the Creator, and performed on Kailāsa before Śiva and Śakti by Bharata and his troupe; see Intro., p. 12.
Dakṣa	'Skill, dexterity'; the power to *fashion*; Aditi, from whom the *devas* were born and Diti from whom the *daityas* were born were his daughters; he had many other daughters—50, 27 are the figures mentioned—from whom sprang all the animals and birds. Dakṣa is therefore the Primal Parent.
Darbha	Sacred grass used in Vedic rituals (still in use in rites and ceremonies).
Daśa-pura	'Ten Cities'—modern Mandasor in western Madhya Pradesh; mentioned in the *Mahābhārata* as one of the sixteen great kingdoms—Mahā-janapada; it was probably a confederation originally, of ten city-states; at the close of the first millennium BC it was headed by a powerful dynasty of rulers.
Daśārṇa	Literally 'Ten Citadels'—the region round modern Bhopal.
Deodar	The Himalayan cedar.
Deva/Devī	The bright or shining ones; gods and goddesses of Light.
Divine Fire	Agni, the Creative Energy; The terms Sacred Fire and Mystic Fire found in the play also refer to Agni.
Dūrvā	Sacred grass, sleek and dark-green; according to Sir William Jones, its tiny flowers 'look like rubies and emeralds'.
Elephant-hide	When illusion in the form of a fierce, demonic tusker (*gaja-asura*) attacked Śiva's devotees

	(and in one variant Śiva himself), Śiva ripped the demon's hide in one clean sweep from trunk to tail and flinging the blood-moist hide over his shoulders, danced in ecstasy. The Śiva concept of godhead is a composite one and complex. One of its constituting elements is of an ancient war-god. In myth, *asuras* or demons, represent brute power, energy running rampant, unguided and uncontrolled by any higher principle, which makes it evil and destructive.
Eyebrow play	The language of coquetry.
Flower cloud	The reference is to the daily temple rituals; to lustrations with holy water and adornment of the deity with flowers as well as adoration using flower-offerings.
Flowers . . . threshold	Flowers offered daily to the divinities of the home. The threshold has sacral associations as it protects the home from the dark forces outside, waiting to enter.
Forest of uplifted arms	The multiplicity of arms represents the omnipotence and the all-embracing, protective nature of godhead. It can also be the iconic representation of many functions or elements that went into the evolution of a composite figure of divinity.
Gambhīrā	'Deep River'; an actual river in Malwa; but it is also a type of woman, a *nāyikā*, one who is high-souled and noble, strong-minded, dignified, yet loving; the opposite of the flashy and shallow woman.
Gandhavatī	'Fragrant stream'; an arm of the River Śiprā; the sacred grove of Mahā-Kāla with its shrine was located beside this stream.
Gāndharva rite	Marriage by rites of mutual love; no ceremony or consent of the family was required; it was

more or less a form of marriage reserved for warriors (Kṣatriyas), but it had to be undertaken with a full sense of the responsibilities involved. It is recognized in *Manusmṛti* as a legal marriage.

Gāṇḍīva — Arjuna's celebrated bow; the swords, clubs, bows, conches of epic heroes had special names; cf. King Arthur's sword, Excalibur.

Gangā — The Ganges is the holiest of India's great rivers and the life-giving river of the northern plains; rises in the Garhwal Himālayas and flows east into the Bay of Bengal. The river has many names; see Appendix II: Myths, for the myth of its descent from heaven.

Gaurī — 'The bright goddess'—one of the names of the mother-goddess, born of the snows of the Himālayas and hence 'Gaurī'; white, brilliant. Pārvatī, another name meaning 'mountain-born'.

Girdles — An important part of the ancient Indian woman's dress: it kept the lower garment in place like a belt but it was also ornamental. Girdles were made of gold or silver, of elaborate filigree-work or were gem-studded and had loops of little bells at the lower edge to make a sweet, tinkling sound as the woman moved around.

Glory — is described as spotlessly white in Sanskrit literature; perhaps, because royal glory is symbolized by the white chowries and umbrella.

Guardian elephants — Colossal elephants in space that guarded the eight points of the compass.

Hara — 'Remover' of illusion and ignorance; one of Śiva's epithets.

Hema-Kūta	'Golden Peak'—a name for Mt. Kailāsa.
Indra	Lord of Heaven; Chief of the Immortals; god of thunder and rain, sustainer of the universe; Indra is with Agni (Fire) the most-invoked deity in the *Ṛgveda.* He is the bountiful giver of riches, *'maghona'*. He is referred to by many names in the play *Śakuntalā,* all of which I have translated.
Indra's bow	The rainbow.
Ingudi	Hermit-tree; its nuts provided ascetics with oil for their lamps and a medicinal salve for wounds.
Jahnu's daughter	The river Gangā; Jahnu was an angry old sage who drank up the waters of the river Gangā brought down from heaven because the river's flow inundated his sacrificial grounds. Relenting, he released the river through his ear; the river is therefore considered as his offspring or daughter, born of his body.
Janaka	King of Videha with its capital Mithilā; father of Sītā of the epic *Rāmāyana.*
Kadamba or Nīpa	A large tree that blooms in the rains; the composite flowers made up of tiny tubular golden florets look like yellow balls; the styles of the florets protrude giving the flower the look of a pin-cushion.
Kailāsa	Holiest of Himālayan peaks; considered the temporal abode of Śiva and Śaktī. Nearby is the sacred lake of Mānasa or Mānasarovar. Kailāsa is described in the Purānas as the fabled mountain of priceless gems and sparkling crystal created as the playground of the divine.
Kāla-nemi	A myriad-headed demon.
Kanakhala	A hill near the gorge through which the Gangā

	rushes into the plains at Hardwar; a village of the same name is a couple of miles down river on the west bank.
Kandalī	A small plant springing up with the first heavy rains, bearing tiny purple flowers.
Karṇikāra	The golden *champa*; has large, showy, flowers with slender petals that twist and curve back; no fragrance.
Kāśa	A tall grass growing by pools and streams, seen mostly in autumn; bears long, silky plumes of pale silver; the fluff floats free like bits of cotton wool carrying tiny seeds; baskets are woven of the grass.
Ketaka, also Ketakī	Screw-pine (Pandanus); the outer leaves are a dark-green, long and tough with serrated edges, sharp as needle-points. The inner leaves are a pale gold, and sheath the creamy efflorescence, both carrying a heavy perfume. Women wear the fragrant leaves stuck in hair knots or plait them into wreaths for their chignon. An essence is made out of the young leaves and efflorescence to be used in perfumes; the essence is also used to scent drinking water, sweets and desserts.
Kimśuka	The Flame-of-the-Forest; a magnificent flowering tree; the scarlet blossoms form spikes; each flower has a curved petal forming a keel which makes it look like a parrot's beak. The word *kim-śuka,* means 'what-a-parrot' or 'what? a parrot?'; *Kim*—what? and *śuka*—parrot.
Kimpuruṣa	A class of divine beings like *yakṣas* and *kinnaras.*
Kinnara (m) Kinnari (f)	A class of divine beings like the *yakśas*; they are the celestial singers. *Kinnari*—woodland nymph.

Kovidāra	Mountain ebony; Bauhinia. The flowers are gorgeous, in colours of white, deep rose, mauve and purple. Sometimes called the Geranium lilac tree; they have no fragrance; the green buds are cooked as a vegetable. Parrots eat the flowers.
Kraunca Pass	Niti Pass; migrating birds are said to fly through it in their annual journeys between India and Central Asia.
Kubera	God of wealth and Lord of the earth's treasures; called the 'King of Kings' because he is the *yakṣa* overlord. See note on *yakṣas*.
Kurabaka	Philippine violet; or amaranth grown as ornamental hedge.
Kuru's Field	Kuru-kṣetra; some 80 miles north of Delhi: celebrated as the battle-field of the Great War in the epic *Mahābhārata* where cousins fought a bloody and bitter war for the throne. The *Gīta* was preached by Kṛṣṇa to Arjuna on the opening day of the war, on this battlefield.
Kuśa	Sacred grass, strewn on Vedic altars; a relic of ancient Indo-Iranian sacrificial ritual.
Kutaja	The tree bears five-petalled, star-shaped white flowers.
Lākṣā	Lac-juice, used to tint the palms and soles of the feet; the juice is a deep rose-red.
Laughter	Is always white in Sanskrit literature, perhaps because of the sparkling whiteness of the teeth visible when laughing.
Lodhra	Blooms in winter; the flower-petals were used to perfume wine; crushed and powdered it became face-powder for the beauties of the ancient world.
Lord of Raghus	Rāma; Raghu was the most famous ruler of the solar dynasty in which Rāma was born as Raghu's great-grandson. Kālidāsa's epic

	Raghuvamśam celebrates the fame and fortunes of the solar dynasty of Raghu.
Lord of Mountains	The Himālayas, also called 'Mountain of Snows'.
Lotus and Conch	Two of the treasures (*nidhi*) of Kubera; they were drawn on entrance doors of mansions and houses as auspicious signs to ward off evil.
Lotus	There are several varieties; those that bloom during the day touched by the sun's rays, and the night-blooming lotuses; they come in many colours; white, pink, deep rose or red, golden and deep blue; the last is really a deep purple shade.
Mādhavī	The spring-creeper, bears white flowers, like the jasmine.
Mahākāla	The name of Śiva in the shrine at Ujjain. Kāla is time; Mahākāla is time projected on to the cosmic plane. It is one of the many epithets of Śiva. The shrine of Mahākāla at Ujjain is of great antiquity; it may have originally been a cave-shrine because at present steps lead down to it. A silver serpent, symbol of Time, circles the *linga*.
Mālatī	A variety of jasmine—most varieties of jasmine bloom at night and fill the night air with their fragrance.
Mirage	The Sanskrit word is *mṛgatṛṣṇā*, the antelope's parching thirst; the poet frames a whole stanza based on the etymology of the word (*R*.:I:II); and uses it again in the play.
Mānasa	'Mind-born'; the sacred lake in the Kailāsa range; haunt of wild geese, swans and flamingos that have their breeding grounds in that region. Both Kailāsa and Mānasa being in Tibet are now in Chinese territory.
Mandāra	One of the five trees of paradise; it has been

identified with the rhododendron, native to the Himālayan valleys. In myth Mandāra flowers are unfading.

Nīcai hill — 'Low Hill'—a long row of low hills lie in the vicinity of Vidiśā (Bhilsa), near Bhopal. There are caves in these hills, some with rock-paintings from neo-lithic times; there are also carved reliefs of the Gupta period, fourth–fifth century AD in the caves.

Nicula — It may be a species of palm with succulent stems.

Nirvindhyā — The Nevaj; rises in the Vindhyas and joins the Chambal.

Pāṭalī
Pāṭala — Identified as the trumpet-tree; the pale, pink blossoms are trumpet-shaped and have a delicate fragrance; a species of Bignonia.

Peacock — The gorgeous bird is the mount of Śkanda, Śiva's emanation and a war-god; the rainy season is the time of courtship for these beautiful birds and one can hear their shrill mating-calls; therefore peacocks and clouds are closely associated in literature. Peacocks and peacock-eyes are seen on Indus valley pottery, symbolizing the human soul; they are held as sacred in many parts of the country. A natural enmity exists between it and the cobra.

Pinākī — Lord Śiva; the *pināka* is the bow that destroys evil and ignorance; the bow is also considered as Time.

Plough-bearer — Balarāma, elder brother of Kṛṣṇa; he is said to have *drawn* the river Yamunā with his plough; this implies some agricultural and irrigation activities. It refers probably to an ancient legend about a cult-hero who harnessed the river for irrigation, digging canals and nurturing agriculture, and who was later deified for

	benefiting his people. Balarāma and Kṛṣṇa are the light and dark aspects of godhead. Being associated with wine, Balarāma may also have cultivated the grape-vine.
Pravaha	Seven winds or air currents are mentioned in ancient cosmo-graphic accounts as circling in space; Pravaha is the current just above the level of clouds.
Preceptor of the Triple-World	Three aspects of Śiva are presented in these two lines—'the holy shrine. . . blue of his throat'; the wrathful, Candeśvara, to punish evil; the preceptor (Guru) to teach and guide the three worlds out of darkness into light; the Protector of the Triple-World, i.e. the universe. The three worlds are: Earth; the world of light above, of *Devas* (Immortals) or Shining Ones; the world below or the underworld. Śiva transcends these and as pure Being is beyond Time.
Priyangu	A vine with slender, dark-bluish stems; it grows into a thicket; the flowers are yellow and fragrant.
Puru	The youngest son of Yayāti of the lunar dynasty, is celebrated for the filial affection and obedience he displayed in exchanging his own youth, beauty and strength for his father's bodily decrepitude brought on by a curse. The Kings of the Paurava (Puru's) dynasty who succeeded him were expected to follow the noble ideal set up by him of putting service for others above his own interests. Puru was rewarded by ultimately succeeding his father as the 'universal monarch' (*cakra-varti*) even though he was the youngest son. King lists are provided in the *Mahābhārata* and in the Purānas of the two celebrated dynasties of India in

ancient times: the Solar and the Lunar, descended from the Sun and the Moon. Rāma, hero of the epic *Rāmāyana* belonged to the former and the heroes of Kālidāsa's two plays based on myth, Purūravas and Duhṣanta, to the latter. The poet's epic *Raghuvamśam* has the solar dynasty for its theme.

Rāma-giri — Rāma's Hill; Rāma spent part of his exile in this region with his wife Sītā and brother Lakṣmaṇa; it is identified with Ramtek, a few rules north-east of Nagpur; a place of pilgrimage; a great fair is held here in December. Its other name is 'the hill of red rock', so called because the rocks when broken are a bright red in colour; a reference to this is seen in *M.*:104.

Ranti-deva — A pious monarch, sixth in descent from Bharata, son of Śakuntalā and Duhṣanta; he is said to have performed so many sacrifices that the blood of the victims flowed as a river—the Carmaṇvatī or Chambal.

Rāvaṇa — A ten-headed demon king in the epic *Rāmāyana*, ruler of Lankā; he abducted Sītā, wife of Rāma and kept her in the Aśōka grove in his palace for a year until Rāma with his brother and a great army of monkeys and bears (obviously tribes of Central India who had monkey and bear totems) fought and killed him. Lankā is traditionally identified with the island of Ceylon (Sri Lanka), but strong arguments have been adduced to prove that Rāvaṇa was the monarch of a large and powerful Gond kingdom in Central India (MP). Rāvaṇa was a great devotee of Śiva; he tried to uproot Mt. Kailāsa with Śiva and Pārvatī on it, and carry it away and fix it in his own gardens, so as to have the sacred presence always close to him and for him alone. When the peak shook from his efforts to uproot it, Pārvatī was frightened; the Lord pressed it down with one big toe to steady it, crushing the intruder who cried for mercy. Repenting, Rāvaṇa cut off one of his ten heads and, hymned the Supreme Power, using the neck and head as a stringed instrument—a drone, in fact—to accompany his singing.

Regal Swans — *Rāja-hamsa*, in Sanskrit; literally King of Swans; it is variously identified as the flamingo, the bar-head goose and the Chinese swan; the last is the most beautiful species of swans, a pure white, with vermilion beak, orange legs and black claws; a splendid looking bird in short, deserving the title of *King of Swans.* It is a rare species.

Ritual baths — Certain ceremonies requires frequent purifying baths during their performance. The rites referred to in this stanza are those performed by the beloved for her husband's safety and speedy return. The hair was washed and knotted, but not dressed.

Revā — River Narmadā, rises in the eastern Vindhya ranges and flows right across the peninsula to fall into the Arabian Sea. The ancient port of Bhṛgu-kaccha (Broach) through which most of the extensive trade between India and Rome via Alexandria passed, was situated near the river's mouth.

Revatī — The beloved wife of Balarāma.

Rohiṇī — The bright star Aldebaran in Taurus.

Rose apple — Hindi—Jamun. A sweet fruit with a big nut, like dark cherries in size, appearance and taste.

Sagara — An ancient mythical king; see Appendix II: Myths, under myth of the Descent of the Gangā.

Sapta-parṇa or Saptacchada	'Seven-leaved'; the leaves grow in groups of seven; small pale clusters of flowers spring from the base of the leaf-whorls.
Śarabha	A fabulous creature with eight legs; probably a species of large locusts. Locusts breed in dry, desert areas and fly in swarms with the prevailing winds; it is likely that rain and thunder scatter and destroy the hordes.
Saras crane	It stands five feet tall with bluish-grey plumage; head and underfeathers are a shining red; they inhabit mostly pools and marshy places and frequent rice-fields; they have a trumpet-like call.
Sarasvatī	'Flowing waters'. The river celebrated as most sacred in the Vedas. The Vedic tribes performed their great sacrifices on its banks. The river loses itself in the sands of the Rajasthan desert. Later the word signifies the Śakti or power of Brahmā, the Creator; the name also symbolizes learning, eloquence, wisdom. Sarasvatī becomes the muse of poetry and the patron-deity of the arts. An ancient civilization, the Sārasvata, believed to have flourished in the Sarasvati Valley. Excavations are in progress.
Sarja	A timber tree; a variety of teak.
Śarmiṣṭṭā	Mother of Puru and Yayāti's queen.
Śephālikā	A tree that bears small, white, six-petalled and fragrant flowers with coral tubes and centres; the flowers bloom late in the evening and lie fallen in the morning on the ground.
Siddha holy Siddhas (plural)	'The perfected one'. Humans who through merit and yogic practices become semi-divine, gaining psychic and super human powers, known as *Siddhis*.
Siddhis	'Perfections'; eight in number: the ability to

become minute, airy and light, enormous, powerful; to attain all wishes; possess self-control; lordship and the ability to move freely at will.

Sindhu — The Kālī Sindh, a river in Malwa.

Single braid — The hair simply twisted or plaited in one braid; the sign of a woman grieving separated from her husband.

Śiprā — The river on which Ujjain is situated.

Śirīṣa — One of the loveliest of Indian flowering trees; the composite flowers are made up of tiny tubular florets, pale cream or deep rose in colour and crested with fine, long, silky filaments, the effect of which is to make the delicate flowers look like miniature power puffs.

Śiva — Literally Good, Beneficent, Auspicious. In Purānic mythology, Śiva is defined as one of the Trinity; its destructive aspect; but in Śaivism or *Śiva-ism* which in its earliest form is perhaps the earliest of the religions in the country, Śiva is the Supreme Being, the Absolute One; and Śakti, its inherent power. It should be remembered that the many names given to the divine are attributes of the unitive godhead or descriptive of its myriad functions; they are not separate gods.

Skanda — An emanation of Śiva created to fight the forces of darkness and therefore imaged as the son of Śiva and Śakti. Śiva's energy was deposited among the reeds on the banks of the River Gangā and when it assumed the form of a child, the six Pleiades nursed it; it grew in strength and size by the minute, soon assuming command of Indra's hosts, the forces of light to fight against the dark forces.

Soma-tīrtha — 'The ford of the moon'—Soma, the moon was said to have been cured of the 'wasting disease' (consumption) which afflicted him when his father-in-law Dakṣa cursed him for showing a preference for one of his twenty-seven wives (the constellations), Rohiṇī (Aldebaran) over the others. This is a myth to explain the waxing and waning of the moon. Soma-tīrtha was a famous place of pilgrimage known as Prabhāsa, in Kathiawad, near the celebrated temple of Somnath. It was believed to be the abode of 'the wind-driven fire' and therefore called the 'mouth of the gods', because all oblations to gods are offered into the Sacrificial Fire; this is implied in Priyamvadā's words to Anasūyā describing Kaṇva's felicitation of Śakuntalā (Act 4). It was probably a place where subterranean gases or vapours emerged, out of the rocks or a fissure near some natural gas deposit.

Son of the wind — Hanumān, the monkey chief who brought Rāma's message of hope with his signet ring to Sītā.

Surabhi — The celestial cow; the fabled cow of plenty.

Śyāmā — The word has three meanings: (i) a slender vine also known as Priyangu, (ii) a young woman who has borne no children, (iii) a young woman with a glowing, pale gold complexion.

Travellers — In ancient India men who travelled on business of various kinds always returned home at the onset of the rains. The rain cloud is therefore a harbinger of hope for the women waiting anxiously at home, as it heralded the return of husbands and sons.

Tree of Paradise — The wish-granting tree. In later myth five trees

(Sanskrit: *Kalpavṛkṣa*)	are described as growing in Nandana, Indra's special grove in Paradise; the bowl containing ambrosia (*Amṛta*), the drink of Immortality, was set at the base of the Tree of Paradise, on its roots; the *Kalpavṛkṣa* is the original of the Tree of Life; the bowl of *Amṛta* was guarded by a serpent, while an archer sat hid in the branches of the tree with his arrow fixed to shoot at anyone trying to steal it. The sun in the form of a golden falcon, stole the bowl, brought it down to earth in a golden boat and placed it on Mujavat, the twin peak of Kailāsa. Through a mythic labyrinth to which I have as yet not found the clue, the bowl in later literature becomes the moon which is also known as Soma; the ancients believed that the life-sap (*Soma*) dripped from the moon on plants at night and from there entered animals and man. But whereas in Paradise the gods who drank from this ever-replenished bowl were ever-young and immortal, once the ambrosia *fell*, that is descended, into the world, this was not so. The trees in Paradise had jewelled leaves, fruits and flowers.
Triple-city	The three cities of gold, silver and iron built for the Titans (anti-gods) in the sky, in the air and on earth; a spark from Śiva's third eye burnt all three to ashes. At a metaphysical level the Triple-city represents the three-fold darkness of human consciousness.
Triple-eyed god	Śiva; the third eye is the eye of inner vision of wisdom.
Triple-world	(i) Heaven the realm of light, (ii) Earth, (iii) Under world.
Udayana, the Vatsa monarch	A famous king of the sixth century BC, contemporary of the Buddha. He ruled over the Vatsa

kingdom, one of the three powerful kingdoms (with Avanti and Magadha); Kosāmbi (Kosam, near Allahabad) was his capital. A cycle of stories gathered round his fame as a hero, celebrating his exploits in love and war. He was also an accomplished musician and his lute was equally famous.

Ujjayinī — Ujjain in Madhya Pradesh; one of the greatest cities in ancient India; see Intro., p. 6. It is also one of the earliest human settlements in the country.

Vetravatī — 'River with reeds'; River Betwa near the modern town of Bhilsa not far from Bhopal.

Vidiśā — Like Ujjayinī, a great and wealthy city, capital of powerful kingdoms in ancient India; on the trade route from the Imperial capital of Pāṭalīputra to the Arabian Sea ports. The Emperor Aśoka's chief queen was the beautiful daughter of a banker of Vidiśā.

Village-shrines — Caityas, simple shrines, sometimes with a small image within and a flag on its roof were built at the base of ancient trees, especially the sacred fig tree, on a raised platform round the base of the tree trunk. A few flowers, fruit were placed there as an offering to honour the tree-spirit. Passers-by stopped to offer flowers, fruit or a few incense sticks. It is part of the *yakṣa-yakṣī* cults of ancient India. Such shrines can still be seen in central and southern India.

Viṣṇu — 'All-Pervader'; originally a sky god; therefore depicted as blue in colour. Viṣṇu, in the earliest conception is a solar deity, the sun that pervades the universe with light and heat and strides across the sky, 'the wide-stepping second stride'. Viṣṇu is believed to be immersed for four months (mid-August to mid-Novem-

	ber) in *yoga-nidrā*, the sleep of contemplation.
Wheel	The water-wheel or Persian wheel; a number of buckets or metal containers were attached to its rim to draw water out of pools and streams.
War of the barons	The *Mahābhārata* war; it is the theme of the epic.
Wearer of the crescent-moon	Śiva
White Bull	Nandi, Śiva's mount.
Yakṣa	Pre-Brahmanic divinities of the ancient people of the country, replaced by Vedic and Purānic gods and fitted into the pantheon in subordinate positions; originally forces of nature and indwelling spirits of trees and pools they were associated with fertility and plenitude. They were worshipped as givers of life and riches. Kubera was their overlord, lord of all the earth's treasures; later assigned the position of regent of the north. Śiva himself probably a pre-Vedic deity is invoked as 'the lord in a *yakṣa*-form'. The Purānas place Kubera's kingdom in the trans-Himālayan region; he is sovereign over many *yakṣa*-rulers whose cities were wealthy, possessing splendid mansions and beautiful gardens—a kind of Earthly Paradise.
Yamunā	River Jamna; one of the three great rivers of the northern Indian plains; it joins the Gangā at Allahabad; the confluence is a very sacred spot. Delhi is situated on the banks of the Yamunā.
Yayāti	Father of Puru and possibly the first 'universal monarch'.
Yuthikā	A large, fragrant variety of jasmine.

born in yoga-nidra, the sleep of contemplation.

Wheel The water-wheel or Persian wheel: a number of buckets or metal containers were attached to its rim to draw water out of pools and streams.

War of the barons The Mahabharata war; it is the theme of the epic.

Wearer of the crescent moon Siva

White Bull Nandi, Siva's mount.

Yaksa Pre-Brahmanic divinities of the ancient people of the country, replaced by Vedic and Puranic gods and slipped into the pantheon in subordinate positions. Originally forces of nature and indwelling spirits of trees and pools they were associated with fertility and plenitude. They were worshipped as givers of life and riches. Kubera was their overlord, lord of all the earth's treasures; later assigned the position of regent of the north. Siva himself, probably a pre-Vedic deity, is invoked as 'the lord in a yaksa-form'. The Puranas place Kubera's kingdom in the trans-Himalayan region; he is sovereign over many yaksa-rulers whose cities were wealthy, possessing splendid mansions and beautiful gardens — a kind of Earthly Paradise.

Yamuna River Jamna; one of the three great rivers of the northern Indian plains; it joins the Ganga at Allahabad; the confluence is a very sacred spot. Delhi is situated on the banks of the Yamuna.

Yayati Father of Puru and possibly the first 'universal' monarch.

Yuthika A large, fragrant variety of jasmine.

Appendix I: Kālidāsa's Dates

To date old texts and ancient writers always pose several problems and in the case of a writer as reticent about himself and his work as Kālidāsa it is not possible to provide accurate and definite dates with the scanty facts we possess at this time. To say that the upper limit might be placed at AD 473, the date of the Mandasor inscription by one Vatsabhatti which reveals some indebtedness to Kālidāsa's poem *Ṛtusamhāram* (*The Seasons*), and the lower limit a few centuries lower than that date, is not very helpful.

To speak of a sense of the poet's writings in general as pointing to a particular period in Indian history, viz. the Gupta period, or to a particular king's reign, Chandra Gupta II (AD 375–414) is by no means proof of conclusive evidence. Franklin Edgerton[1] makes a very valid point about the subjectivity underlying such conclusions. We cannot say with any certainty that the opulence and splendour or the peace and prosperity of the Gupta period is reflected in Kālidāsa's work. The manner in which a writer's work relates itself to its age and times is complex. The ominous shadow of the French Revolution with its consequences writ large in history hardly falls on the pages of Jane Austen's novels. Kālidāsa's plays and poems move in many worlds—mythic, epic and historic. Do the descriptions of Alakā reflect the splendour of cities—Ujjayinī, Vidiśā, Pātalīputra—of the Gupta period, or of an earlier period? Are they in part allusive of epic descriptions of the splendours of Indraprastha, Ayodhya and Lanka? Raghu's 'conquest of the quarters' (*digvijaya*) may or may not be inspired by Samudra Gupta's similar conquest in the early fourth century AD, but the conquests of the Pāndava brothers as detailed in the *Mahābhārata* are certainly part of the literary consciousness of the poet's epic, *Raghuvamśam* (*Raghu's Dynasty*).

Tradition holds that Kālidāsa was the court-poet of Vikramāditya who ruled at Ujjain; a king who was a great conqueror and hero, a munificent patron of the arts, learned, wise and accomplished; a king who embodied the ideal of kingship in himself; who drove the invading Śakas out of Malwa presumably and established the Vikrama or Samvat (still used) era, in 57 BC to commemorate his victory. Story-cycles have gathered round his name and fame: the *Vetālapancavimśati* (*Twenty-five Tales of the Goblin*), *Vikramāditya-Charitra* (*Life and Stories of Vikramāditya*). Such story-cycles centre round the name of many ancient kings such as the Emperor Aśoka and Udayana, King of the Vatsas, who ruled at Kauśāmbi during the time of Gautama Buddha, in the sixth century BC. We find a reference to the Udayana-tales in *Meghadūtam* (32). None has been as popular and widespread in the country as the Vikramāditya stories. But historicity has been denied to this Vikramāditya by some scholars who relegate him to the realm of legend and romance.[2]

The name, Vikramāditya which appears to have been the personal name of an ancient king, legendary or historic, occurs frequently in history. Three kings of that name ruled at Ujjayinī at various times; one of the most famous was Yaśodharman of Malwa who defeated the Huns in the sixth century AD. Some rulers assumed the name Vikramāditya, meaning The Sun of Valour, as a title representative of their heroic exploits and achievements as rulers, the most celebrated of these in history being Chandra Gupta II. Other great rulers have been identified with the Vikramāditya of tradition, such as Gautamī-putra Śātakarni (first century AD) the greatest of the Śātavahana emperors, who is recorded to have been a very handsome man, a great conqueror and a just and compassionate ruler, the qualities attributed to the traditional Vikramāditya. But this identification has also been disputed. The question is to determine which of the many Vikramādityas that history parades was the patron of Kālidāsa. Who is the *real* Vikramāditya?

Western Sanskritists after Sir William Jones and beginning with A.B. Keith, favour the identification of the Gupta emperor, Chandra Gupta II, as *the* Vikramāditya, patron of Kālidāsa, and place the poet accordingly in the fourth–fifth century AD. But this is open to challenge.

Kālidāsa's patron is identified by some scholars[3] as King Vikramāditya, son of Mahendrāditya of the Pramara dynasty ruling at Ujjain in the first millennium BC. This dynasty belonged to the Malwas mentioned in history as one of the clans following a republican form of government. It has also been suggested that the description of the Asura Tāraka and his evil forces in Kālidāsa's long poem *Kumārasambhavam*, is a veiled reference[4] to the invading Śakas[5] who were then in occupation of Sind and were pushing into Malwa. This would be at the close of the first millennium BC and accord with the first century BC date of 57 BC for the poet and of his association with the Vikramāditya who defeated the Śakas.

Another veiled reference in the epic, *Raghuvamśam* is seen as evidence of a first century BC date for the poet. Devabhūti, the last of the Śunga emperors, who was a weak and dissolute monarch, was assasinated in his bed in the dark by a slave girl dressed as his queen; he is taken as the model for Agnivarṇa the last of the rulers with whom Raghu's dynasty came to an ignoble end, who was also a weak, self-indulgent and dissolute monarch as Kālidāsa portrays him in the last chapter of the epic; and he seems to have died also in suspicious circumstances though the epic itself speaks of a wasting disease as the cause of his death.[6] This dating places Kālidāsa at the close of the first millennium BC; Devabhūti ascended the throne in 82 BC and was assasinated in 73 BC on the orders of his minister Vāsudeva[7] who proclaimed himself emperor establishing the Kaṇva dynasty.

One of the three dates put forward for Kālidāsa places the poet in the second century BC during the period of the Śunga Empire (182–73 BC) and makes him the court-poet of Agnimitra Śunga, son of Puṣyamitra Śunga, the emperor, ruling at Pātalīputra, the ancient capital of the northern empires of India. Agnimitra was his father's viceroy for the western part of the empire ruling with the title of Mahārāja at Ujjayinī which had been the second and western capital from Mauryan times. Kālidāsa's first play *Mālavikāgnimitram* is about this monarch and has for its theme the romance between him and Mālavikā, princess of Vidharba (Berar). Certain historical events that are referred to in the play relate to the two main power struggles of the period: the conflict in the north-western region of the empire with the Bactrian Greeks and the struggle for control over the southern boundaries against the expanding power of the Śātavahanā empire in the south. In the last act of the play certain interesting facts are contained in a letter from the emperor to his son Agnimitra that might have some bearing on the problem of Kālidāsa's dates. Puṣyamitra refers to himself in the letter as *Senāpati* (Commander-in-chief) writing from 'within the sacred enclosure of the Horse-Sacrifice (*Rāja-Sūya Yajna*), already consecrated for its performance' and invites his son and daughter-in-law to the ceremony requesting them to 'attend without delay' and 'setting aside all feelings of anger' (*vigata-roṣa-chetasah*). Now, this is a curious phrase that indicates that relations were somewhat strained between the emperor and his son. We know from Śunga coins unearthed in this century, that the Śunga emperors used their hereditary title of Senāpati or Senāni even though Puṣyamitra had performed two Horse-Sacrifices to legitimize and signify his accession to the throne at Pātalīputra after he had assassinated the last Mauryan emperor in public. The Śungas had been hereditary commanders-in-chief of the Imperial Mauryan armies. It is somewhat extraordinary that a poet who lived and wrote more than 500 years after the events referred to here, which would be the case if Kālidāsa were to be placed in the fourth–fifth century AD as many Western and some Indian Sanskritists do, should refer to the small details contained in the letter, particularly to the fact of the strained relations between Agnimitra and his father. As Indians of the past are alleged to be sadly lacking in the historical sense (in the Western sense of the term) this would be even more extraordinary. The letter itself is not structurally important in the play, *Mālavikāgnimitram*; it serves to glorify the future emperor, Vasumitra, 'the mighty bowman', son of Agnimitra who had defeated the Greek cavalry that had captured the sacred horse on the banks of the river Sindhu after bitter fighting and brought back that 'king of horses' to his grandfather. Vasumitra is glorified in the passage by a comparison to Amśumat, a mythic hero who had also released the sacrificial horse of his grandfather, Sagara, from captivity and brought it back to the sacrificial enclosure. A fallout of Vasumitra's bravery in his fierce encounter with invading Bactrian Greeks is that his mother, Queen Dhāriṇī, is assured of her position as Chief Queen, even though Mālavikā had taken the King's affections away from her. The introduction of the letter into the play therefore seems to suggest a reference to events that were either contemporaneous with the dramatist or within living memory.

Considering these facts, viz. the letter in the last act of the play, *Mālavikāgnimitram*; the striking resemblance between the events in the life and death of Agnivarṇa in the poet's epic poem and the last Śunga emperor, Devabhūti; and the veiled references to the Śakas that are perceived in canto 2 of *Kumārasambhavam*, where the Immortals pray for deliverance from the atrocities of the Asura Tāraka, it is plausible to argue that Kālidāsa lived and wrote at the close of either the middle of the second or the first century BC.

Claims have been made that the feel and tone of Gupta art of the fourth–fifth century AD indicate that it was contemporaneous with the great poet and dramatist. A strong case can be equally made out that the flowering in stone of the art of the Śunga-Śātavāhana period (second century BC to second century AD) reflects the flowering in the verbal arts of Kālidāsa's poetry. The great friezes of Bharhut and Sanci and the carvings on the great gateways of the stupa in the latter reveal that same juxtaposition of the natural and human worlds seen in Kālidāsa's poetry, rendered in loving detail and exactitude, but stylized (Sanci—north gate, lowest beam).[8] In Bharhut and Sanci and in the very recently unearthed Sanghol sculptures in red sandstone belonging to the Mathura School, are carved *yakṣis* and *vṛkṣikas* (tree-nymphs) standing under flowering trees and vines, embracing them, leaning against them, clasping flowering sprays, kicking a tree with the left foot[9] ornamented with anklets or holding a wine cup in one hand. We see a beautiful example of the former motif in the figure of the *yakṣi* (unfortunately mutilated) who adorns the East Gate bracket at Sanci; she seems to be swinging gracefully in space, kicking the tree (probably an Aśoka) with her left foot loaded with anklets, and clasping a flowering spray with her left hand, while the right is turned around another blossoming branch hanging down.[10] This sculptured beauty reminds us of the beloved in *Meghadūtam* (74) standing next to the Mandara tree she had nurtured and whose clusters of blossoms 'bend . . . within reach of her hand', like a son bowing in respect to a mother and offering her flowers as a gift. The latter motif referred to, of lovely women holding a wine cup in their hands, perhaps to sprinkle the Kesara tree with the wine from their mouths to make it bloom (again the dohada-idea, also referred to in the poem, st. 77) is sculpted in the Sanghol figures. A flowering in stone depicting the teeming energies of nature delineated and placed side by side with curving voluptuous figures of women with swelling breasts—a symbol of the maternal—and a smile and inscrutable look on their faces that seem to convey their awareness of their own youth, beauty and power to enchant men, it can be perceived as parallelling the flowering in verse of that age. Kālidāsa often uses the word '*pramadā*' to convey this self-conscious feeling of young women exulting in their youth and beauty. The *yakṣis* and *devatās* of Bharhut, the Mathura *yakṣī*[11] and the Sanghol figures[12] (also belonging to the Mathura school, though found near Chandigarh) are all *pramadās* with that same inscrutable smile and look as if all lit within with happiness (*Ṛtu.*: 3:20); lovely women aware of and exulting in their own youth and beauty. A close-up of one of these lovely *yakṣis*,[13] is that of Chūlakoka at Bharhut, displaying intricate patterns drawn with sandal paste on her cheeks; she reminds us of the lady in *Ṛtu.*: 6.7. In the Sanghol group we also find a depiction of young women intent on looking at themselves in a mirror and adorning themselves (*Ṛtu.*: 4:13–16) and consciously exulting in their husbands' love for them. A *yakṣa-yakṣi* couple[14] seated in a rocky niche (she is seated on his lap) and a deer (?) on one side, are chiselled behind a pair of jugate peacocks, with a melting tenderness in their faces as if lost in love for each other. A definite feeling of kinship, of unity of the arts is evident. Needless to say, that conclusions of this nature can only be drawn tentatively; we have, as already noted, no definite proof of the poet's dates.

In the final analysis, Kālidāsa's 'dates' are perhaps not that important. Fixing them might bring the satisfaction that solving a mathematical problem which has teased one into deep thought might; but does it add at all to the understanding of the poet's consummate art or enhance in any way the appreciation of his poetry to vex our minds with this problem, when the time and thought spent on it could be more profitably used in exploring the complexities of his works? The poet himself has chosen not to reveal anything about his life and work. So we might as well leave it at that.

Names and dates in ancient Indian history can be bewildering; the following note and table should be of some help.

Of the sixteen great kingdoms (*mahā-janapadas*) mentioned in the epic, Magadha with its capital at Rājagṛha (very close to the later capital of Pātalīputra—Patna), emerged as the most powerful around 600 BC. The sixth century BC is very important in ancient history, politically and culturally, because it saw not only the rise of Magadha (Bihar) as a power well on its way to becoming an empire, but also the rise of Jainism and Buddhism founded by Mahāvīra and Gautama Buddha as rival religions and systems of thought to Vedic Brahmanism. The empire under Chandra-gupta Maurya (325–298 BC) and his grandson Aśoka the Great (273–236 BC) included almost all of India, excepting the deep south and extended into Afghanistan and up to Khotan. The capital of the northern empire was at Pātalīputra and later, at Ujjayinī; Chandra Gupta II is mentioned as having shifted his capital from Ujjayinī to Ayodhyā which was more central. But there seemed to have always been four capitals to facilitate the administration of a farflung empire with princes of the royal blood in charge and Ujjayinī had been the western capital from very early times.

In the south the Śātavāhana rulers who are believed to have originated in Mahārașțra (some historians think that they belonged to Āndhra-deśa and that they are the Āndhras mentioned in late Vedic texts prior to 600 BC), with their capital at Pratișțțāṇa (near Aurangābad) gradually spread east consolidating their power in the peninsula, excepting the traditional Chola-country in the deep south. Their kingdom grew into an empire (third century BC to third century AD).

The two powers, as was inevitable, met and clashed along the River Narmadā (Kālidāsa's Revā) and the encounter of their armies is referred to in Kālidāsa's *Mālavikāgnimitram* (Act 5).

We can see that the descriptive phrase that Kālidāsa uses with reference to his heroes, 'rulers of the earth' (the world known to the ancients) 'from sea to sea', i.e. the eastern and western oceans bounding India may apply equally to the Śunga, Śātavāhana and Gupta emperors. The mythic rulers in his plays, Purūravas and Duhșanta actually ruled over a very small part of the country between the rivers Sindhu (Indus) and Sarasvatī-Dṛṣadvatī, celebrated in the *Ṛgveda.* Hastināpura across the river from Delhi was founded by Hasti, the King descended from Bharata, son of Duhșanta. The line of descent in the lunar dynasty is as given on page 314.

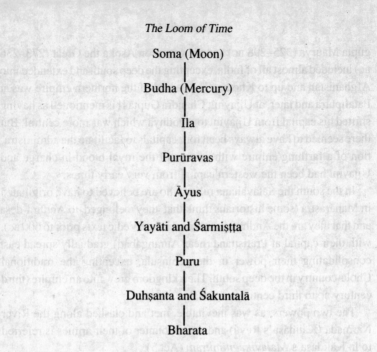

Soma (Moon)
|
Budha (Mercury)
|
Ila
|
Purūravas
|
Āyus
|
Yayāti and Śarmiṣṭa
|
Puru
|
Duhṣanta and Śakuntalā
|
Bharata

Approximate dates: Second century BC to fifth century AD (as having a bearing on Kālidāsa's dates)

Mauryan Empire: 325-187 BC; the last emperor was assassinated in public by Puṣyamitra Śunga, C-in-C, at a review of the Imperial armies.

Śunga: 187-72 BC — Śātavāhana (Andhra) Empire—third century BC–third century AD

Puṣyamitra	187-149 BC	
Agnimitra	149-141 BC	
Vasumitra	133-128 (?) BC	
Three kings		Gautamī-putra Śātakarni 70 (?)–AD 95
Devabhūti	assassinated in 72 BC	

Śaka rule; rule of Śaiva Kings, Bhara Sivas and Nāgas and Śātavāhana emperors in Malwa and the surrounding regions—'the Kālidāsa-country'; followed by Gupta rule fourth to sixth century AD.

Imperial Guptas

Samudra Gupta	AD 335–375
Chandra Gupta II	AD 375–414
Kumāra Gupta	AD 415–455

Appendix II: Myths

The Descent of the River Gangā

Gangā is a river-goddess. Flowing originally in heaven, and therefore called Svar-Gangā (M: 45), the Heavenly Gangā, the river was brought down to earth by the severe penances of Bhagīratha, great-grandson of the mythic monarch Sagara.

Sagara wishing to attain the title of universal monarch arranged to perform a Horse-Sacrifice. Consecrating the right horse he loosed it to wander free all over the earth, guarded by his sixty thousand sons. The roaming of a sacrificial horse for a year, symbolized the sovereignty of a monarch over all the lands the horse wandered unchallenged. Indra, Lord of Heaven, jealous of the power and glory that Sagara would gain by the successful completion of the sacrifice and afraid that the King might seek for dominion in heaven itself, carried the horse away and left it to graze in the underworld near the hermitage of Kapila, a mighty sage who having adopted a vow of complete silence was performing austerities.

Searching high and low on earth and not finding the horse, the sixty thousand princes went down into the underworld and seeing Kapila asked if he had seen their father's sacrificial horse. When annoyed by the sage's silence they insulted him, Kapila opened his eyes in anger and burnt them all to ashes. After waiting for several years, the old king sent his eldest grandson Amsumat in search; Amsumat recovered the horse and brought back news that the ashes of his uncles were lying unconsecrated for want of the proper funeral rites and that only the holy waters of the heavenly river could purify them so that their souls would go to heaven. His son Bhagīratha undertook the task of bringing Gangā to earth, performing hundreds of years of severe penance in the Himālaya mountains, until the goddess, pleased, agreed to come down, if someone could support her fall so that its force would not shatter the earth's surface and destroy all life. Nobody could be found fit to do this except Śiva, who, as the Lord of Beings, possessed the power to support Gangā's descent. Bhagīratha went back to the mountains to perform more austerities, this time to please Śiva. Śiva agreed to bear the river on his head and let her flow down gently on to the earth. But Gangā exulting in her own power fell on Śiva's head with such force that the god, infuriated, bound her up in his matted locks (*M*: 52). Bhagīratha left his kingdom and once more began a series of penances to make Śiva relent, and succeeded. The great god unbound one of his locks to allow part of the river to flow down gently. Chastened, Gangā followed Bhagīratha to where the unconsecrated ashes of his ancestors lay in the underworld in a pile. But that was not the end of Bhagīratha's trials and tribulations. On her way, the river inundated the sacrificial grounds of another irascible sage, Jahnu, who was performing sacrificial rites at that moment, and was swallowed up in one mouthful by him. It was yet another bout of hardship and penance for Bhagīratha. The sage, pleased with his dedication and loyalty to the family, relented and let the river out through one ear. Hence the river was reborn as it were, as the daughter of Jahnu (*M*: 52). Her waters inundated and purified the ashes of Sagara's sixty thousand sons, who were then able to reach heaven (*M*: 52). The huge concourse of waters formed the deep ocean and to honour Sagara, it was named, Sāgara, after him. And to honour that long-suffering and pious monarch, Bhagīratha, Gangā was named, Bhāgirathī. The name is still used for one of the three Himālayan rivers that join to form the great river Gangā, before it comes bursting through the gorge at Hardvar (the gateway of Hara or Śiva). The other two rivers are known as Mandākinī and Alaka-nandā (*M*: 65). Gangā is described as triple-streamed (*S*: 7: 6) because one stream still flows in heaven, one on earth and the third in the underworld.

Bali and Viṣṇu's Triple-Stride

Aditi and Diti were sisters, daughters of Dakṣa, both married to Kaśyapa, the Primal Parent. Their sons were for ever fighting for supremacy over the universe. The sons of Aditi were the Devas or gods, Immortals, with Indra as their overlord; the sons of Diti were Daityas, Titans or anti-gods. Bali was a famous Daitya king, who through devotion and penance had defeated Indra in battles, humbled the gods and extended his dominion the over the Triple-World. He was virtuous, a just ruler and magnanimous to a fault; no one who came to him asking for alms went away empty-handed. The gods and Indra were disconsolate; Aditi, their mother wept in sorrow at their pitiable state and prayed to Viṣṇu, who out of compassion for her promised to be born as her son, Vāmana (dwarf) to humble Bali and restore their pristine glory to her sons (*Śak*. 7.27).

Bali once performed a great sacrifice on the banks of the river Narmadā and gave wealth in crores, and lands and gifts to any one who came to him pleading need and distress. Vāmana arrived there and asked for some land just sufficient to cover three strides. Bali, though warned by his Preceptor, readily agreed. The dwarf put his foot out, grew in size and covered the whole earth in one stride. Growing enormously in size, he covered the whole of the heavens with a second stride, standing poised with uplifted foot to take the third and final stride. Bali, to keep his word meekly bent down and offered his head, saying 'This is all I have left, O All-Pervading Lord (Viṣṇu).' Viṣṇu-Vāmana put his foot on Bali's bowed head and pushed him down to Pātāla. In later mythological accounts, Pātāla signifies the nether world and Bali, therefore, became the King of the nether world. But, *Pātāla* was a big port in the estuary of the river Indus which together with *Broach* at the mouth of the Narmadā handled the extensive trade between India and the Mediterranean lands—Alexandria, Rome and earlier with Greece. A war of two peoples seems to underlie this mythological tale of two peoples or two great confederations of tribes who fought for the land between the Himālayas and the river Narmadā in the peninsula.

A solar myth is also involved in this tale. Viṣṇu—literally, All-Pervader—was originally the sun (*Ṛgveda*). The triple-stride represents the path of the sun across the sky with three clearly marked stations: dawn, noon, sunset. Vāmana, the dwarf, is the early morning sun that grows and waxes in power and pervades the whole universe, except the nether world (the antipodes), which then became Bali's realm or darkness. Obviously this myth belongs to the period in proto-history when the earth was conceived of as flat, prior to the round-earth theory (earth as a sphere) suggested in parts of the *Ṛgveda*.

Churning of the Ocean

In the Beginning, Devas and Asuras (or Daityas), gods and anti-gods strove to obtain *Amṛta*, the elixir of immortality (the water of life). Viṣṇu advised them to throw in bits of all the great medicinal herbs into the Milky Ocean (Milky Way in the space-ocean) and churn it, using the cosmic mountain, Mandara as the stick, and Vāsuki, the serpent Time, as the rope. After great toil many wondrous things emerged out of the frothing ocean. First rose Surabhi, the cow of plenty, who granted all wishes to the good; then Vāruṇi, Wine; third, the Tree of Paradise emerged, bearing innumerable, unfading flowers, whose fragrance perfumed the whole world; then rose the *Apsarās* in all their beauty; followed by the cool-rayed moon that Śiva placed as a crest jewel on his topknot of matted locks. The ocean then spewed out deadly poison that Śiva immediately swallowed to preserve the universe, retaining it in his throat which turned blue-black. Beauty (Sri) herself, seated on a lotus then rose in glory and was followed by the archetypal physician Dhanvantari holding the bowl containing the Water of Life (*Amṛta*) in his hands. The story continues with the fierce battle for the *Amṛta* and the stratagem of Viṣṇu, by which only the Devas (gods) got to taste the ambrosia and gained immortality, the Daityas or Asuras being defeated.

The lotus is the symbol of the blossoming world that rose out of the still waters of the space-ocean. There are contradictions and inconsistencies in the many versions of the basic myths of *origins*, because they are layered, with different strands coming out of several ethno-cultural sources that reflect the heterogeneity of the people and the cultures that made up India and her civilization in the past. They are all fitted together to form a rich mythological mosaic but the joints sometimes show.

Appendix III: Sources for the Play

***Śakuntalā and Duṣyanta: Mahābhārata*: Book 1: chs 62–69**

The bard Vaiśampāyana tells this story to the monarch Janamejaya, descendant of Bharata, at the Great Sacrifice that the monarch was performing.

Duṣyanta,* out on a great hunt, arrived at Kaṇva's Hermitage, deep in the forests by the river Mālinī, to pay his respects to the revered sage. There he met Śakuntalā who was alone, her father having gone out of the hermitage to gather fruit. She offered the King due hospitality and in response to his questions about herself, told him the story of her birth as she had heard it from her 'father's own lips'. The Apsarā Menakā, had abandoned her as soon as she was born and some birds (*śakunta*) taking pity on the new-born babe had protected and fed it, until Kaṇva found the child and brought it up as his own daughter.

The King enamoured of Śakuntalā's uncommon beauty and grace, wanted to marry her according to the Gāndharva mode of marriage—a recognized form of marriage based on love and mutual agreement. Śakuntalā demurred, asking him to wait for her father's return, 'When my father returns, O King, he will himself give me to you.' But the infatuated Duṣyanta wanted to marry her instantly and began persuading her that according to the Law, she had complete right over herself and did not need parental permission to dispose of herself. Śakuntalā replied that if it was not against the Law, she would become his wife on one condition, that the son born to her would be the heir-apparent and succeed him as King. The King agreed and took her as his wife, and then left for his capital promising to send for her with the proper retinue accompanied by a detachment of his army. Kaṇva on his return to the Hermitage soon after was pleased, and

* Same as Duhṣanta. Duṣyanta is the form used in the Mahābhārata.

felicitated Śakuntalā on her excellent choice of a husband. But Duṣyanta, apprehensive about how the sage Kaṇva would react to this union contracted during his brief absence from the Hermitage did not send for her.

A son was born, blazing like fire; years went by until Kaṇva noticing the extraordinary strength and energy that the boy displayed, advised Śakuntalā that it was time to take him to his father and get him consecrated as the heir-apparent, and sent her with her son in the company of some hermits to the capital. Śakuntalā arriving at Duṣyanta's palace had herself announced, and having duly honoured him, presented her son to him. 'Here, O King, is the son, resembling a god, born of your strength; now accept him and carry out the promise you made.'

Duṣyanta, although he remembered his promise and every detail of their meeting and marriage, pretended to remember nothing and in the cruellest and most insulting words asked her to take her boy and get out.

Śakuntalā, shattered by Duṣyanta's treatment of her, stood dumbfounded, but being a girl of great spirit and courage decided to fight for her son's rights. Even though she could have destroyed him by the power of her penance, she remained calm and explained the Law to him and laid out what his duties and obligations were under the Law to her and his son. Seeing that all her arguments were of no avail, she flung these last words at him, that she would not have anything to do with a man like him, but that in the end her son would be sovereign, and prepared to leave. At that point, an aerial voice spoke testifying to the truth of Śakuntalā's words and demanded that the King keep his promise to her. The nobles, ministers and priests at the Court heard the aerial voice and accepted its testimony. Relieved, Duṣyanta welcomed her with costly gifts and received her and his son with honour, making Śakuntalā Queen and consecrating the boy as heir-apparent.

The story ends with Duṣyanta explaining to Śakuntalā as to why he had acted as he did. The marriage having been a secret one, unwitnessed, his ministers and people would have doubted the legality of the marriage and the legitimacy of the prince. 'I forgive you all the unpleasant words you spoke to me, my beloved, because I love you,' he says welcoming her and accepting his son as the heir.

Appendix IV: Interpolated Stanzas

The following verses, not included in the Bharata Mallika text of *Meghadūtam*, are found in Mallinātha's text:

1

Countless pearl-garlands
with lustrous gems flashing at the centres,
conches, mother-of-pearl and coral branches,
emeralds green as young grass
with fiery rays of light shooting up, lie
spread out for sale in Ujjayinī's marts.
Seeing, one wonders if the oceans lie
bereft of all its treasures save their waters.

2

Here, in this city,
the Vatsa-monarch carried off
King Pradyota's beloved daughter:
and here, in this very spot
stood that same king's grove
of golden palm-trees:
here too, his elephant, proud Nalagiri
crazed with frenzy
tore up
its strong tying-post
to run wild—
thus recounting old tales
skilful story-tellers entertain their visiting kin.

Mallinātha places these two stanzas after st. 33; the verses that follow are part of his *Uttaramegham*, the Alakā-section of the poem and he places them after st. 68. These six stanzas, part of the Alakā-section of *Meghadūtam* are not found in all recensions; some old commentators considered some or all of them, interpolations.

Where the hum of intoxicated honey-bees
fill the ever-blossoming trees;
Where rows of wild-geese like jewelled girdles stretch
across pools ever full of lotus-blooms;
where garden-peacocks whose trains ever gleam
resplendent, raise their necks up to call:
where evenings are beautiful, always bright
with moonlight keeping darkness at bay.

Where tears are shed only from an excess of joy,
and no other cause; where pain is caused
only by the God of Love's arrows of flowers,
easily assuaged by union with the beloved;
where parting comes only through lovers' little quarrels:
Indeed! Do the lords of wealth know
of no other time of life than youth?

Where maidens sought for as brides by gods
and waited upon by breezes cooled
by Mandākinī's waters, shaded from the heat
by Mandāra-trees growing on her banks,
play hide-and-seek with gems held tight in fists
thrust deep into her golden sands.

Where Yakṣas with inexhaustible treasure-troves
enjoy banquets each day accompanied
by Apsarās, choicest courtesans,
in the Gardens of Light in Alakā's outskirts,
while Kinnaras sing of the glories of the Lord of Wealth
in high, sweet voices.

An array of richly-dyed cloths,
wine that expertly instructs lovely eyes in graceful play;
sprays of blossoms bursting out of tender shoots,
varied jewels, decorations,
glowing juices worthy of tinting red
the soles of lotus-feet; all things of adornment
for lovely women are brought forth
solely by the Tree of Paradise.

Where horses sleek, glossy, dark, as Palāśa-leaves
rival those that draw the chariot of the sun,
and elephants massive as mountains,
drip streams of rut that pour like your rain;
where the foremost warriors steadfastly face
ten-faced Rāvaṇa in battle fierce—
the scars of their wounds, his gleaming scimitar made
put to shame the lustre of jewels they wear.

Notes and References

Introduction

1. The Vāg-Sūktam or hymn of the *Word* is one of the great poems of *Origins* in the Vedas; in it *Vāc* or *Vāk*, the creative Word (also meaning speech, voice), announces herself (the word is in the feminine) and speaks in images that combine power and beauty, of bringing the universe into being and establishing communion between human and divine. *Vāc* is the *Śakti* or inherent power of the creator as envisaged in the *Ṛgveda*.

2. *Anon*: The Sanskrit word for the ring finger is *a-nāmikā* (the nameless).

3. Bāṇa Bhatta, lived and wrote in the seventh century AD.

4. Kumarila Bhatta, the philosopher, AD 590–650 quotes two lines from *Śakuntalā*:1:20, in his *Tantra-vārtika*; cited in Nandargikar's edition of *Meghadūtam*, 1893, Intro., p. 31.

5. The Aihole inscription AD 634 of Pulikesena II, the powerful Chalukyan monarch who ruled over what is now Maharāṣṭra; the poet is here mentioned by name.

6. AV. 19:53, 54.

7. Śiva is the silence. Quoted from Śaiva sacred texts; see I. P. Radhakrishnan, vol II, p. 727.

8. *Vāc* is later personified as Sarasvatī (flowing waters), goddess of wisdom and eloquence and the patron deity of the arts. In the Vedas, the *waters* are the infinitude of potentialities which is the origin of the universe, the space-ocean that forms the waters of creation.

9. 'The seers with wisdom searching within / discovered the bond of being in non-being.' *RV*. 10:129:4.

10. 'Let us in well-wrought songs proclaim the origin of the gods / that may be seen when chanted in the ages to come.' *RV*. 10:71:1.

11. 'I reveal the Father at the World's highest peak.' *RV*. 10:125:7.

12. *Kalpanā*, the poetic imagination, is the reflection of *Māyā*, the cosmic imagination; *Māyā* derived from the root 'mā', 'to form, measure, display', is the shaping power of the Supreme.

13. The caves in the low hills near Bhilsa (Vidiśā) and on the way to Sanci contain ancient rock-paintings and sculptured reliefs.

14. The Gangā was an important waterway with fleets of barges carrying merchandise up to Indra-prastha (Delhi) which was the last ford.

15. Rām: *Sundara Kandam*: canto 7.

16. *Harṣa-charitram*: ch. 6. See p. 192 of trans. by Cowell and Thomas.

17. Veda is literally wisdom; the Vedic texts are regarded as revelation.

18. *RV*. 10:108.

19. *RV*. 10:95.

20. *RV*. 10:125.

21. *RV*. 7:86.

22. *RV*. 10:100; the refrain is: 'For our boon we ask for felicity full and boundless.' And in 10:134: 'The glorious Mother gave you birth, / the blessed Mother gave you birth'.

23. D.D. Kosambi, *The Culture and Civilization of Ancient India*, p. 199.

24. A.B. Keith, *The Sanskrit Drama*, pp. 36, 37.

25. *NS*. 1:44.

26. *NS*. 4:9,10.

27. *NS*. 4:13,14.

28. *Sūta* in Sanskrit.

29. Kuśī-lavas are bards, singers, actors.

30. These recitations have continued right to this day, performed in temples and village squares; the Sanskrit texts are explained in the vernaculars and the message expounded in simple language, and often accompanied by music and dance; such recitals are called Hari-Kathā or Kathā-Kalakṣepa. In Madhya Pradesh, the Pandavani is a re-telling by one or more persons with musical and drum accompaniments, of episodes from the Pāndava story in the epic *Mahābhārata*.

31. Indus Valley Civilization, circa 3000 BC; the figures are housed in the National Museum, Delhi.

32. Matthew Arnold writes in *The Function of Criticism*, p. 4. (Every-

man's): '. . . for the creation of a master-work of literature, two powers must concur, the power of the man and the power of the moment.'

33. *Bharata-Nātya-Manjarī*, G.K. Bhat, Intro., pp. liii–liv and *NS.* 2: 76–80.

34. The Woman-tree motif has a continuous history in Indian art and literature; beginning with the Indus Valley goddess amid the leaves of a tree, through the art of Bharhut, Sanci, Mathura and the recently excavated Sanghol sculptures down to the dreaming Gyaraspur Vṛkṣakā (Gwalior Museum).

35. *Rātri Sukta: RV.* 10:127

36. *Araṇyānī Sukta. RV.* 10:146

37. *RV.* 10:85

38. *Pṛthvī Sūkta. AV.* 12:1

39. It is difficult to sustain an argument that nothing in the way of long poems was composed after the epic period, until we get to Aśvaghosa and Kālidāsa. But nothing has survived. A few stanzas from Pāṇiṇi's *Jāmbavati-Vijaya* and solitary stanzas from the works of other poets have survived, chiefly as quotations in other works.

40. He, covering the Earth on all sides
dwells within, in ten fingers' space;
Puruṣa alone is all this:
What has been and what is to come,
The Lord of Immortality
and of that here which grows by food.
(*RV*: 10:90:2)

(*Puruṣa* is the Primal Being)

41. Corresponds to the present Holi Festival, though the dates are slightly different.

42. Mahākāla—Great Time or Sacred Time or Time projected onto a cosmic plane.

43. *Umā* (mother), *Devī* (shining one), *Pārvatī* (mountain-born), are all epithets given to Śakti, Śiva's inherent shaping power.

44. Ananda-vardhana: *Dhvanyāloka* 1:8

45. Gunādhya's *Bṛhat-Kathā,* The Great Story, is the earliest to be mentioned, but only late adaptations of it, of the ninth–tenth centuries survive, like the *Kathā-Sarit-Sāgara.* The story-cycles narrate the life and

exploits of Udayana's son; perhaps the *Bṛhat-Kathā* also contained the tales of King Udayana of Kauśambi referred to in *Meghadūtam* (32). These are probably part of the lost body of popular tales.

46. *SB*: 13:5:4:15

47. Puṣpa-danta, a *gaṇa,* or attendant of Śiva, is cursed and banished to earth as a mortal, because he overheard the Lord telling Pārvatī a story never told before, never heard before and recounted it to his own wife, who in turn repeated it to her mistress, Pārvatī, as a brand-new story. Pārvatī was angry and cursed Puṣpa-danta for overhearing a private conversation between herself and Śiva and for repeating it. She also cursed another *gaṇa* who interceded. Śiva out of pity set a period and a condition for the release of the two *gaṇas* and their return to Śiva-loka (Śiva's world), which was for Puṣpa-danta to tell the same tale that he had overheard to a *yakṣa* cursed by Kubera to be born on earth as a goblin (*pisāca*). At the end of the tale, Puśpa-danta would be released from the curse and return to Śiva's heaven and the *yakṣa* by telling the tale to the second cursed *gaṇa* would be also released from the curse and return to his celestial home. The third person in the frame-story (the second *gaṇa*) would be released from his curse when he published the tale to the whole world for every one to listen to. The tale told by all three, is the *Bṛhat-Kathā* and the author of it, Gunādhya, is the second *gaṇa,* the last to find release. *Gaṇas* are divine beings like *yakṣas, gandharvas and apsarās.* (*Kathā-Sarit-Sāgara:* ch. I)

48. Intro., translation of *Śakuntalā* by Laurence Binyon.

49. De and Dasgupta, *History of Sanskrit Literature*, p. 144.

50. *Urvaśī*:.3:19

51. *Raghuvamśam,* 8:32–95.

52. J.B. Chaudhuri mentions hundreds of *Dūta-kāvyas* as still existing: p. 12 of Intro. to his edition of *Meghadūtam* with Bharata Mallika's commentary.

53. *Nātyaśāstra, KS*: 25:10–11

54. *RV.* 10:108

55. *Mbh.*, 3:70: 18–31

56. Rām. *Sundara Kandam.* Hanumān shows Rāma's signet ring to Sītā in canto 36.

57. As theriomorphic forms of divine effluence; e.g. Śiva's Bull, Nandi,

Skanda's peacock. Such forms are believed to have the power of mediating between human and divine.

58. A conversation poem has an auditor who is silent but has a clear identity and fully characterized personality.

59. *Kṛṣṇa-Yajur Veda, Maitrāyani Samhita.* 1:10:13

60. The Purānas in the form we have them now might be later than Kālidāsa, but the material contained in them is of great antiquity; earlier versions have been edited and written over.

61. *Sandhyā* (the meeting point), the points in time when day and night meet.

62. His form is everywhere: all-pervading is His Śiva Śakti.
Chidambaram is everywhere: everywhere His dance . . .
. . . He dances with Water, Fire, Wind and Ether.
(*Tirumūlar*—The Vision of the Divine Dance)

63. The *NS* lists eight *nāyikas* (heroines); they represent the emotional state of a woman and the attitudes she adopts to her lover (husband): angry and scornful, jealous and quarrelsome, feeling betrayed and bitter, secure in her husband's affections, waiting for her husband, all dressed to kill.

64. Certain words in the text indicate this: *Śyāma* is a young woman who has not yet given birth to a child; *bālā* is a young girl sixteen years of age (82); *prathama-viraha* (93) is the very first parting.

65. Wilson edition of *The Cloud Messenger*, 1843, fn. p. 14.

66. Ten stages in the emotional state of grief caused by separation from the loved one are described in the *NS* (24:160-62); the last being death.

67. Keats, *Hyperion*, 1:35–6

68 and 69. The enumeration of the ten stages in the *NS* is confusing, occurring as it does in a passage that is repetitive and obviously corrupt. They are: longing or craving, thinking or dwelling upon the beloved, recollection, enumeration of his virtues, anguish, lamentation, being distraught, sickness, stupor (withdrawal) and death. (*KS*. 24:160 ff & *MNG* 24:168 ff). The *NS* text characterizes these stages as the manner in which a maiden, inexperienced, expresses her emotional state—i.e. it treats of the stages of *first falling in love* if it remains *unfulfilled.* But two things have to be kept in mind:

(i) there are interpolations in the *NS* text and some verses way have been put in, modelled on descriptions of persons in love as *portrayed* in literature—the *NS* description as already noted, applies to a maiden falling in love and not of a woman grieving separated from her husband.

(ii) Bharata (the author of *NS*), has placed these descriptions in the chapter where he deals with histrionic representation of emotions—it is part of his aim to instruct actors *how* to portray emotional states. We should not view the enumeration of these ten states as describing how a woman ought to feel in a state of *love-in-separation* or of *unfulfilled* love.

70. *Poetics* as a formal discipline came later in the history of Sanskrit literary criticism. Drama was the form first to be treated.

71. Harisvāmin.

72. Reading between the lines of the *SB* text, the story was probably recited during the sacrifices but the *SB* being mainly a ritualistic text has just this cryptic indication; the story itself of Śakuntalā, the Apsarā who married the King of the lunar dynasty of Puru would have been part of the literary inheritance of Kālidāsa but unfortunately it is lost to us in its original form. We have only a very earthy version of it as one of the epic tales.

73. The Queen in *Mālavikā*.

74. The Queen in *Urvaśī*.

75. The Queens in *Raghuvamsam*.

76. The four *aśramas* or stages in a Hindu's life are: *Brahmacarya*, the student's, when a young man gets instruction and is trained and equipped for a profession (and perhaps also apprenticed to some trade in other cases); *Gṛhastha*, the householder's, when the man gets married, manages his career and gets children; *Vāna-prastha*, retirement to the forest, a kind of retreat from an active life in the world; *Śanyāsa*, total abandonment of the world. The second *aśrama* or stage of life, the householder's, is considered the most meritorious, because the person is in the world, doing good, helping others and generally sustaining society and the state.

Ṛtusamhāram (*The Gathering of the Seasons*)

1. This is one of the brilliant conceits in the poem, beautifully controlled and hinged on a single word—pales—*pāndutā* (paleness), in Sanskrit. The moon staring all night like some peeping-tom, at the lovely women sleeping on terraces, grows *pale* at the first light of dawn as if struck with

guilty shame at being caught out staring secretly at other men's wives. Other striking conceits are in sts. 24–26 and 3:7 where every adjective refers to the young girl as well as the night who are compared.

2. *Mṛgatṛṣnā*: literally the antelope's parching thirst; signifies a mirage. The poet frames a whole stanza based on the etymology of this word without in the least looking pedantic.

3. Night grows imperceptibly longer day by day in autumn, like a young girl gradually growing into womanhood. The first three lines of the text are descriptive of the young girl (*bālā*—a girl just turned sixteen) and the autumn night, which it is not possible to convey in a translation, because each compound word that forms an adjective has to be split and separated differently to give the separate meanings. The moon *is* Night's face; once it is free of clouds Night wears its radiance like a mantle; the young girl's face is like the moon free of obscuring cloud. Moonlight *is* Night's robe; the young girl wears a garment, silvery white like moon-light. The star-clusters correspond to the girl's jewels or to sparkling white flowers she adorns herself with. In both cases the beauties concealed within are gradually revealed. The word used for woman is *pramadā,* one who is exultant and aware of her youth and beauty and power to enchant men.

4. A brilliant word-picture brings sky and water together in an image drawn from a keen observation of nature. Fine emeralds when set, glow a very deep bluish-green. The waters of the pool reflect the deep, deep blue of clear autumn skies; but the dark blue is tinged with the dark green of the foliage at the water's edge, and the exact shade of a fine emerald is caught. The spotlessly white swan floating on the waters like the moon floating in space completes this exquisite picture. Kālidāsa sees nature and woman with the eye of a painter and sets down what he sees with the skill of a great poet whose language is musical. He was probably a painter and musician. Those days, poets as well as rich and cultivated young men and women were accomplished in many arts.

5. Lover, invariably refers to the husband. Kālidāsa does not treat of illicit relationships. *Ṛtusamhāram* is a celebration of married love.

6. Fumigation to get rid of tiny pests like mosquitoes and the like.

7. This stanza is a good example of a distinctive feature of Kālidasa's style—the multi-layered image. A number of elements go into building this image: it is also an example of the interweaving of human emotion with

nature's beauty. Coral is usually shaded; so are the Aśoka's cluster of blossoms, ranging from pale orange to scarlet depending on the age of the flower. The blossoms completely cover the branches and twigs to suggest branching coral—a forest of coral. The Aśoka grove wears the mysterious beauty of a coral reef. Kālidāsa was a much-travelled poet; in *Raghuvamśam*, he describes the pearl and coral fisheries of the deep south. The word used for coral here is *vi-druma; druma* is tree. Sanskrit is rich in synonyms and Kālidāsa's choice of words is always dictated by the needs of the imagery, not by the exigencies of the metrical pattern. To give the latter as a reason for the choice of one word rather than another is to betray a lack of close reading of the text.

Both the trees in the Aśoka grove and the girls watching their beauty, are *budding* into youth; the delicate beauty of the leaf-shoots—*pallava*—suggests the fresh and delicate charm of young girls just stepping into womanhood. Poetic convention perceives the Aśoka blossom as one of the five flower-arrows of Kāma, god of love; and the girls are filled with vague stirrings of emotion. But the poet uses the convention in a fresh manner. The girls are filled with a gentle sadness. The internal rhyme of *a-śoka* (free from sadness) which is the name of the flower and *sa-śoka* (filled with sadness) of the human emotion links the two words and sets them off against each other. The 'tree of no sorrow'—Aśoka—induces not a real sorrow but the make-believe sadness of adolescence—*nava-yauvana.*

The compound word, *vidruma-rāga-tāmram,* is made up of three colour-words: coral–red–rich copper. *Rāga*, in addition, has the double meaning of redness of colour and of passion. The flowers are 'impassioned' and transmit their emotion to the nubile girls. Further it is the colour of the red Aśoka blossoms that attracts the bees, leading to pollination and fruiting. The flower–bee relationship symbolizes love and union.

Meghadūtam (The Cloud Messenger)

1. *Prakṣaniyam= pra + īkṣaniyam,* to view with eagerness, see intently; *pra* is a prefix that possesses the senses of 'going forth', as if the eye darts forward, and of intensity and excess. The word expresses the idea of seeing something striking or spectacular; it also suggests the *viewing* of a show, a spectacle or a play; *prekṣāgṛha* is a theatre. The speaker of the poem may

therefore be seen as presented as a spectator, viewing a canvas that unrolls or a play presented on a stage. This is an interesting way of looking at the poem. (st. 2)

2. The unseen lady of the poem is first referred to as *kāntā* (st. 1), the beloved, a word derived from the root *kam* 'to desire; to be enamoured of'—a sexual undertone is present. Here, another aspect of the lover-beloved, *yakṣa-yakṣi* relationship is indicated by the use of the word *dayitā*, from the root meaning 'to have sympathy, compassion'; companionship rather than a sexual relationship is conveyed.

3. *Santapta*—applies to the burning of the sun's heat and the burning anguish of love and passion. The cloud gives relief from both, by providing shade and by heralding the return of the menfolk to their grieving women. In ancient India men who had to travel on business of various kinds invariably returned home at the onset of the monsoon.

4. *Gandha* in *sa-gandha*, has the double meaning of pride and kinship. The cātaka is kin to the cloud, because it drinks only rainwater, however thirsty; the disdain for any other water characterizes the bird as proud.

5. *Mekhalā*—girdle; it is also the name of a range of hills in the eastern part of the Vindhya mountains—the Maikal Hills.

6. *Bhavatah*—genitive form of the pronoun 'you' or more correctly 'Your Honour', qualifies both *samyogam* (union) and *sneha-vyaktih* (display of affection). A variant of the word in other recensions is *bhavatā*, the instrumental of the pronoun, meaning 'with you': this multivalence allows for more than one reading of the stanza; I give below the alternative rendering and lines 3, 4 of the stanza.

Kāle-kāle bhavati bhavatah yasya samyogam etya
sneha-vyaktih cira-virahajam muncato bāṣpam uṣṇam (12)

Note the wordplay of *bhavati* (becomes) and *bhavatah* (Your Honour's).

Embrace and bid farewell to your loving friend,
this lofty peak in the Mekhalas, marked
by the holy feet of the Lord of Raghus
adored by the world: reuniting with whom
time and again your affection is displayed
by the fall of burning tears born of long separation.

In one case what results from the meeting of cloud and hill, is a shower of warm rain; in the other, the mists and vapours exhaled by the hill during the rains. To the reader of Sanskrit both meanings are present simultaneously.

7. *Hālām abhi-mata-rasām Revatī-locānankām*—'the cherished wine marked by Revatī's eyes'; the compound word *Revatī-locānankām* suggests a number of meanings: Revati's eyes, amber or wine-coloured are reflected in the wine in the cup; the wine itself is the colour of her eyes; it produces the joy and exhilaration that Revati's eyes did; and by implication, the *yakṣa* had to abandon, as Balarāma did, the joys of drinking in the company of his beloved.

8. The actual confluence of the rivers Yamunā and Gangā is some 400 miles downstream at Prayag (Allahabad).

9. *Tryambaka = tri-ambaka*; *ambaka* has three meanings; the word therefore has three meanings: triple-eyed, Śiva's Third Eye is the inner eye of wisdom; parent of the Triple-World; the Lord who utters the triple sound of the Primal Word OM—A-U-M. Śiva is known a Omkāra-nātha, the Lord whose form is OM.

10. *Kuliśa* means lightning, i.e. the sparks off Indra's thunderbolt and also diamond, are hard, sharp and bright. In the latter meaning the sense we get is that the sharp and bright points of the diamond bracelets worn by the celestial maidens pricks the cloud and makes the water jet out. The former meaning that I have used in the translation seems more appropriate.

11. *Jyotis-chāyā-kusuma-racanāni* (variant *racitāni*—formed of) literally star-reflection-flower-forms; this word gives us and suggests the following: star-shaped flowers are strewn as decorations on the terrace-floors; star-shaped designs in brilliant gems decorate the terrace-floors, flower-shaped stars are reflected on the gem-inlaid terrace-floors, which because they are gem-inlaid sparkle like stars.

Abhijnānaśākuntalam (*The Recognition of Śakuntalā*)

1. Bard or rhapsode, also charioteer to the King; originally one of the seven persons in a kingdom who was closely associated with the choice and consecration of a king. For this reason, I have retained the Sanskrit word *Sūta* instead of charioteer. *Sūtas* were honoured persons; the most celebrated of charioteers in literature is Kṛṣṇa, who in the epic *Mahābhārata*,

drives Arjuna's chariot and preaches the *Gītā* on the battle-field.

2. The blackbuck is a very sacred animal; there is a close relationship in the play between Śakuntalā and the blackbuck; Śakuntalā's purity and gentleness as well as her delicate beauty are suggested.

3. The lunar dynasty; see glossary under Puru.

4. Solar associations are present in this image; the chariot wheels of a universal monarch—*cakra-vartī*—roll over the whole earth (the known world) just as the sun's wheel (the solar disc) rolls through space. The wheel is also associated with Buddha, who turned the wheel of a spiritual empire.

5. A significant phrase; Śakuntalā is pictured as a goddess of the woodland. For her associations with sylvan goddesses like *yakṣis* and guardians of sacred pools, see intro., section ix, 57–59.

6. Throbbing of the right arm in a man indicates the prospect of meeting a beautiful woman and love and marriage. Throbbing of the right eye or arm is a good omen in a man and of the left in a woman.

7. According to Manu a man should marry in his own class or below it; a woman in her own or in a class above her. If Śakuntalā's parents were both of the Brahmin class, then she was hierarchically above the King who was a Kṣatriya (class of warriors and rulers). If her mother were not Brahmin, i.e. of the same class as the sage Kaṇva, she would not be a pure-bred Brahmin girl and the King could marry her. As it happens her real father was a Kṣatriya and hence named a royal sage, as Duhṣanta himself is in Act 2.

8. According to Manu concealing one's true identity is reprehensible; on the other hand kings and high state officials often went around incognito to see for themselves how things were in the kingdom.

9. For the chase as a significant metaphor in the play, see 'A Note on Texts and Translations' of this book.

10. Misfortunes do not come singly.

11. The Sanskrit word *kubja* stands for a hunchback as well as an aquatic plant that bends and waves buffeted by the force of the current.

12. Hunting is one of the four most pernicious vices of the ten that kings are warned against, the other three being: drink, whoring and dicing.

13. A kind of crystal believed to glow and even catch fire when struck by the sun's rays.

14. A sixth of all kinds of income and produce were paid into the treasury as taxes.

15. Sages inspired reverence as repositories of holiness, but they were also easy of approach (Durvāsā is an exception to the rule).

16. 'The Concealer'—the demon of drought or darkness.

17. Indra and Agni are the two oft-invoked deities in the *Ṛgveda*.

18. See n. 9. The *cakra-rakṣi* is used for those warriors who rode by the side of the King's war-chariot; lit. 'protectors of the wheels'.

19. Lit. one who should live long.

20. A king who wished to go to heaven bodily and decided to perform sacrifices to ensure this. Viśvāmitra (Śakuntalā's real father) undertook to officiate at these sacrifices, at the end of which Triśanku began to make his bodily ascent to heaven; the gods pushed him down and Viśvāmitra pushed him up with the result that Triśanku hung suspended in space between heaven and earth.

21. A prelude provides information about events not presented on the stage; a prelude may be brief like this one or long like the one in Act 4, where a number of events that have taken place over a length of time are recounted.

22. *Man-matha*—Churner of the mind; one of the many names for Love (Cupid).

23. See Glossary under Bodiless one.

24. Love; like the Greek Eros, the Indian god of love, Kāma, is associated with dolphins.

25. Refer to the Glossary.

26. Since she refers a few lines earlier to a song, Śakuntalā may at this point sing rather than speak these lines.

27. The King refers to his descent from the moon.

28. The secluded and well-guarded part of the palace which formed the residence of the queens.

29. A king who is paramount sovereign is said to be wedded to the earth.

30. Double meaning indicated here: (i) Śakuntalā is thinking of parental consent; (ii) she considers it disrespectful to place her feet on the lap of the King and whom she has chosen as husband.

31. The word *Kumārī* means a very young girl, one in her pre-teens, and also a virgin; in the context the second meaning is more appropriate.

32. See glossary.

33. *A-mṛta,* lit. deathless, i.e. the waters of immortality.

34. The two friends are not far and warn Śakuntalā. Sheldrakes—*cakravāka* and *cakravākī*—said to be parted at night because of a curse.

35. i.e. the prayers were accepted by the deity.

36. The eldest son of the Chief Queen becomes the Heir-Apparent.

37. These are two upper garments, one probably a veil and the other a kind of mantle.

38. This verse is reminiscent of a very celebrated one in the Vedas: '*Madhuvāta ṛtāyate. . .*'

39. Kaṇva's message is subtly-worded; the King is expected to behave in a manner worthy of his noble lineage and keep his promises to Śakuntalā; he was chosen by her (by the Gāndharva rite), giving him her love freely without any pressure from family and friends; the King has esteemed the sage highly to contemplate marriage with his daughter; finally, Kaṇva is rich not in material goods as Duhṣanta is, but in holiness and self-restraint—a veiled reminder of the sage's 'holy power'.

40. St. 23 has an air of finality in closing the gate of the 'green world' to Śakuntalā; her return is placed in the distant future, when she and the King might return to the Hermitage in their last days, entering *vāna-prastha,* 'retreat from the world', the third stage in a Hindu's life.

41. The Chamberlain like the court jester is a stock figure in drama.

42. Śeṣa, the Great Serpent that is believed to hold the earth up on its hood.

43. The old-fashioned umbrella, a cumbrous contraption with a long and heavy handle, is meant. It is carried by servants who held them over princes, nobles, the wealthy and whoever could afford a servant to perform this service.

44. The Sanskrit word for a spray of flowers is *manjari,* in the feminine; hence the feminine pronoun in the next line, which refers to the singer Hamsavatī whom he has loved and left; and it suggests the King's love for another, Śakuntalā, which is already forgotten.

45. The lotus is described as *vasati-matram,* a one-night halt or mere stay overnight. In the Devanāgari recension, the King's reply to Mādhavya's query reads differently—'She taunts me with spending all my time with Queen Vasumati. . .' implying that the King's interest in the crowned

queen is in the nature of an enforced overnight stop.

46. A king's conduct affects the well-being of his kingdom; the reverse is also true, that the King bears responsibility for offences committed in his kingdom, because he is the ruler and has to keep order.

47. The two ascetics are different in temperament and behaviour. Śārṇgarava is an irascible man and somewhat contemptuous of secular authority and of Brahmins who are hangers-on at the royal court. He is quick to anger but sympathetic. Śāradvata on the other hand is most unlikeable, cold and hard, rather sanctimonious; cleanliness of all kinds is very much on his mind. The three ascetics that Kālidāsa portrays with gentle irony, Durvāsā, Śārṇgarava and Śāradvata exemplify three undesirable qualities that ascetics above all others should not possess: Anger, pride and self-love.

48. These are formal greetings; it is important that the penances of sages should prosper and that a king needs all the good fortune he can have for he carries his life on the point of his sword.

49. A reference to the proverbial mismatching of married couples. Note that what Kaṇva's pupil actually says to the King is totally different from the message that the sage had entrusted to him.

50. Śacī is Indra's consort and Queen of the Immortals.

51. The teachings of Real-Politik.

52. Ancient methods of punishment.

53. Royal honours.

54. The Spring Festival in honour of Kāma, the god of love.

55. The Himālayas; Gauri is Śakti, Śiva's consort or inherent power.

56. A ceremony performed in the third month of pregnancy to ensure that the child in the womb is a male.

57. The section of Act 5 beginning with the entrance of Caturikā with Śakuntalā's portrait and ending with the King swooning is interesting for a couple of insights; and also important. Up to the receipt by the King of the letter about the shipwreck and death of a wealthy merchant who was childless, it is a re-enactment of the events of Act I—the initial meeting of the King and Śakuntalā. Duhṣanta seems almost to relive these events in an attempt to *will* a change in their course and outcome and wipe off the repudiation of his wife from his mind, until the comment of Mādhavya who has no use for illusions makes it impossible for the King to do so. The re-

enactment that the King attempts is also part of the process of penitence that leads to the restoration of wife and son. Recognizing the sorrow of childlessness and the danger to the kingdom and the dynasty left without an heir, the King swoons. And when he regains consciousness he is a new and better man and King.

58. I have translated the word here as missile for this reason: a certain class of weapons, arrows, discus, etc. were released after a charm or invocation was pronounced over it, directing it to a specific target. Similarly, another charm or sacred word was spoken to recall it; for this I have used the term 'de-activate'.

59. The unitive godhead, Śiva-Śakti.

Appendix I

1. Intro. to the *Vikramāditya-charita*, Harvard Oriental Series.
2. D.C. Sircar, *Ancient Malwa and the Vikramaditya Tradition.*
3. Shermbavanekar: Date of Kalidasa, p. 233 J.U.B. Part VI, May 1933.
4. Ksetresachandra Chattopadhyaya, *AUS* Vol. II, 1926
5. Sakas or Scythians.
6. See intro.
7. *Harsa-charitra,* p.193, trans. Cowell and Thomas.
8. Kramrisch, *The Art of India*, pl. 22, 23
9. Known as *dohada* (see glossary under blossoming-time): referred to in *Meghadūtam* (77).
10. Pl. 74, p. 74, Mario Bussagli and Calembus Sivaramamurti, *5000 Years of the Art of India*, See also ch. 4 on the art of Bharhut and Sanci.
11. Pl. 39, Kramrisch, op. cit.
12. National Museum, New Delhi.
13. Pl. 67, p. 64, *The Art of India*, Bussagli and Sivaramamurti.
14. Pl. 21, Kramrisch, op. cit.

A Short Bibliography

Sanskrit Texts and Translations

Abhijnāna-Śākuntalam, ed. S.K. Belvalkar, Sahitya Akademi, Delhi, 1963.

——, ed. M.R. Kale, Motilal Banarsidass, Delhi, 1969.

——, ed. R. Pischel, Rev. Carl Capellar, Harvard Oriental Series, No. 16, 1922.

——, ed. Rajaraja Varma with Abhirama's comm., Trivandrum, 1913.

——, Nirnaya Sagar Press edition with Raghava Bhatta's comm., Bombay.

——, ed. Gauri Nath Sastri. Sahitya Akademi, Delhi, 1983.

Abhijnāna-Śākuntalam: A Reconstruction, ed. D.K. Kanjilal, Calcutta Sanskrit Research Series, Calcutta, 1980.

Atharva Veda, ed. Devichand, Munshiram Manoharlal, Delhi, 1982.

Dhvanyāloka, Ānanda Vardhana, ed. K. Krishna Moorthy (with Eng. trans.), Motilal Banarsidass, Delhi, 1980.

Harṣa-Charitram, Bāṇa, translated by E.B. Cowell and F.W. Thomas.

Kṛṣṇa-Yajur-Veda: Maitrāyaṇi Samhitā, ed. Devichand (with Eng. trans.), Munshiram Manoharlal, Delhi, 1980.

Mahābhārata, Critical Edition, BORI, ed. by several scholars.

Manu Smṛti, ed. Pt. Hargovinda Sastri with Kulluka Bhatta's comm. Chaukhambha Sanskrit Samsthan, Varanasi, 3rd edition, 1982.

Megha-Dūtam, ed. S.K. De, Sahitya Akademi, Delhi, 1957.

——, ed. J.B. Chaudhuri, with Bharata Mallika's comm., Subodhā, Pracya Vani Mandira Series, Calcutta, 1952.

——, ed. G.R. Nandargikar, with Mallinātha's comm., 1893.

——, ed. H.H. Wilson, (with a free metrical trans. into English), London, 1843.

Nātyaśāstra of Bharata Muni, ed. M.M. Batuk Nath Sharma and M.M. Baldeva Upadhyaya, Kashi Sanskrit Series, Chaukhambha, Varanasi, 1929.

———, ed. M. Ghosh (with Eng. trans.), (ch I–XXVII only), Bibliotheca Indica, No. 272, Calcutta, 1950.

Nīti-Sāra of Kāmandaki, ed. Rajendra Lala, 1861, Revised by Sisir Kumar Mitra (with Eng. trans.), The Asiatic Society, Calcutta, 1964.

Rāmāyaṇa of Vālmīkī, Critical Edition in several volumes, BORI, 1966.

Ṛg Veda, ed. Max Muller, Kashi Sanskrit Series, Chaukhambhi, Varanasi, reprinted in 2 vols. by Motilal Banarsidass, Delhi, 1965.

Ṛtusamhāram of Kālidāsa, Nirnaya Sagar Press, with Manirama's comm., 8th edition, Bombay, 1952.

———, ed. M.R. Kale, with Śastri Vyankatācharya Upadhye's comm., Motilal Banarasidass, Delhi, 2nd edition, 1967.

Śata-patha Brāhmana, with the commentaries of Sāyana and Hariswaṃin, Ganga Viṣṇu and Srikishandass, Bombay, 1940.

The Complete Works of Kālidāsa, ed. V.P. Joshi, E.J. Brill, Leiden, 1976.

Books referred to or consulted

Ali, S.M., *The Geography of the Puranas*, Peoples Publishing House, Delhi, 1966.

Bhat, G.K. *Bharata-Nātya-Manjarī*, BORI, 1975.

Bhattacharya, P.K., *Historical Geography of Madhya Pradesh from Early Records*, Motilal Banarsidass, Delhi, 1977.

Bussagli, Mario and Calembus Sivaramamurti, *5000 Years of the Art of India*, Harry N. Abrams, New York, n.d.

Chattopadhyaya, K.C., *The Date of Kalidasa*, reprint AUS.

Coomaraswamy, A.K., *Yaksas*, Washington, 1931.

Cowen, D.V., *Flowering Trees and Shrubs in India*, Thacker & Co., Bombay, 1950.

Dave, K.N., *Birds in Sanskrit Literature*, Motilal Banarsidass, Delhi, 1985.

De, S.K. and S.N. Dasgupta, *History of Classical Sanskrit Literature*, University of Calcutta, 1977.

Keith, A.B., *Sanskrit Drama*, Oxford University Press, 1924.

Keith, A.B. , *A History of Sanskrit Literature*, Oxford, 1920.

Kosambi, D.D., *The Culture and Civilization of Ancient India in Historical Outline*, Vikas Publishing House, 1970.

Kramrisch, Stella, *The Art of India through the Ages*, Phaidon Press, London, 1954.

Mirashi, V.V., *Sanskrit Studies*, Vol. 1.

Panikkar, K.M., *A Survey of Indian History*, The National Information and Publications Limited, Bombay, 1947.

Radhakrishnan, Sarvapalli, *Indian Philosophy*, 2 vols., George Allen and Unwin, London, Indian edition, 1940.

Shembavanekar, K.M., *The Date of Kalidasa*, Reprint, JUB, 1933.

Sircar, D.C., *Ancient Malwa and the Vikramaditya Tradition*, Munshiram Manoharlal, Delhi.

Upadhyaya, B.S., *India in Kalidasa*, Allahabad, 1947.

Zimmer, Heinrich, *The Art of Indian Asia* (completed and edited by Joseph Cambell), Bollingen Series XXXIX, Princeton University Press, Princeton, 1955.

MORE ABOUT PENGUINS

For further information about books available from Penguins in India write to Penguin Books (India) Ltd, B4/246, Safdarjung Enclave, New Delhi 110 029.

In the UK: For a complete list of books available from Penguins in the United Kingdom write to Dept. EP, Penguin Books Ltd, Harmondsworth, Middlesex UB7 0DA.

In the U.S.A.: For a complete list of books available from Penguins in the United States write to Dept. DG, Penguin Books, 299 Murray Hill Parkway, East Rutherford, New Jersey 07073.

In Canada: For a complete list of books available from Penguins in Canada write to Penguin Books Canada Ltd, 2801 John Street, Markham, Ontario L3R 1B4.

In Australia: For a complete list of books available from Penguins in Australia write to the Marketing Department, Penguin Books Australia Ltd, P.O. Box 257, Ringwood, Victoria 3134.

In New Zealand: For a complete list of books available from Penguins in New Zealand write to the Marketing Department, Penguin Books (N.Z.) Ltd, Private Bag, Takapuna, Auckland 9.